CASTLE

RICHARD CASTLE'S

DEADLY STORM

A DERRICK STORM MYSTERY

Writers
BRIAN MICHAEL BENDIS & KELLY SUE DECONNICK

Breakdowns
LAN MEDINA
WITH TOM RANEY (pages 73-82)

Finishes
SCOTT HANNA
WITH DAN GREEN (pages 73-82)

Colorists
SOTOCOLOR
WITH VAL STAPLES (pages 50-69)

Letterer
VIRTUAL CALLIGRAPHY'S CHRIS ELIOPOULOS

Cover Art
CARLO PAGULAYAN, DANNY MIKI & RICHARD ISANOVE

Editor
SANA AMANAT

Senior Editor
RALPH MACCHIO

Special Thanks
Andrew Marlowe & Noreen O'Toole

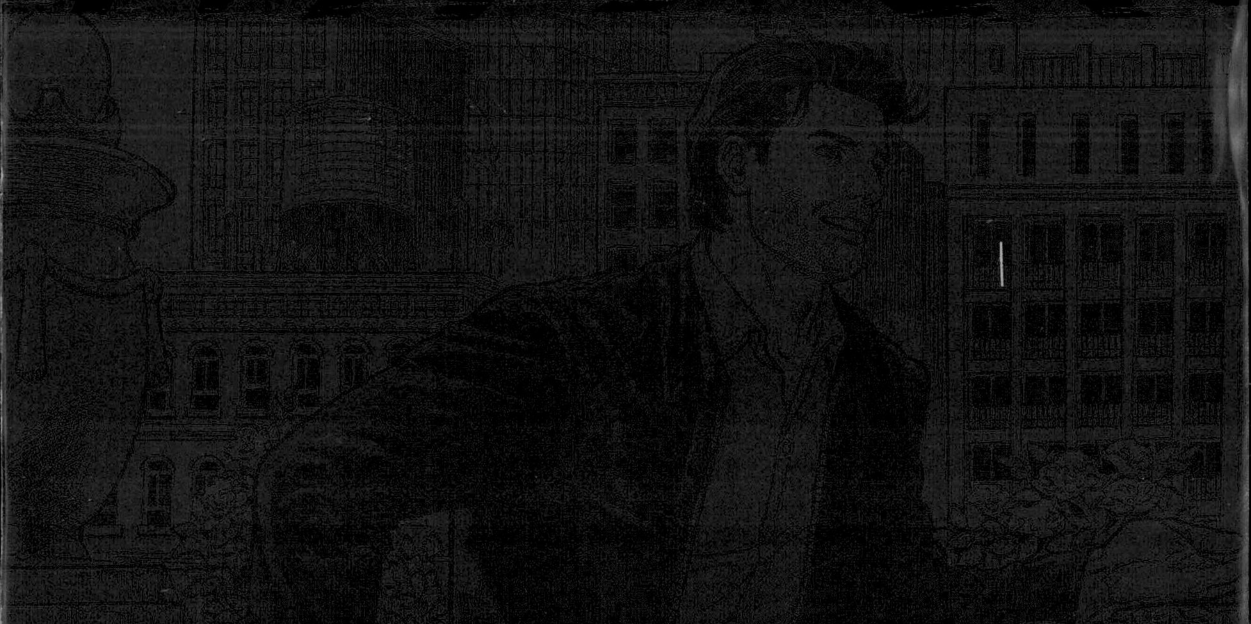

Collection Editor **Jennifer Grünwald** **Alex Starbuck & Nelson Ribeiro**
Mark D. Beazley **Jeff Youngquist**
David Gabriel **Jeff Powell**
Axel Alonso **Joe Quesada** **Dan Buckley**

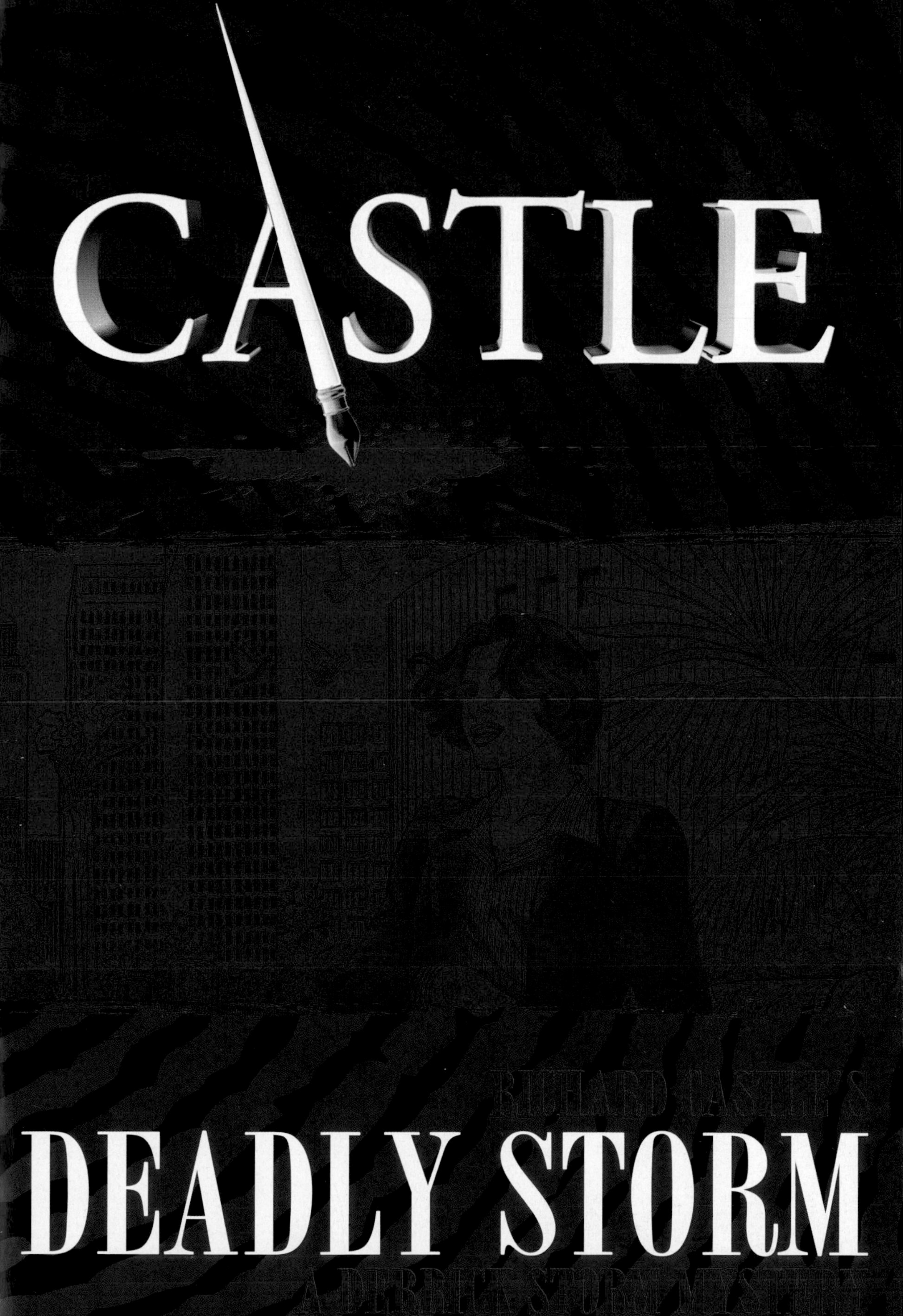
CASTLE
RICHARD CASTLE'S
DEADLY STORM
A DERRICK STORM MYSTERY

INTRODUCTION

daptation. It's a word most authors hate. It conjures images in their minds of their beloved perfect prose being hacked to pieces by literary infidels. I'm sure it happens, but if it does, this graphic novel stands as a startling exception. Seeing my book "Deadly Storm" be translated into comic form has been a remarkable joy, and here's why:

Growing up without a father, my first real male role models were found in the pages of comic books. From a young age, I aspired to be one of those complicated, hard-charging heroes driven by circumstance and fate to do what was right, no matter the personal cost. During the raging storms of tumultuous youth, these characters provided me a grounded moral compass that I could turn to again and again, even as they, like me, struggled with their flaws.

I don't think it's an exaggeration to say that my early love of these comic characters had a huge influence on me during the creation of Derrick Storm. There's no doubt that Derrick, my rugged and morally complicated Private Investigator turned CIA spy who fights the forces of darkness and conspiracy at every turn, owes much to those rainy days I spent buried beneath an avalanche of dog-eared comics, living out adventures far beyond my imagination. So when the good folks at Marvel approached me about turning "Deadly Storm" into a graphic novel, I truly felt like I'd come home.

I can think of no better folks to have entrusted my beloved character to than the remarkably talented Brian Michael Bendis and Kelly Sue DeConnick. Their sure hands have steadied my nervous heart. The magic they've conjured together has been brought to life beautifully by Lan Medina's artwork. For fans of the Derrick Storm novels, I think you'll be thrilled by how much these guys have honored their spirit. To them, and everyone at the Marvel organization, I give my heartfelt thanks.

And now, stop wasting time on a boring foreword. Turn the page. A deadly Storm awaits!

Richard Castle
New York, 2011

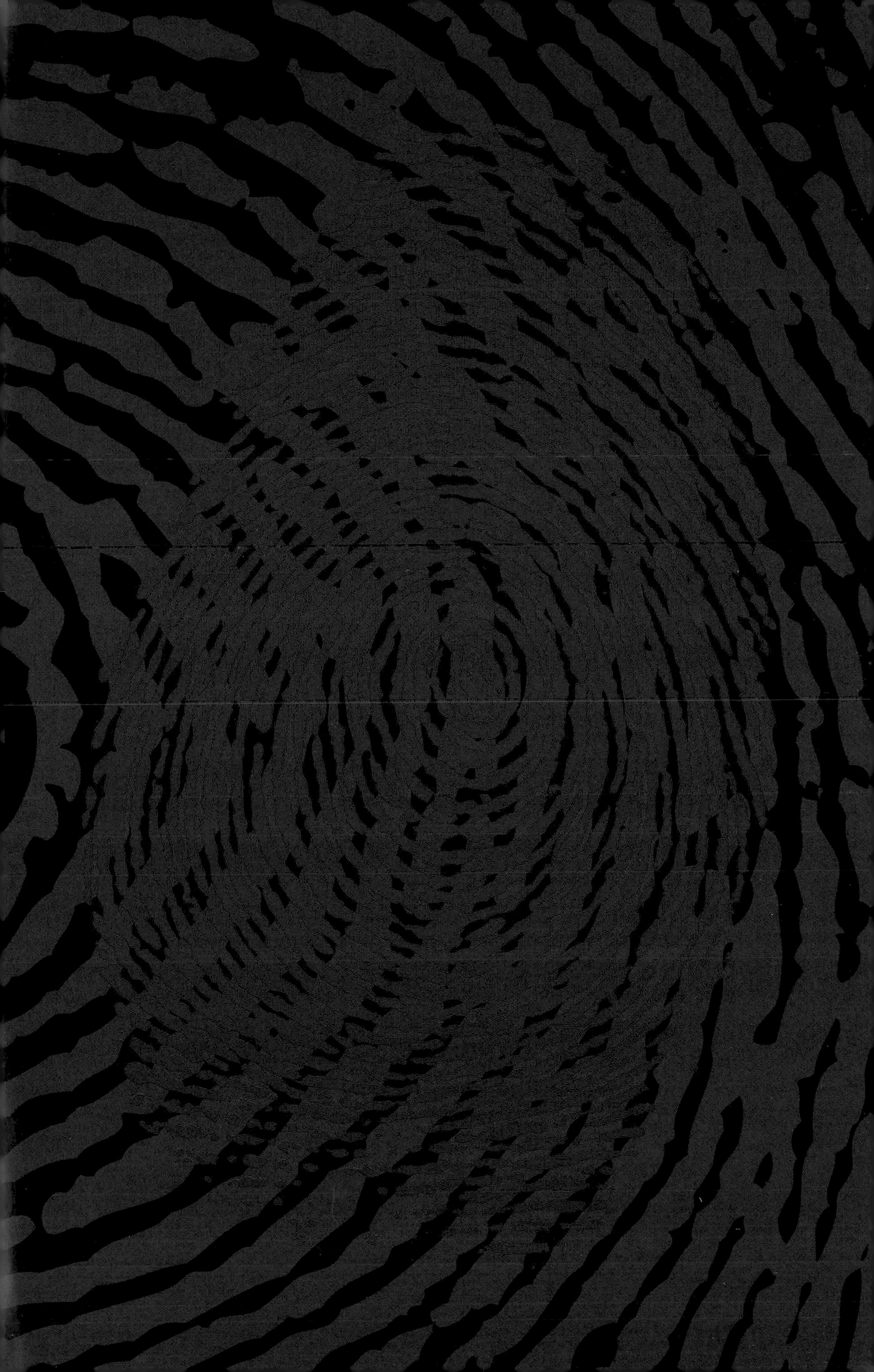

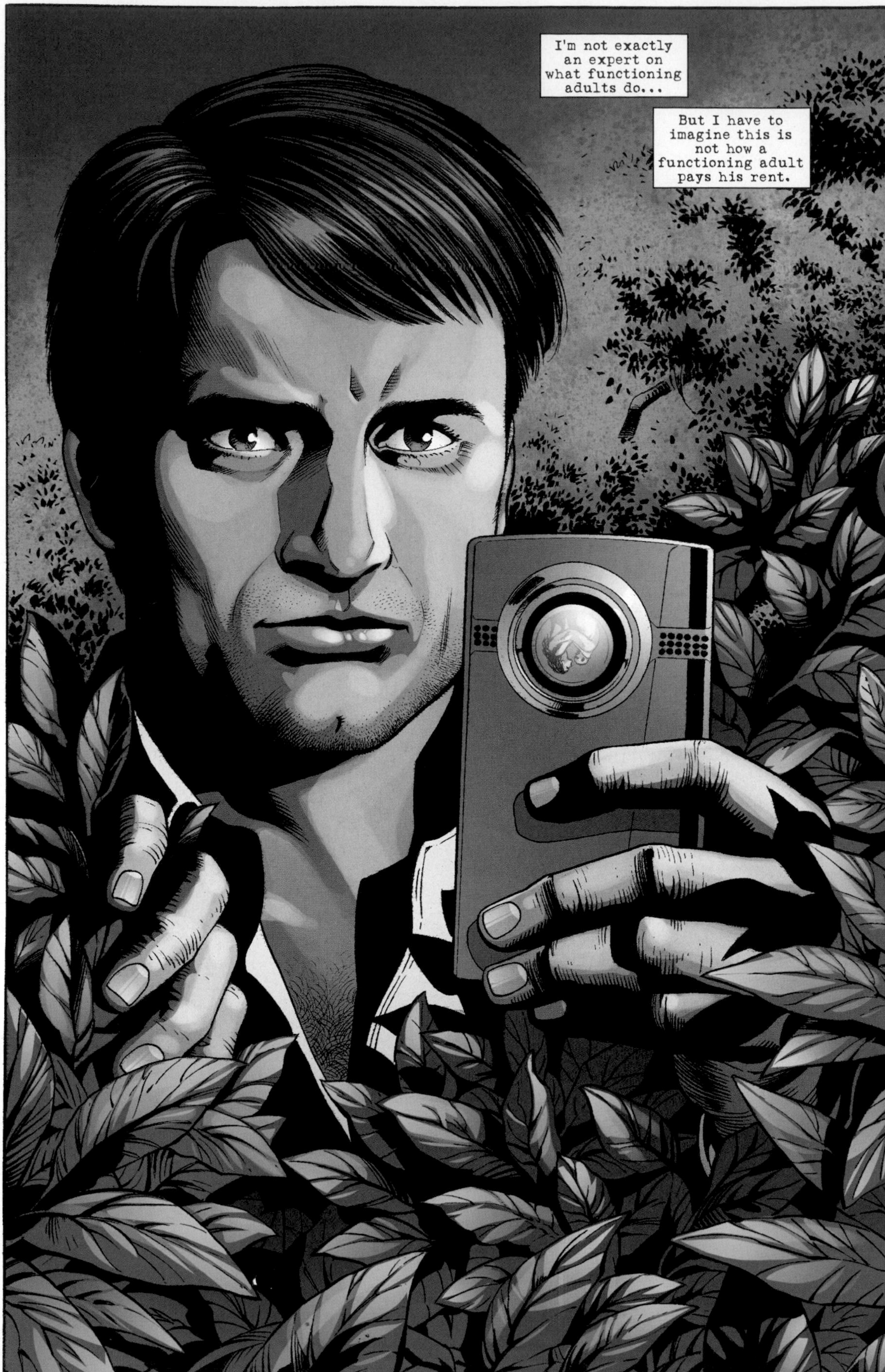
I'm not exactly an expert on what functioning adults do...
But I have to imagine this is not how a functioning adult pays his rent.

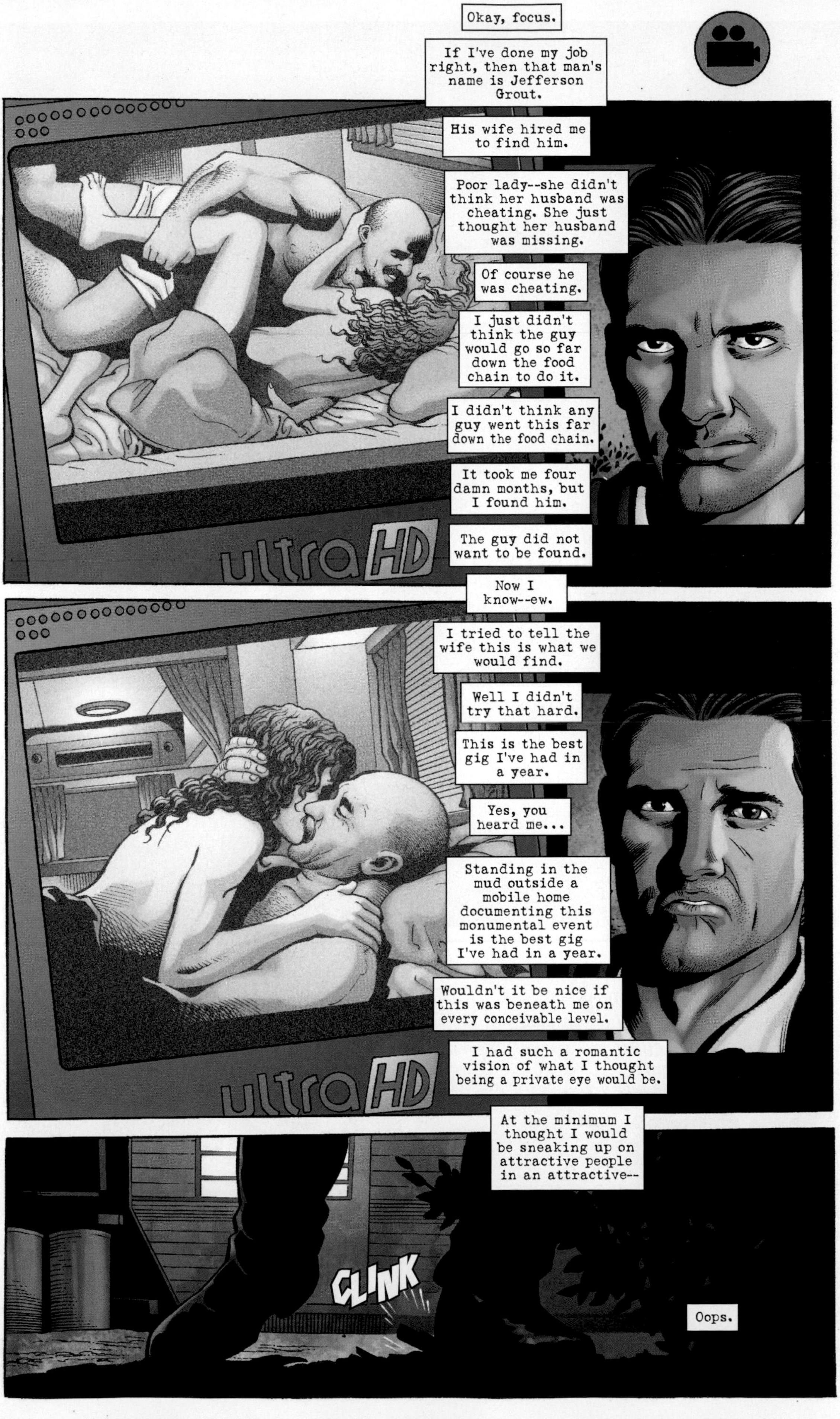
Okay, focus.
If I've done my job right, then that man's name is Jefferson Grout.
His wife hired me to find him.
Poor lady--she didn't think her husband was cheating. She just thought her husband was missing.
Of course he was cheating.
I just didn't think the guy would go so far down the food chain to do it.
I didn't think any guy went this far down the food chain.
It took me four damn months, but I found him.
The guy did not want to be found.
ultra HD
Now I know--ew.
I tried to tell the wife this is what we would find.
Well I didn't try that hard.
This is the best gig I've had in a year.
Yes, you heard me...
Standing in the mud outside a mobile home documenting this monumental event is the best gig I've had in a year.
Wouldn't it be nice if this was beneath me on every conceivable level.
I had such a romantic vision of what I thought being a private eye would be.
ultra HD
At the minimum I thought I would be sneaking up on attractive people in an attractive--
CLINK
Oops.

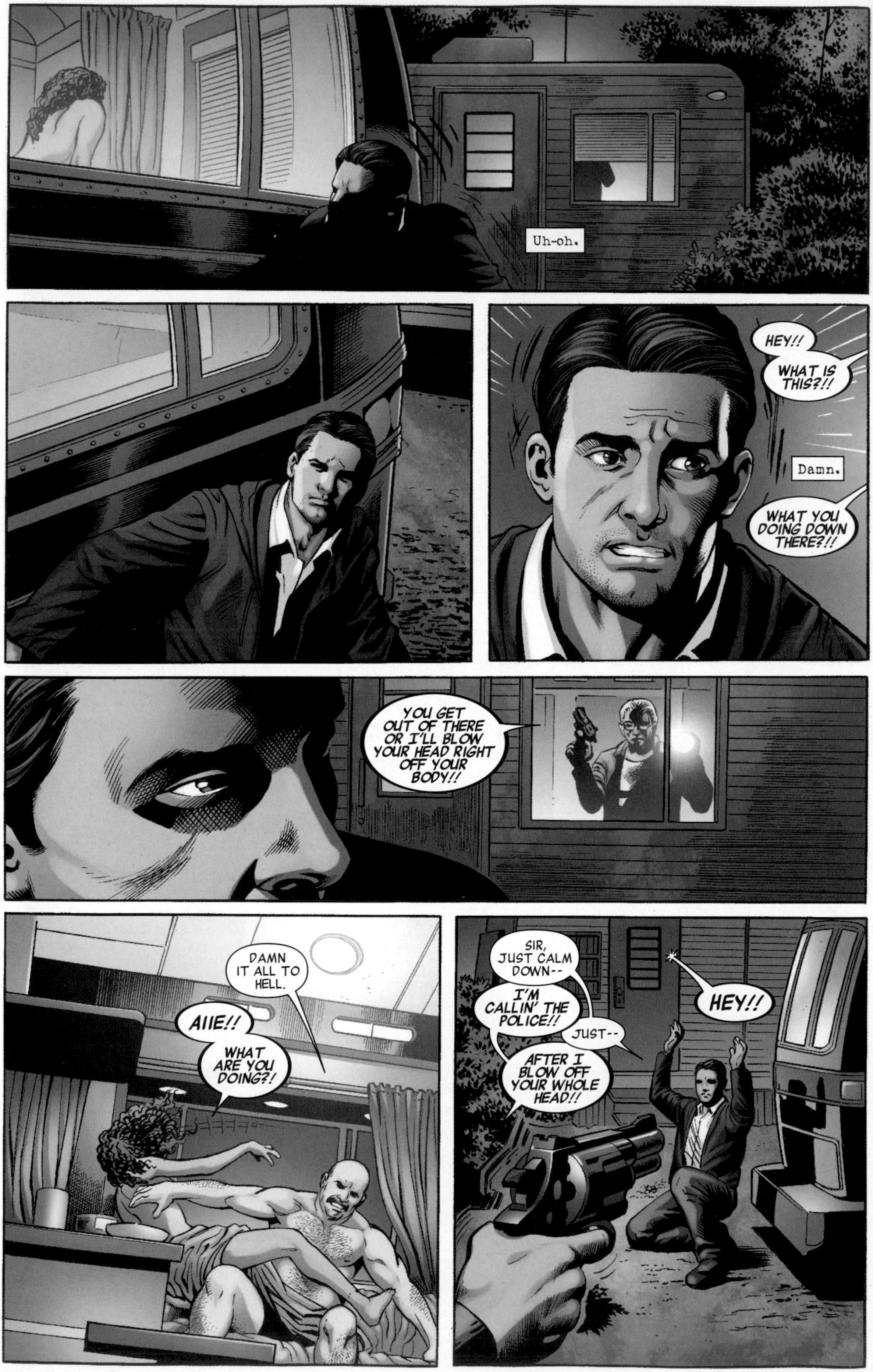
Uh-oh.
HEY!!
WHAT IS THIS?!!
Damn.
WHAT YOU DOING DOWN THERE?!!
YOU GET OUT OF THERE OR I'LL BLOW YOUR HEAD RIGHT OFF YOUR BODY!!
DAMN IT ALL TO HELL.
AIIE!!
WHAT ARE YOU DOING?!
SIR, JUST CALM DOWN--
I'M CALLIN' THE POLICE!!
JUST--
AFTER I BLOW OFF YOUR WHOLE HEAD!!
HEY!!

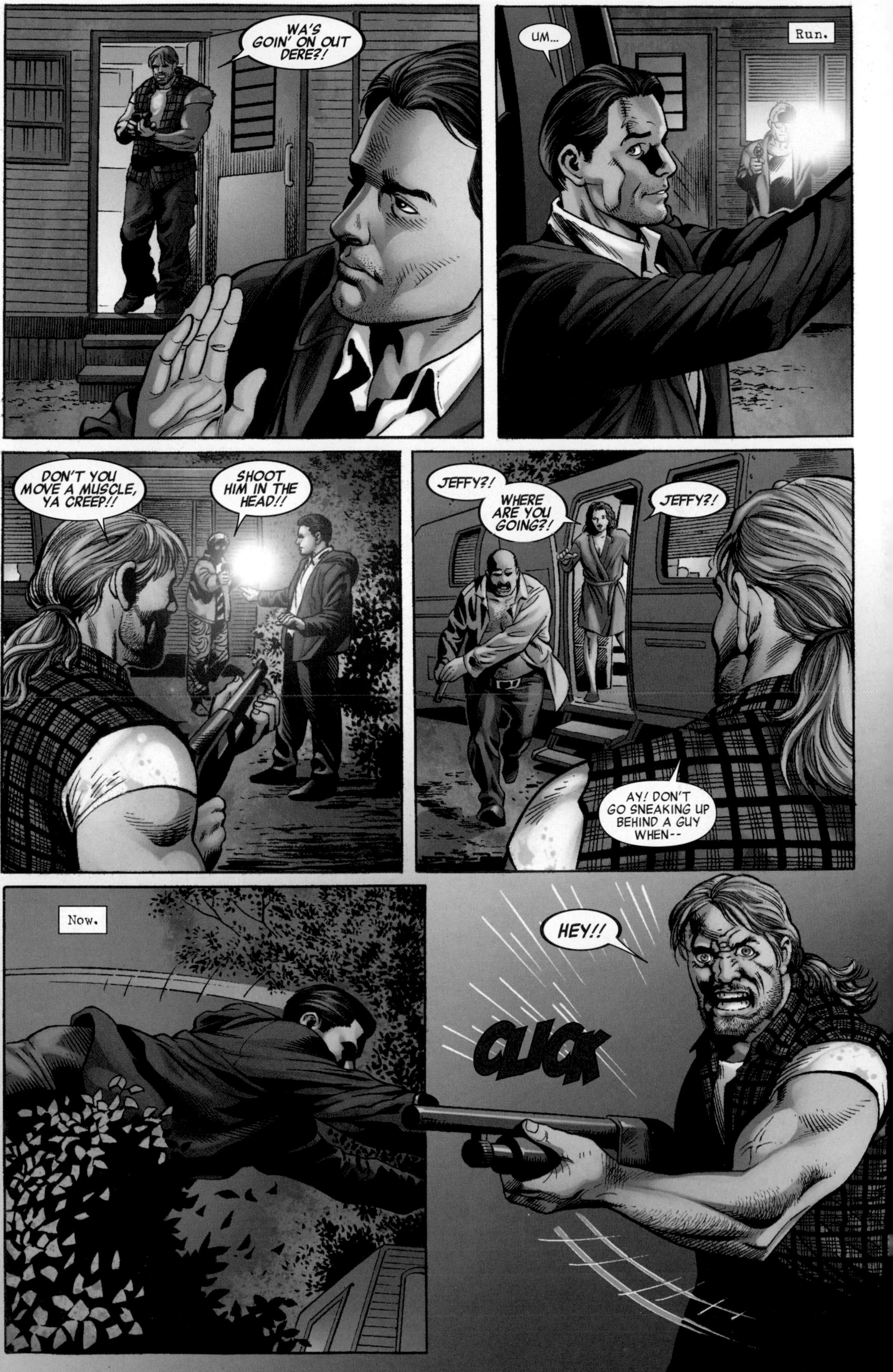
WA'S GOIN' ON OUT DERE?!
UM...
Run.
DON'T YOU MOVE A MUSCLE, YA CREEP!!
SHOOT HIM IN THE HEAD!!
JEFFY?!
WHERE ARE YOU GOING?!
JEFFY?!
AY! DON'T GO SNEAKING UP BEHIND A GUY WHEN--
Now.
HEY!!
CLICK

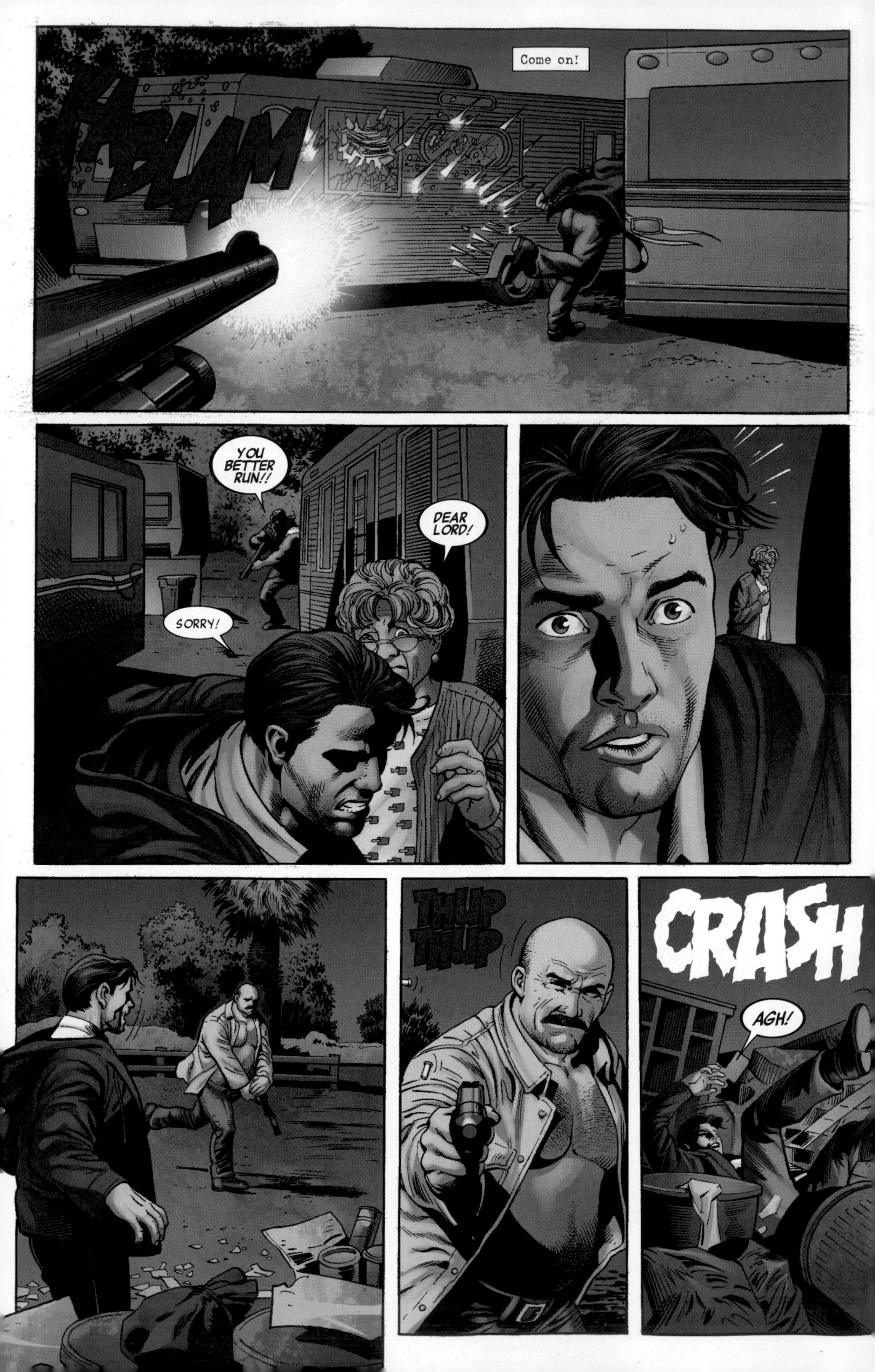

BLAM
Come on!
YOU BETTER RUN!!
DEAR LORD!
SORRY!
THUP THUP
CRASH
AGH!

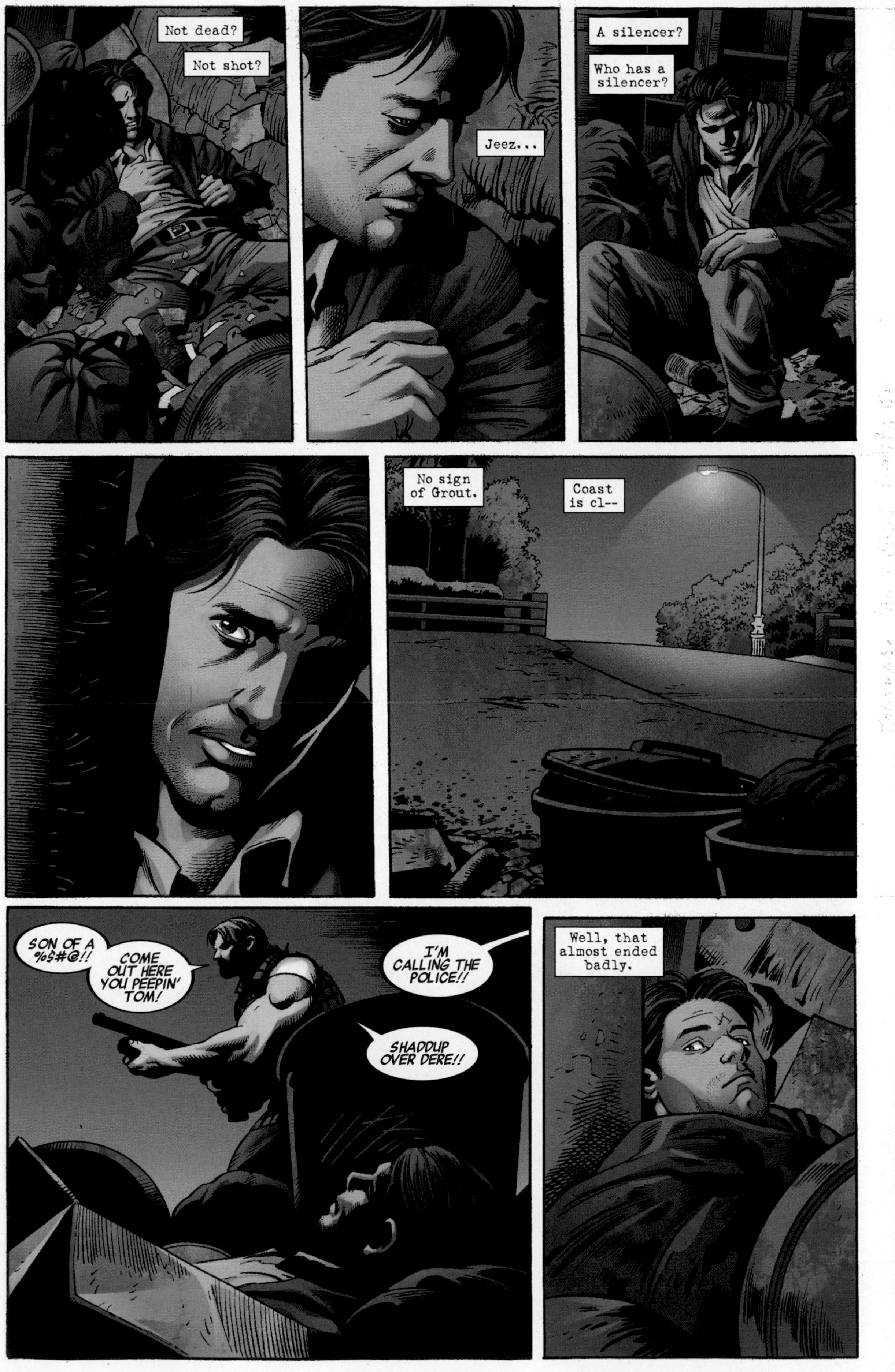

Not dead?
Not shot?
Jeez...
A silencer?
Who has a silencer?
No sign of Grout.
Coast is cl--
SON OF A %$#@!!
COME OUT HERE YOU PEEPIN' TOM!
I'M CALLING THE POLICE!!
SHADDUP OVER DERE!!
Well, that almost ended badly.

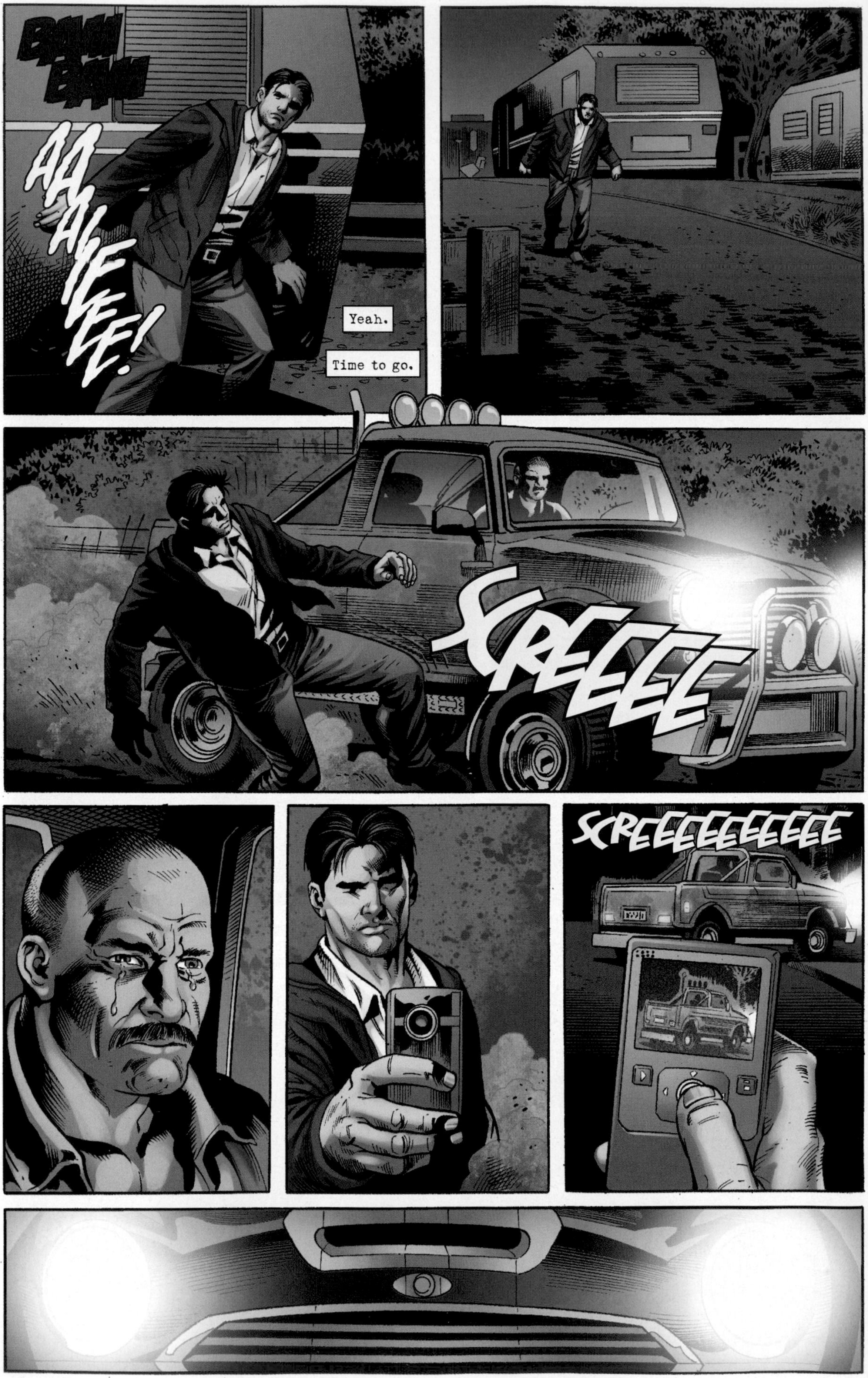
BAM BAM
AAAHEEEE!
Yeah.
Time to go.
SCREEEE
SCREEEEEEEEEEE

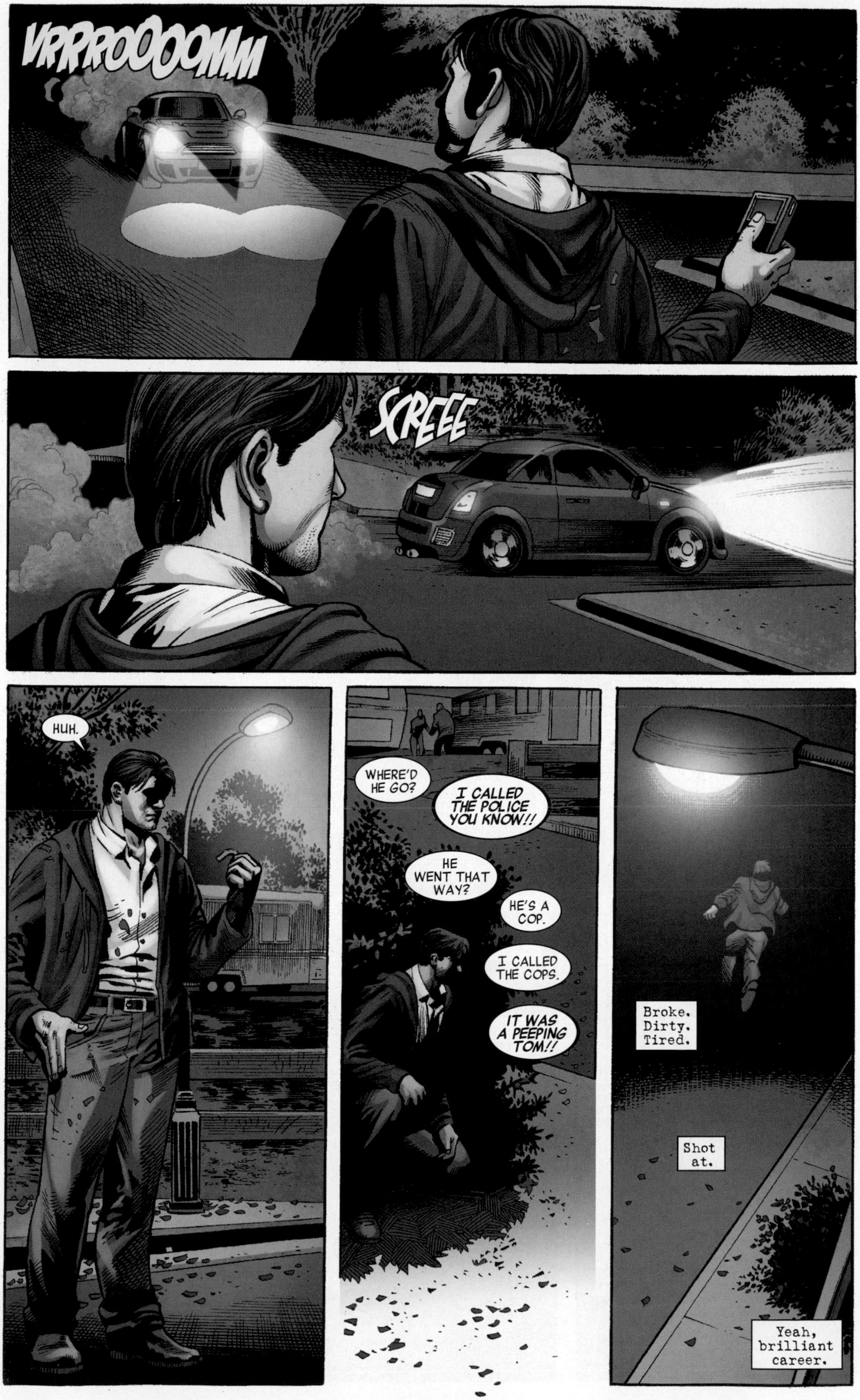
VRRROOOOMM
SCREEE
HUH.
WHERE'D HE GO?
I CALLED THE POLICE YOU KNOW!!
HE WENT THAT WAY?
HE'S A COP.
I CALLED THE COPS.
IT WAS A PEEPING TOM!!
Broke. Dirty. Tired.
Shot at.
Yeah, brilliant career.

But I have my footage.

Now all I have to do is break this poor lady's heart and she'll pay me for the--

Same car as last night.

Little turd of a car, but a car nonetheless.

They were chasing after our mysterious Jefferson Grout.

Maybe I led them to him.

Whoever he is.

And now they're up my butt.

But if I don't get my client's info from my office, I don't get PAID.

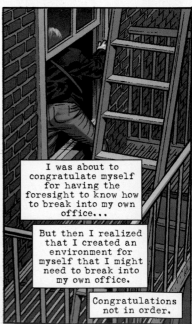

I was about to congratulate myself for having the foresight to know how to break into my own office...

But then I realized that I created an environment for myself that I might need to break into my own office.

Congratulations not in order.

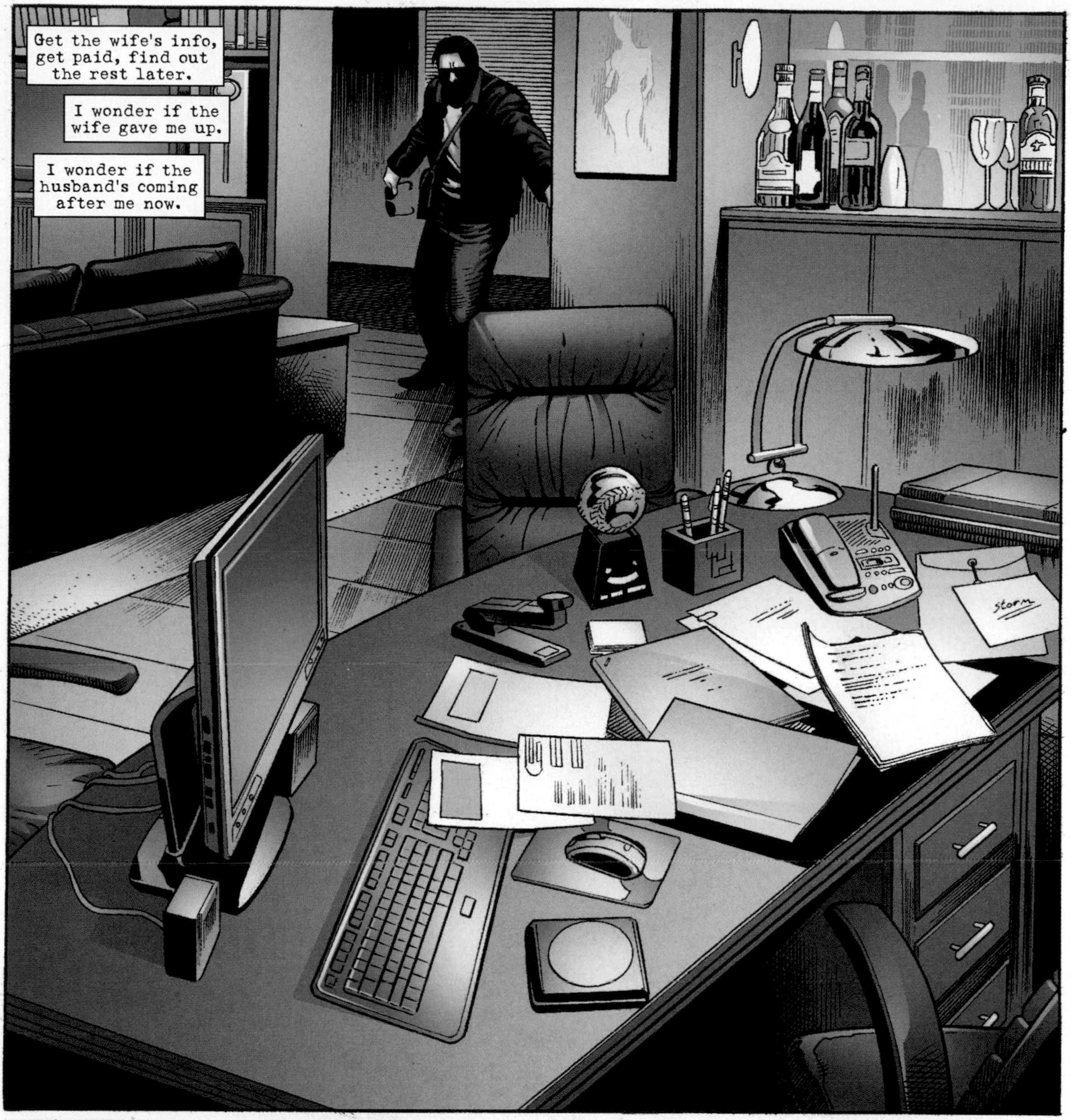
Get the wife's info, get paid, find out the rest later.
I wonder if the wife gave me up.
I wonder if the husband's coming after me now.
storm

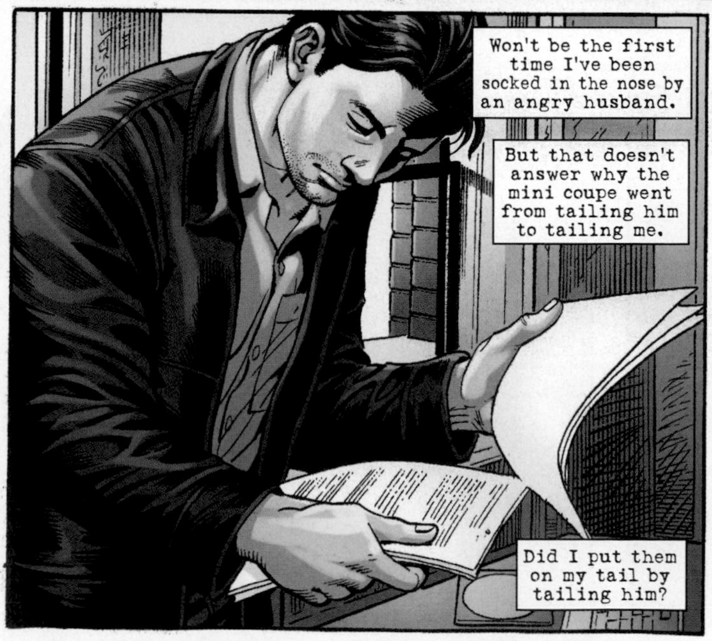
Won't be the first time I've been socked in the nose by an angry husband.
But that doesn't answer why the mini coupe went from tailing him to tailing me.
Did I put them on my tail by tailing him?

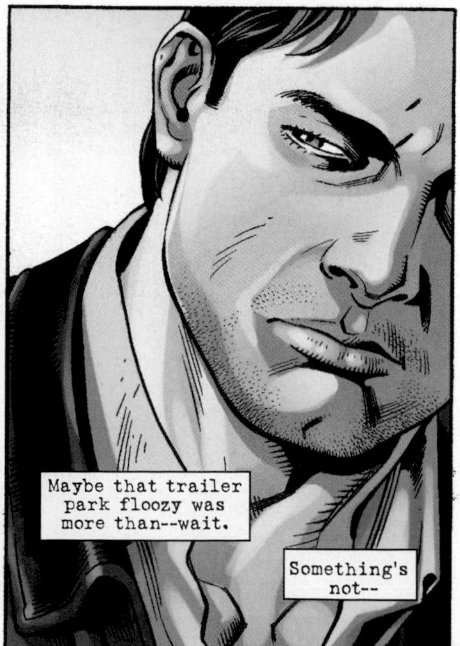
Maybe that trailer park floozy was more than--wait.
Something's not--

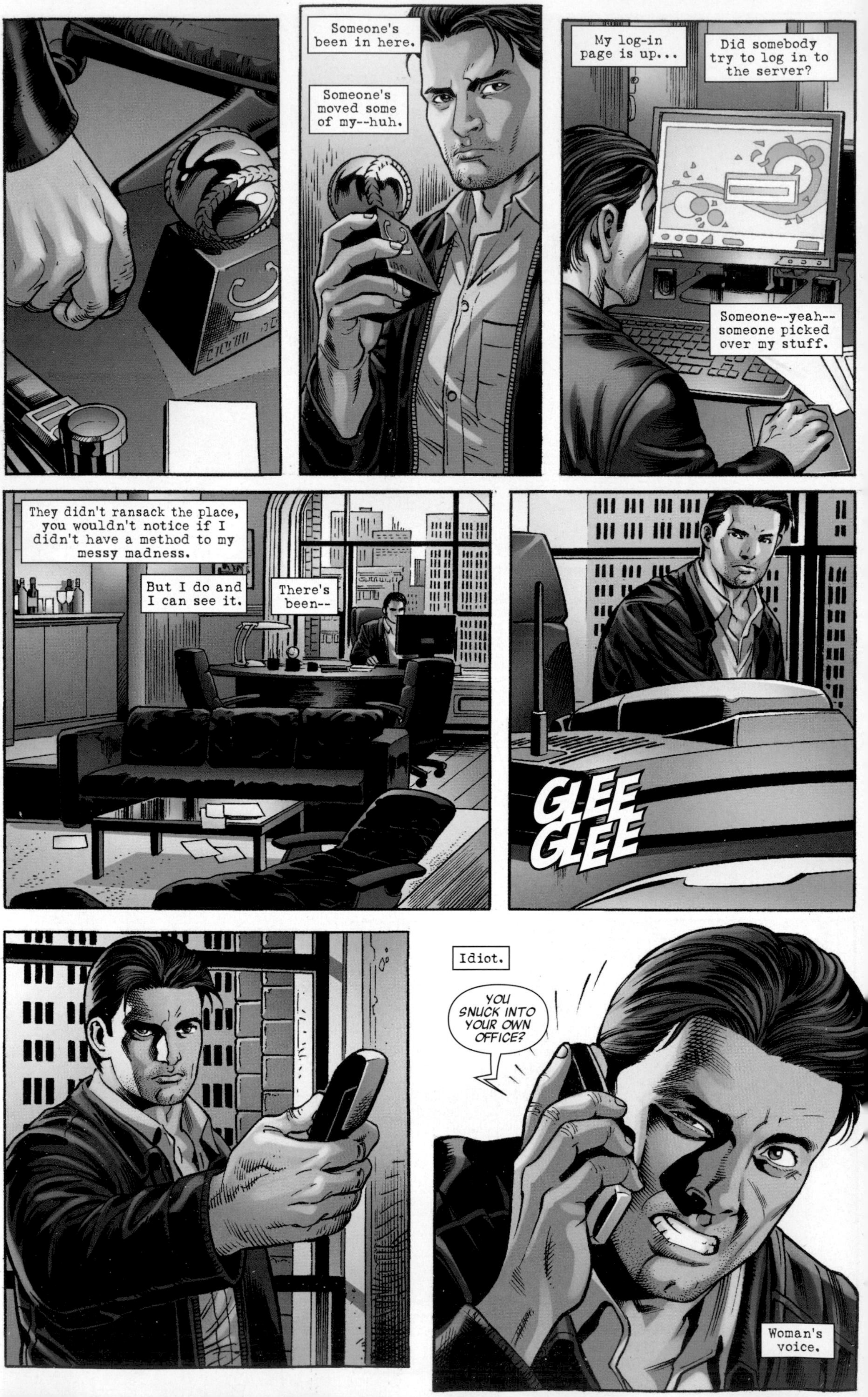
Someone's been in here.
Someone's moved some of my--huh.
My log-in page is up...
Did somebody try to log in to the server?
Someone--yeah--someone picked over my stuff.
They didn't ransack the place, you wouldn't notice if I didn't have a method to my messy madness.
But I do and I can see it.
There's been--
GLEE GLEE
Idiot.
YOU SNUCK INTO YOUR OWN OFFICE?
Woman's voice.

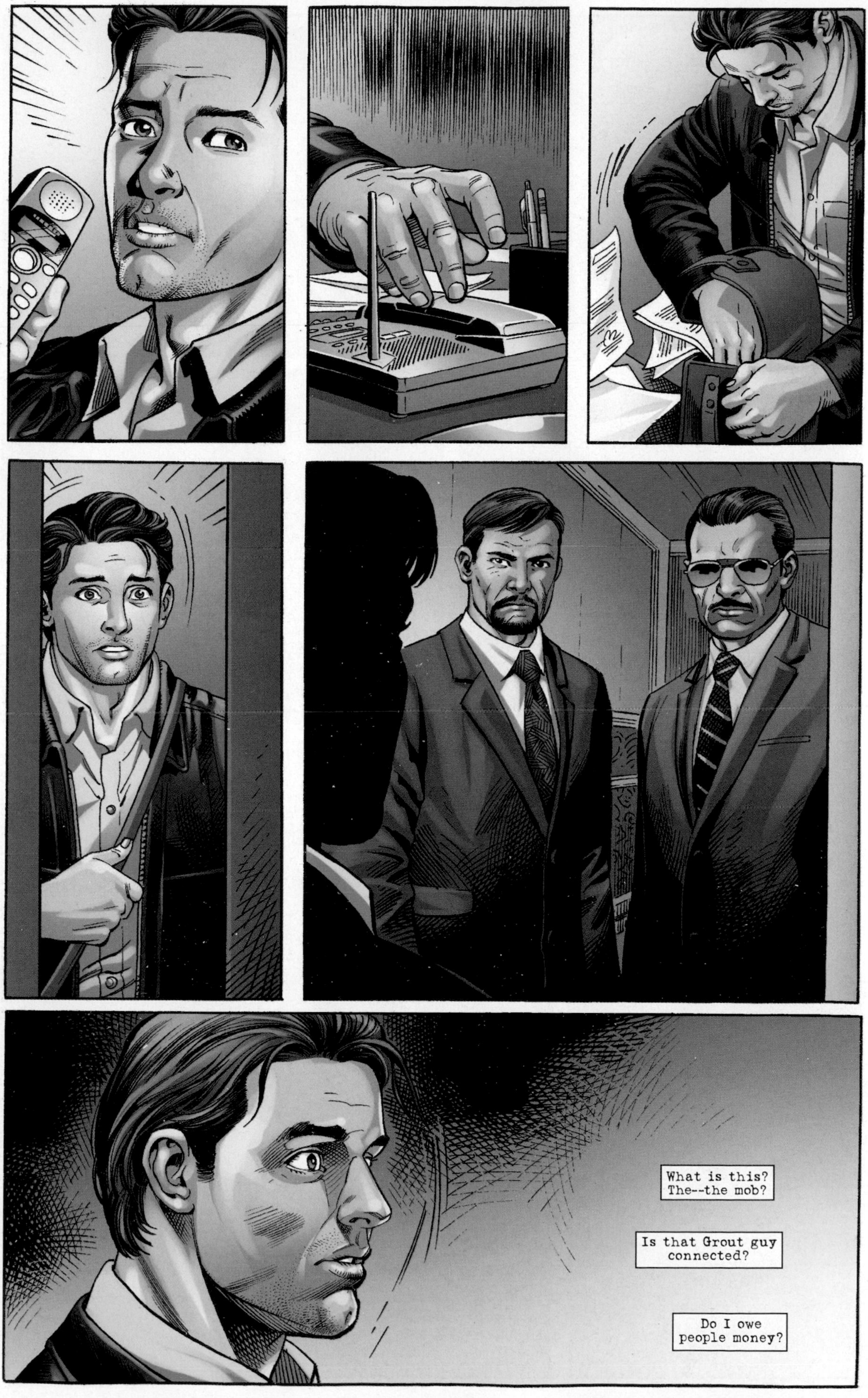
What is this? The--the mob?
Is that Grout guy connected?
Do I owe people money?

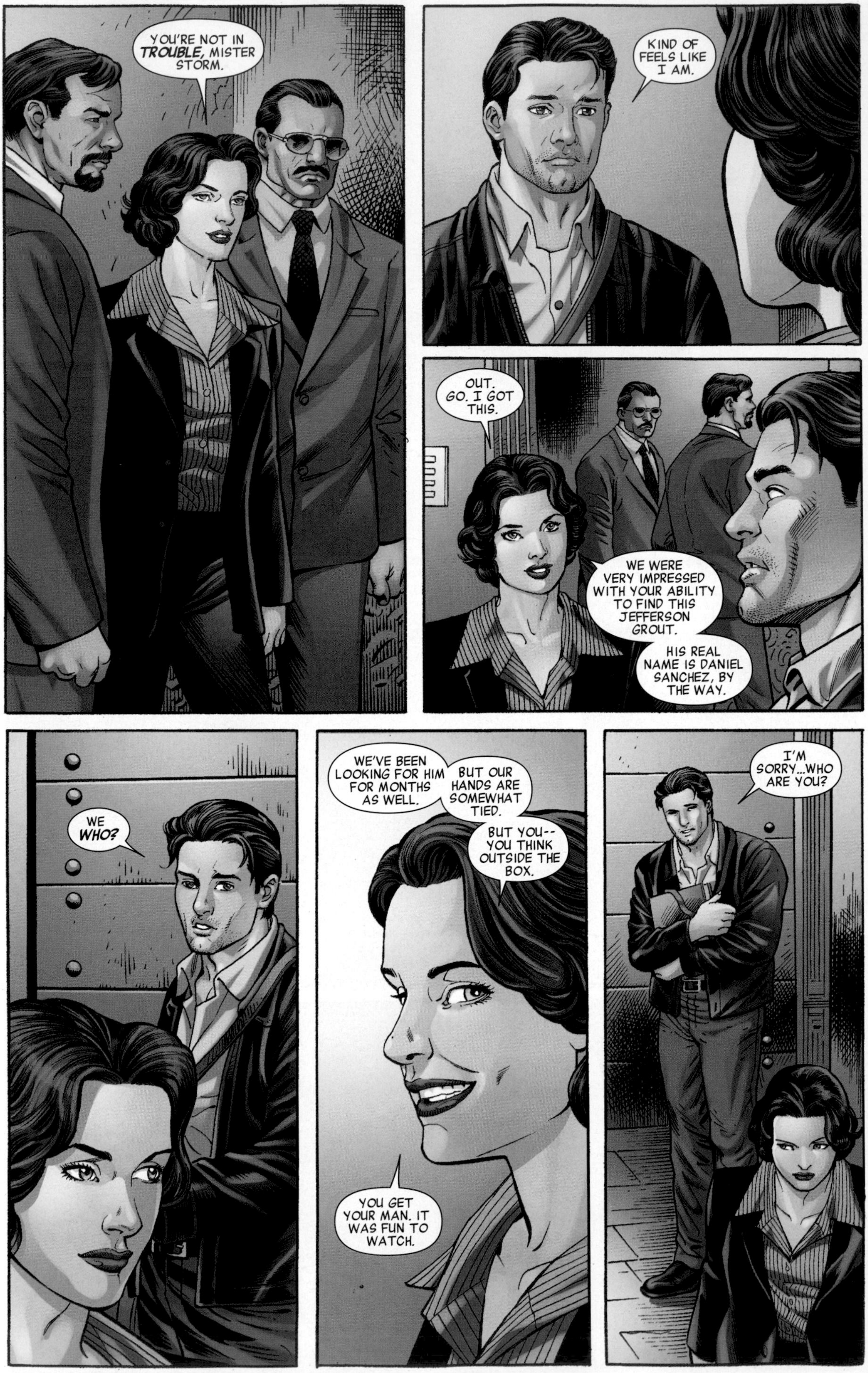
YOU'RE NOT IN TROUBLE, MISTER STORM.
KIND OF FEELS LIKE I AM.
OUT. GO. I GOT THIS.
WE WERE VERY IMPRESSED WITH YOUR ABILITY TO FIND THIS JEFFERSON GROUT.
HIS REAL NAME IS DANIEL SANCHEZ, BY THE WAY.
WE WHO?
WE'VE BEEN LOOKING FOR HIM FOR MONTHS AS WELL.
BUT OUR HANDS ARE SOMEWHAT TIED.
BUT YOU-- YOU THINK OUTSIDE THE BOX.
YOU GET YOUR MAN. IT WAS FUN TO WATCH.
I'M SORRY...WHO ARE YOU?

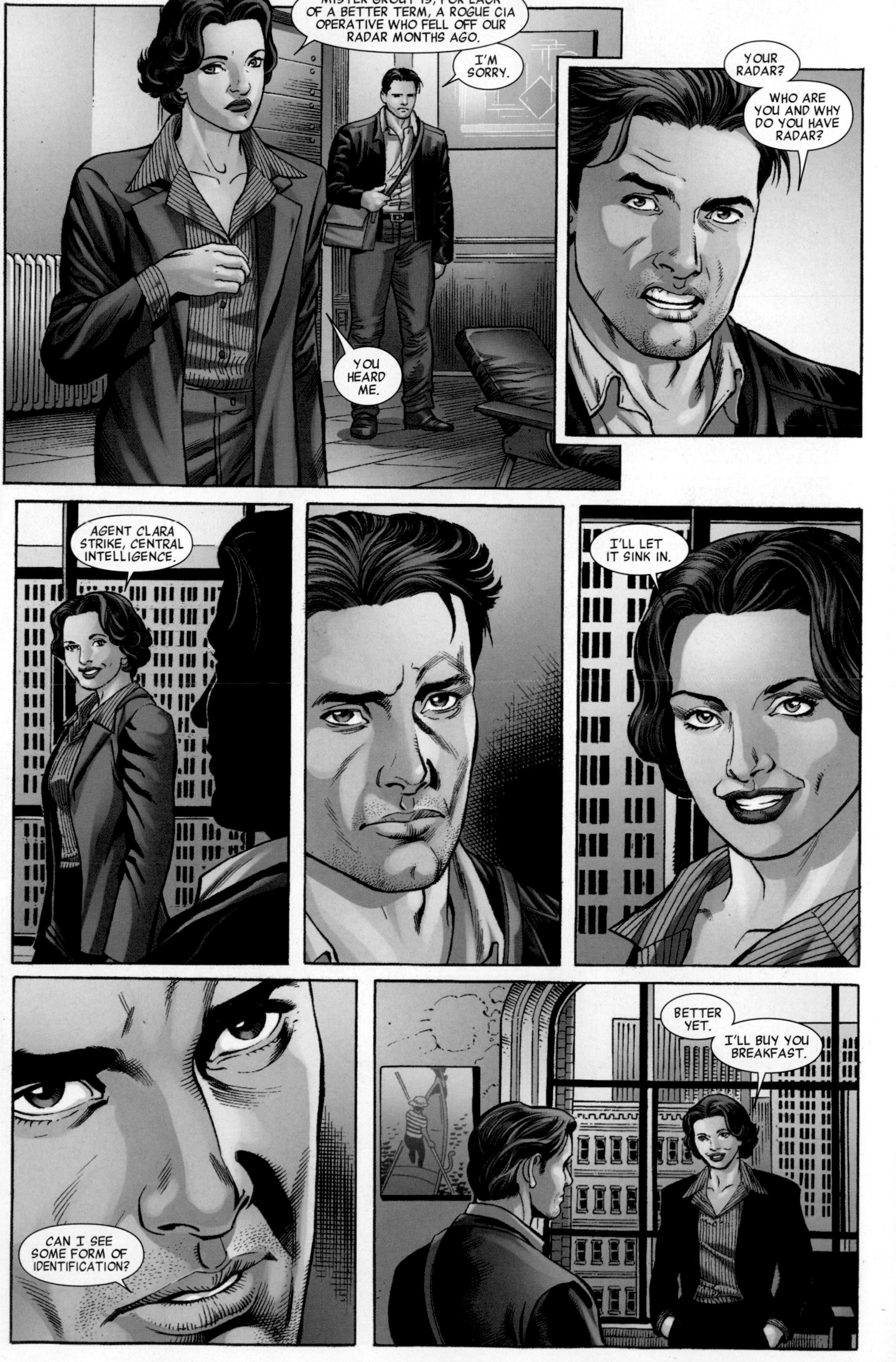

MISTER GROUT IS, FOR LACK OF A BETTER TERM, A ROGUE CIA OPERATIVE WHO FELL OFF OUR RADAR MONTHS AGO.
I'M SORRY.
YOU HEARD ME.
YOUR RADAR?
WHO ARE YOU AND WHY DO YOU HAVE RADAR?
AGENT CLARA STRIKE, CENTRAL INTELLIGENCE.
I'LL LET IT SINK IN.
CAN I SEE SOME FORM OF IDENTIFICATION?
BETTER YET.
I'LL BUY YOU BREAKFAST.

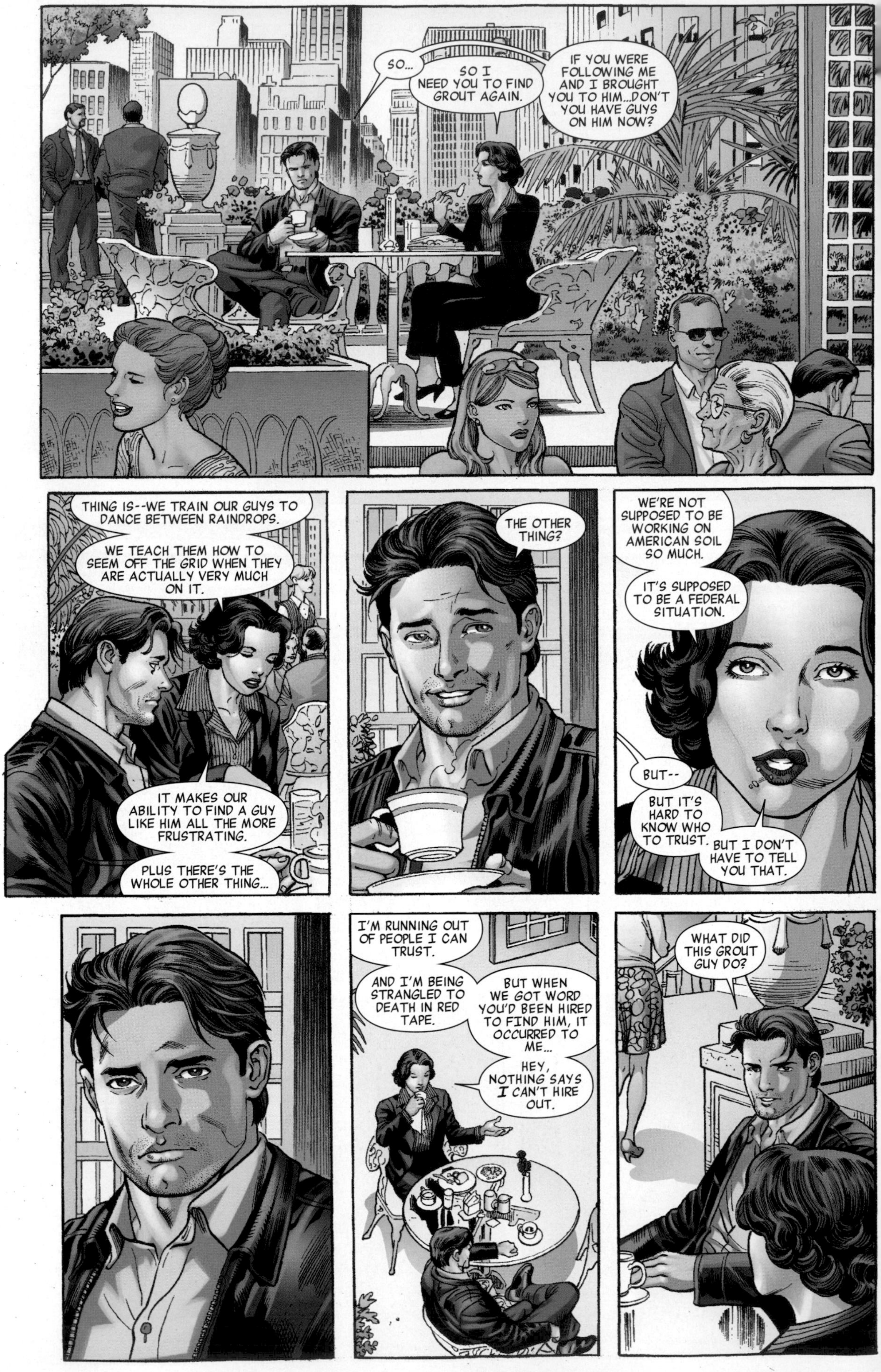
SO...
SO I NEED YOU TO FIND GROUT AGAIN.
IF YOU WERE FOLLOWING ME AND I BROUGHT YOU TO HIM...DON'T YOU HAVE GUYS ON HIM NOW?
THING IS--WE TRAIN OUR GUYS TO DANCE BETWEEN RAINDROPS.
WE TEACH THEM HOW TO SEEM OFF THE GRID WHEN THEY ARE ACTUALLY VERY MUCH ON IT.
IT MAKES OUR ABILITY TO FIND A GUY LIKE HIM ALL THE MORE FRUSTRATING.
PLUS THERE'S THE WHOLE OTHER THING...
THE OTHER THING?
WE'RE NOT SUPPOSED TO BE WORKING ON AMERICAN SOIL SO MUCH.
IT'S SUPPOSED TO BE A FEDERAL SITUATION.
BUT--
BUT IT'S HARD TO KNOW WHO TO TRUST.
BUT I DON'T HAVE TO TELL YOU THAT.
I'M RUNNING OUT OF PEOPLE I CAN TRUST.
AND I'M BEING STRANGLED TO DEATH IN RED TAPE.
BUT WHEN WE GOT WORD YOU'D BEEN HIRED TO FIND HIM, IT OCCURRED TO ME...
HEY, NOTHING SAYS I CAN'T HIRE OUT.
WHAT DID THIS GROUT GUY DO?

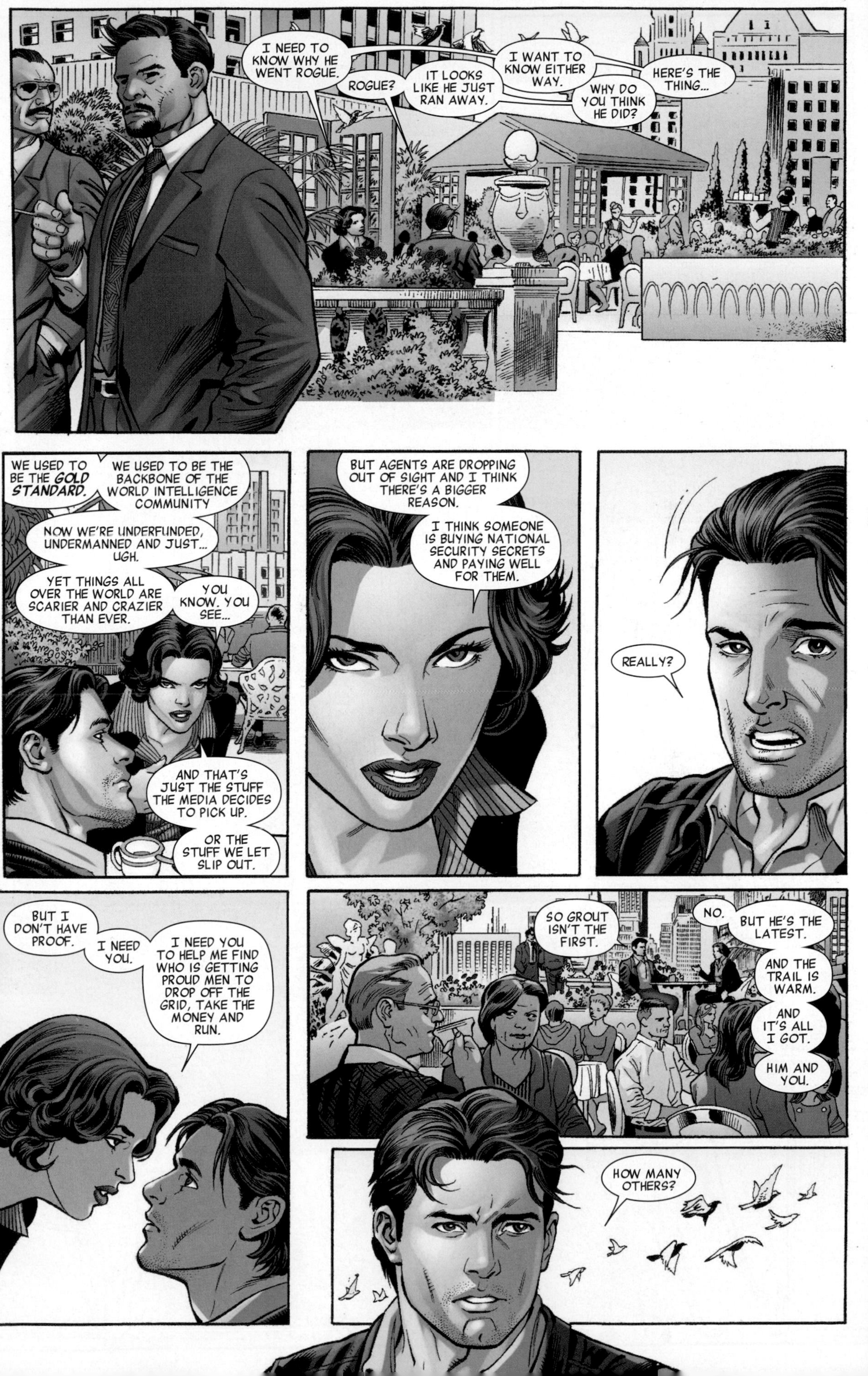

I NEED TO KNOW WHY HE WENT ROGUE.
ROGUE?
IT LOOKS LIKE HE JUST RAN AWAY.
I WANT TO KNOW EITHER WAY.
WHY DO YOU THINK HE DID?
HERE'S THE THING...
WE USED TO BE THE *GOLD STANDARD.*
WE USED TO BE THE BACKBONE OF THE WORLD INTELLIGENCE COMMUNITY
NOW WE'RE UNDERFUNDED, UNDERMANNED AND JUST... UGH.
YET THINGS ALL OVER THE WORLD ARE SCARIER AND CRAZIER THAN EVER.
YOU KNOW. YOU SEE...
AND THAT'S JUST THE STUFF THE MEDIA DECIDES TO PICK UP.
OR THE STUFF WE LET SLIP OUT.
BUT AGENTS ARE DROPPING OUT OF SIGHT AND I THINK THERE'S A BIGGER REASON.
I THINK SOMEONE IS BUYING NATIONAL SECURITY SECRETS AND PAYING WELL FOR THEM.
REALLY?
BUT I DON'T HAVE PROOF.
I NEED YOU.
I NEED YOU TO HELP ME FIND WHO IS GETTING PROUD MEN TO DROP OFF THE GRID, TAKE THE MONEY AND RUN.
SO GROUT ISN'T THE FIRST.
NO.
BUT HE'S THE LATEST.
AND THE TRAIL IS WARM.
AND IT'S ALL I GOT.
HIM AND YOU.
HOW MANY OTHERS?

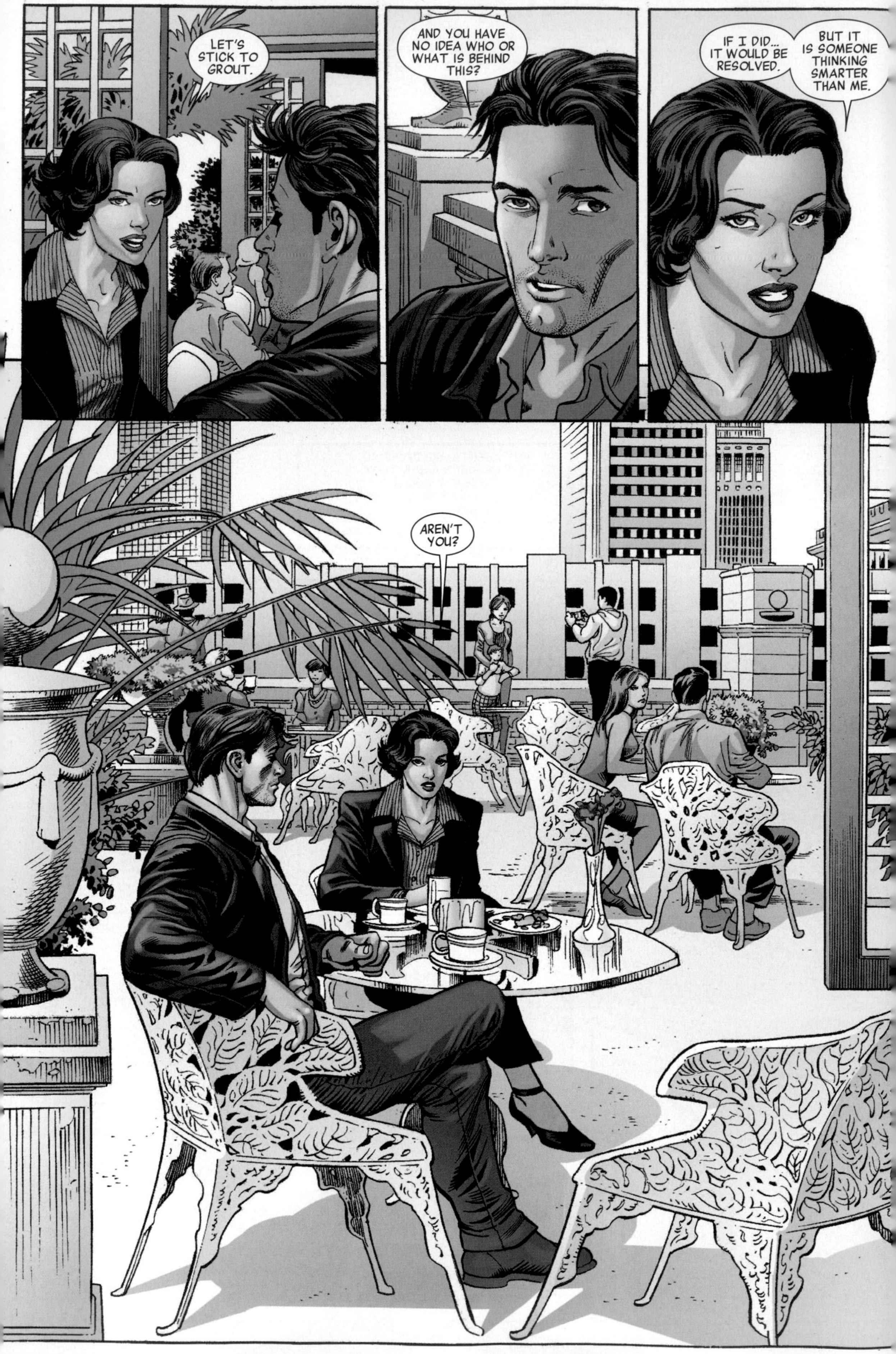
LET'S STICK TO GROUT.
AND YOU HAVE NO IDEA WHO OR WHAT IS BEHIND THIS?
IF I DID... IT WOULD BE RESOLVED.
BUT IT IS SOMEONE THINKING SMARTER THAN ME.
AREN'T YOU?

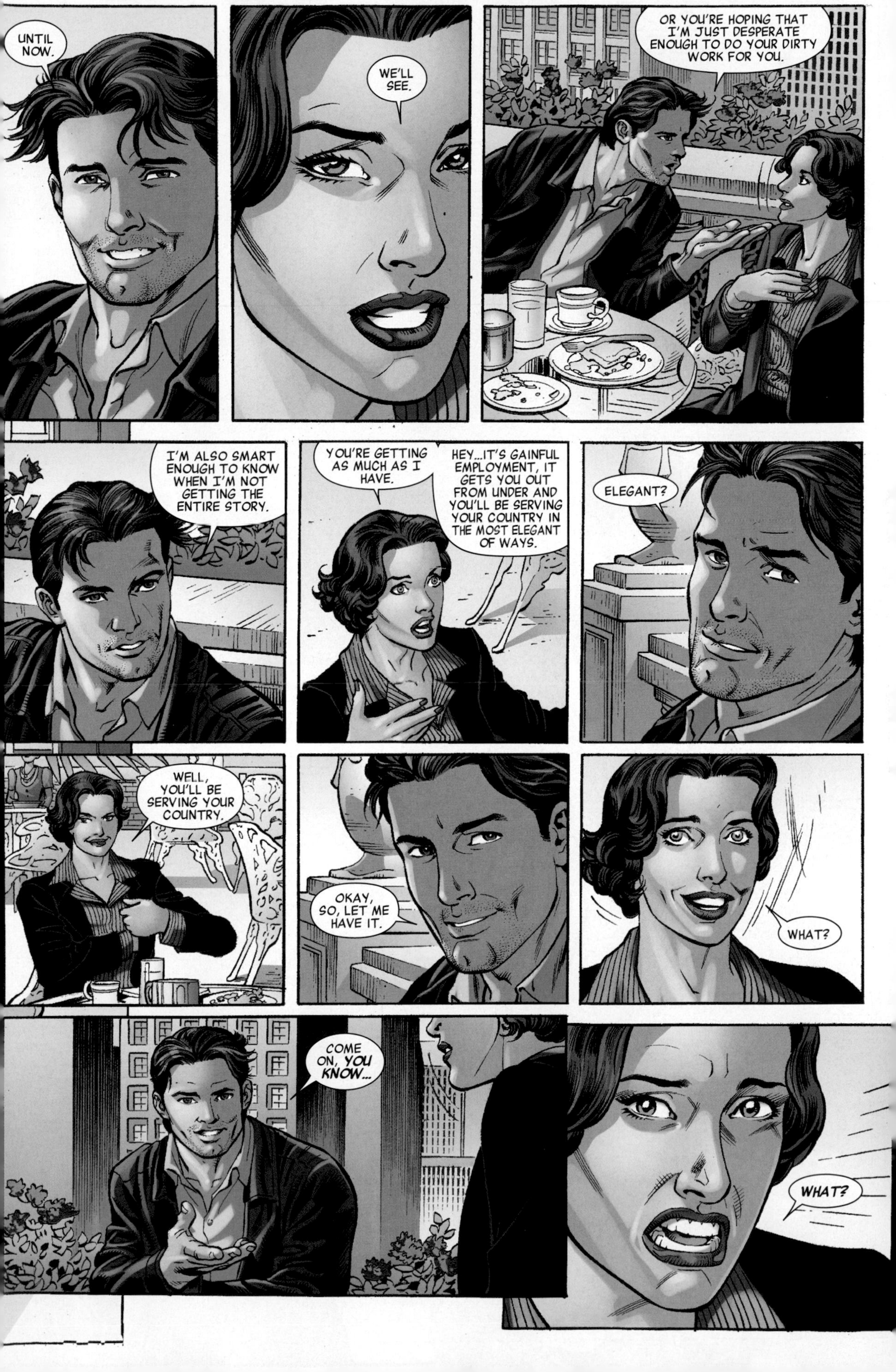
UNTIL NOW.
WE'LL SEE.
OR YOU'RE HOPING THAT I'M JUST DESPERATE ENOUGH TO DO YOUR DIRTY WORK FOR YOU.
I'M ALSO SMART ENOUGH TO KNOW WHEN I'M NOT GETTING THE ENTIRE STORY.
YOU'RE GETTING AS MUCH AS I HAVE.
HEY...IT'S GAINFUL EMPLOYMENT, IT GETS YOU OUT FROM UNDER AND YOU'LL BE SERVING YOUR COUNTRY IN THE MOST ELEGANT OF WAYS.
ELEGANT?
WELL, YOU'LL BE SERVING YOUR COUNTRY.
OKAY, SO, LET ME HAVE IT.
WHAT?
COME ON, YOU KNOW...
WHAT?

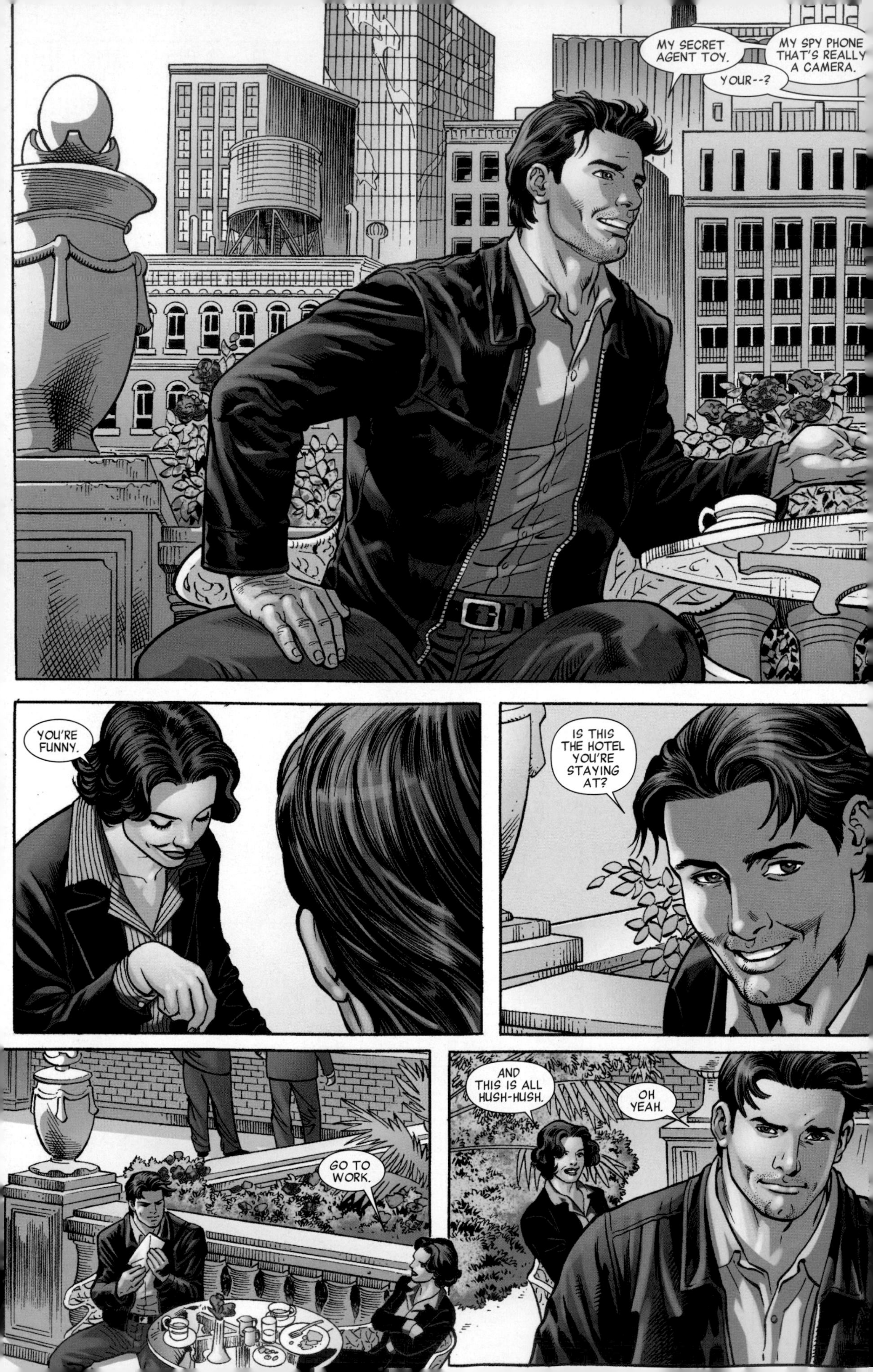
MY SECRET AGENT TOY.
YOUR--?
MY SPY PHONE THAT'S REALLY A CAMERA.
YOU'RE FUNNY.
IS THIS THE HOTEL YOU'RE STAYING AT?
GO TO WORK.
AND THIS IS ALL HUSH-HUSH.
OH YEAH.

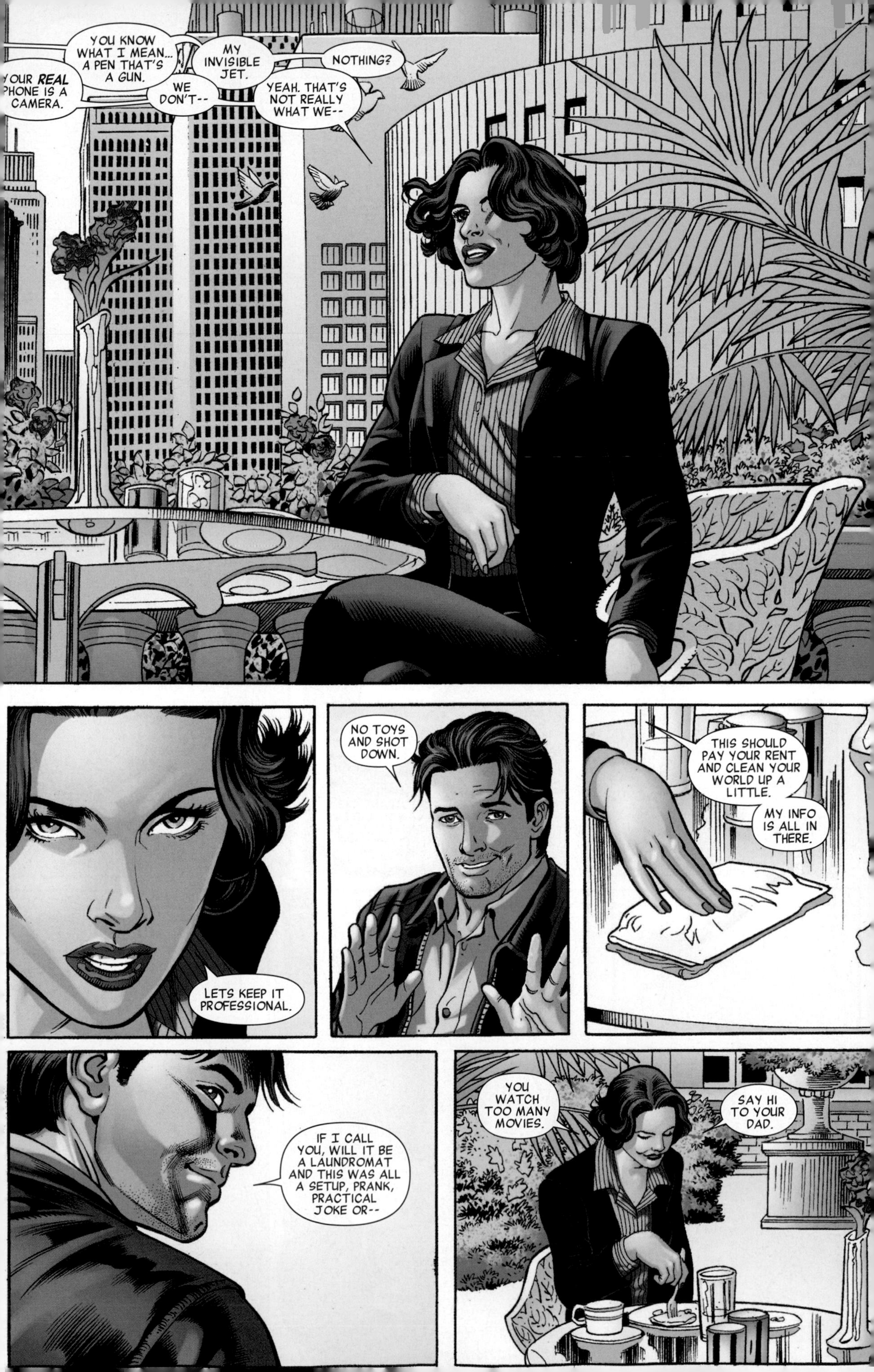
YOUR REAL PHONE IS A CAMERA.
YOU KNOW WHAT I MEAN... A PEN THAT'S A GUN.
WE DON'T--
MY INVISIBLE JET.
YEAH. THAT'S NOT REALLY WHAT WE--
NOTHING?
LETS KEEP IT PROFESSIONAL.
NO TOYS AND SHOT DOWN.
THIS SHOULD PAY YOUR RENT AND CLEAN YOUR WORLD UP A LITTLE.
MY INFO IS ALL IN THERE.
IF I CALL YOU, WILL IT BE A LAUNDROMAT AND THIS WAS ALL A SETUP, PRANK, PRACTICAL JOKE OR--
YOU WATCH TOO MANY MOVIES.
SAY HI TO YOUR DAD.

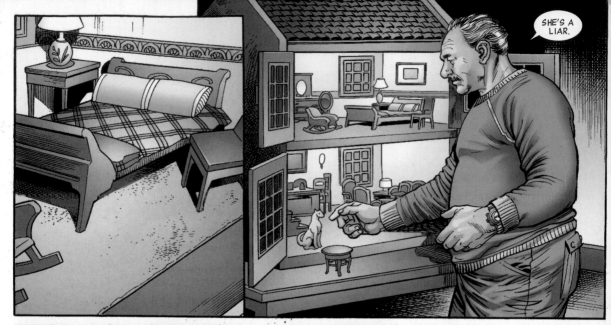

SHE'S A LIAR.

YOU SAY THAT ABOUT EVERY WOMAN, DAD.

AND I'M ALWAYS RIGHT.

SHE KNEW ABOUT YOU.

OF COURSE SHE DID.

SHE'S C.I.A. AND SHE'S A LIAR AND SHE'S WORKING YOU OVER.

WHAT DID SHE SAY?

SHE SAID SAY HELLO TO YOUR FATHER.

I ASSUME THAT MEANS SHE KNOWS YOU ARE EX-F.B.I. AND I COME TO YOU FOR MY HARD-TO-FINDS.

OF COURSE THAT'S WHAT SHE MEANT.

LEAVE TOWN.

WHY?

BECAUSE YOU'RE INVOLVED IN SOMETHING.

NO, I'M NOT.

WHAT THE HELL IS WRONG WITH YOU?

WHY CAN'T SHE BE HIRING ME BECAUSE I'M GOOD?

OH, OKAY... ON A SCALE OF ONE TO TEN...

WHAT?

HOW HOT IS SHE?

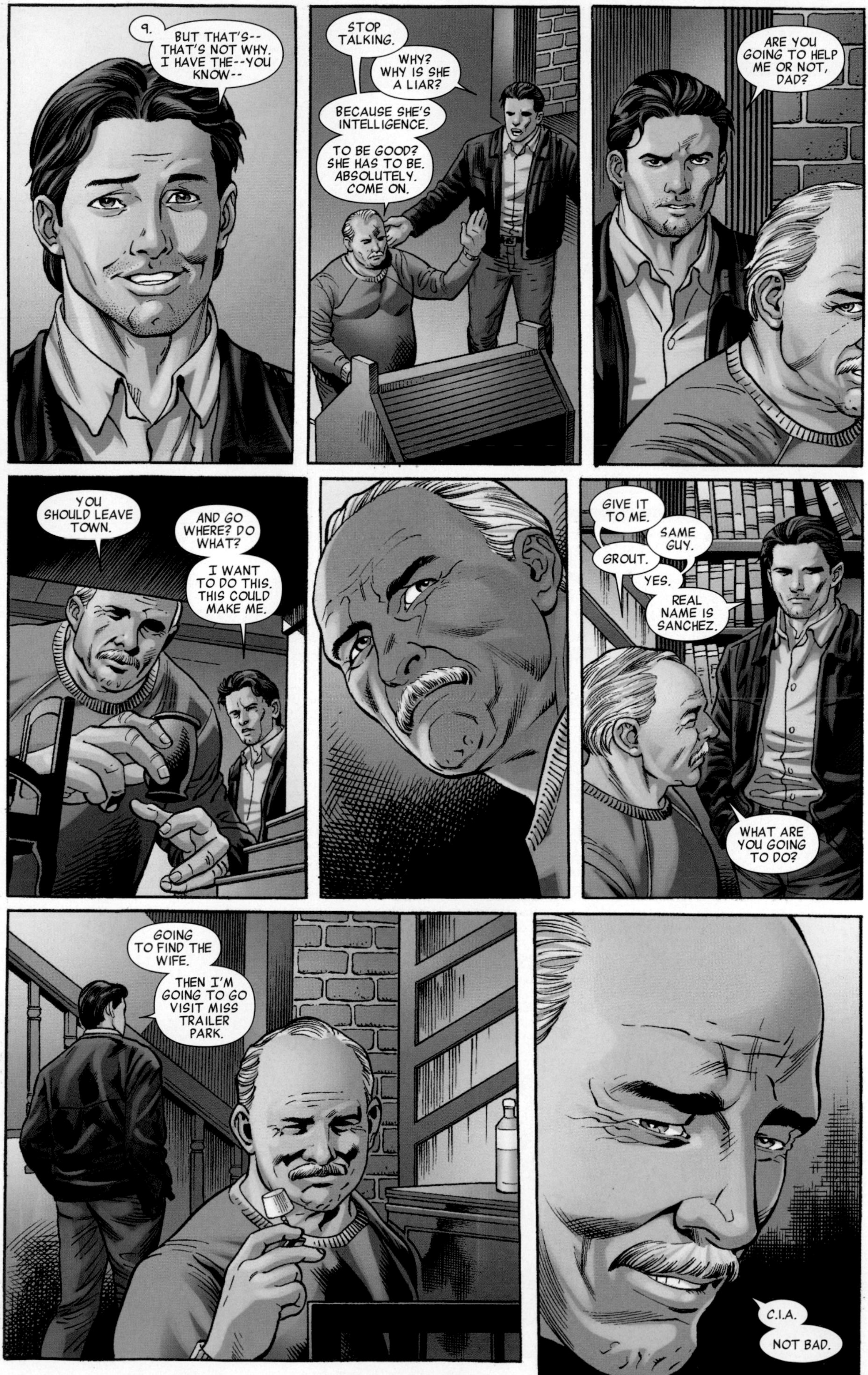
9.
BUT THAT'S--THAT'S NOT WHY. I HAVE THE--YOU KNOW--
STOP TALKING.
WHY? WHY IS SHE A LIAR?
BECAUSE SHE'S INTELLIGENCE.
TO BE GOOD? SHE HAS TO BE. ABSOLUTELY. COME ON.
ARE YOU GOING TO HELP ME OR NOT, DAD?
YOU SHOULD LEAVE TOWN.
AND GO WHERE? DO WHAT?
I WANT TO DO THIS. THIS COULD MAKE ME.
GIVE IT TO ME.
SAME GUY.
GROUT.
YES.
REAL NAME IS SANCHEZ.
WHAT ARE YOU GOING TO DO?
GOING TO FIND THE WIFE.
THEN I'M GOING TO GO VISIT MISS TRAILER PARK.
C.I.A.
NOT BAD.

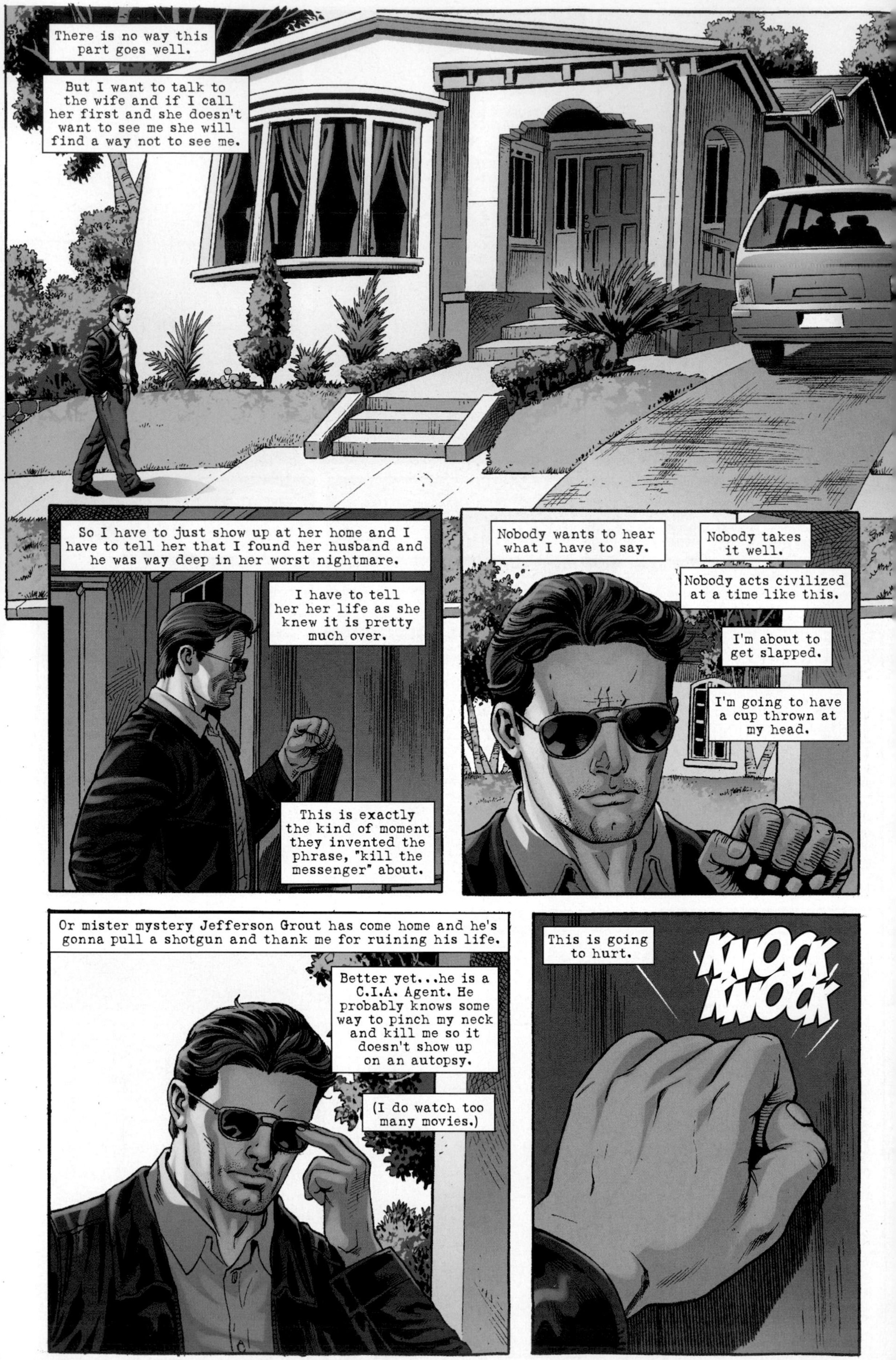
There is no way this part goes well.
But I want to talk to the wife and if I call her first and she doesn't want to see me she will find a way not to see me.
So I have to just show up at her home and I have to tell her that I found her husband and he was way deep in her worst nightmare.
I have to tell her her life as she knew it is pretty much over.
This is exactly the kind of moment they invented the phrase, "kill the messenger" about.
Nobody wants to hear what I have to say.
Nobody takes it well.
Nobody acts civilized at a time like this.
I'm about to get slapped.
I'm going to have a cup thrown at my head.
Or mister mystery Jefferson Grout has come home and he's gonna pull a shotgun and thank me for ruining his life.
Better yet...he is a C.I.A. Agent. He probably knows some way to pinch my neck and kill me so it doesn't show up on an autopsy.
(I do watch too many movies.)
This is going to hurt.
KNOCK KNOCK

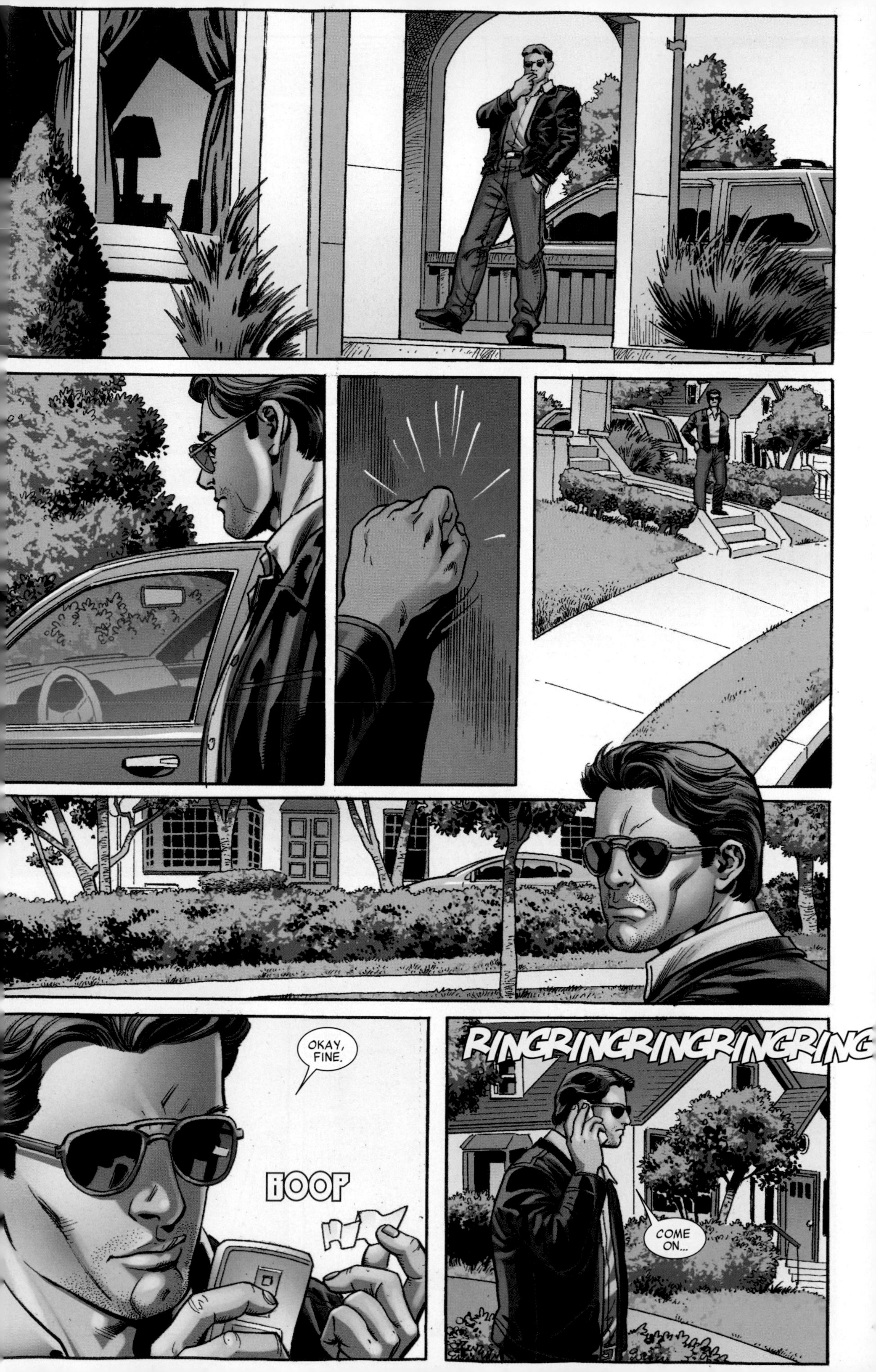
OKAY, FINE.
BOOP
RINGRINGRINGRINGRINGRING
COME ON...

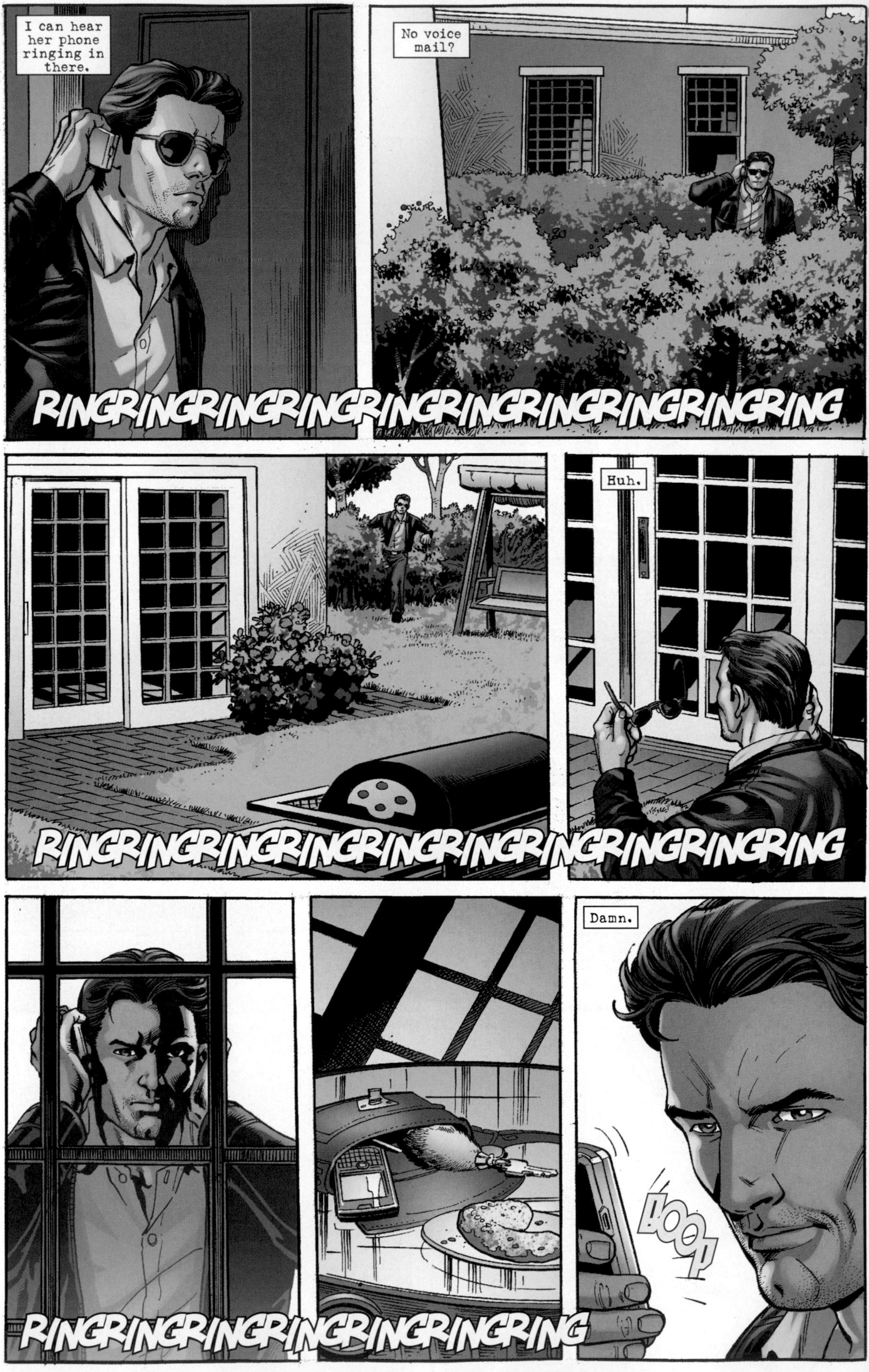
I can hear her phone ringing in there.
No voice mail?
RINGRINGRINGRINGRINGRINGRINGRINGRINGRING
RINGRINGRINGRINGRINGRINGRINGRINGRINGRING
Huh.
RINGRINGRINGRINGRINGRINGRINGRING
Damn.
BOOP

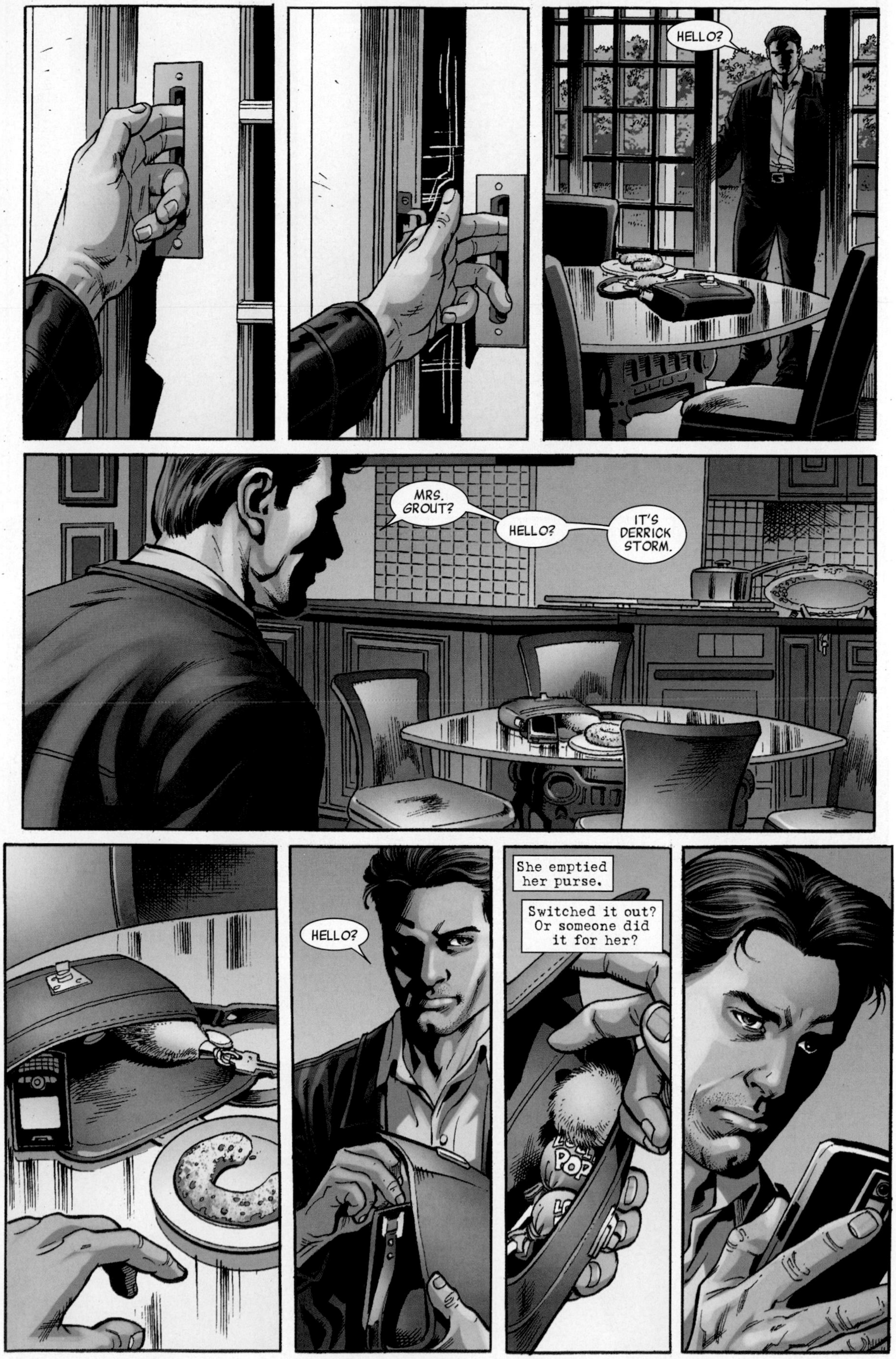
HELLO?
MRS. GROUT?
HELLO?
IT'S DERRICK STORM.
HELLO?
She emptied her purse.
Switched it out? Or someone did it for her?
POP

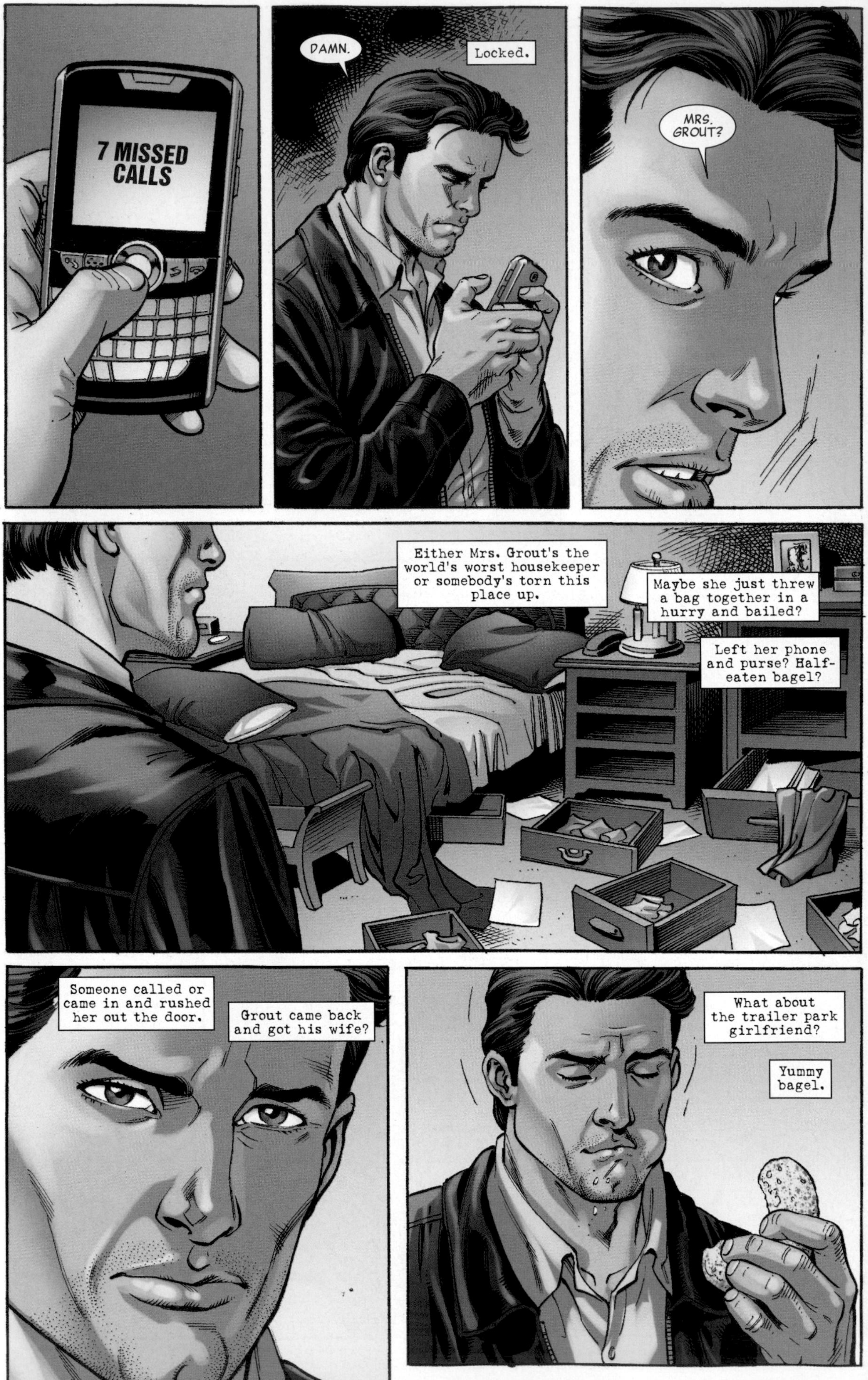
7 MISSED CALLS
DAMN.
Locked.
MRS. GROUT?
Either Mrs. Grout's the world's worst housekeeper or somebody's torn this place up.
Maybe she just threw a bag together in a hurry and bailed?
Left her phone and purse? Half-eaten bagel?
Someone called or came in and rushed her out the door.
Grout came back and got his wife?
What about the trailer park girlfriend?
Yummy bagel.

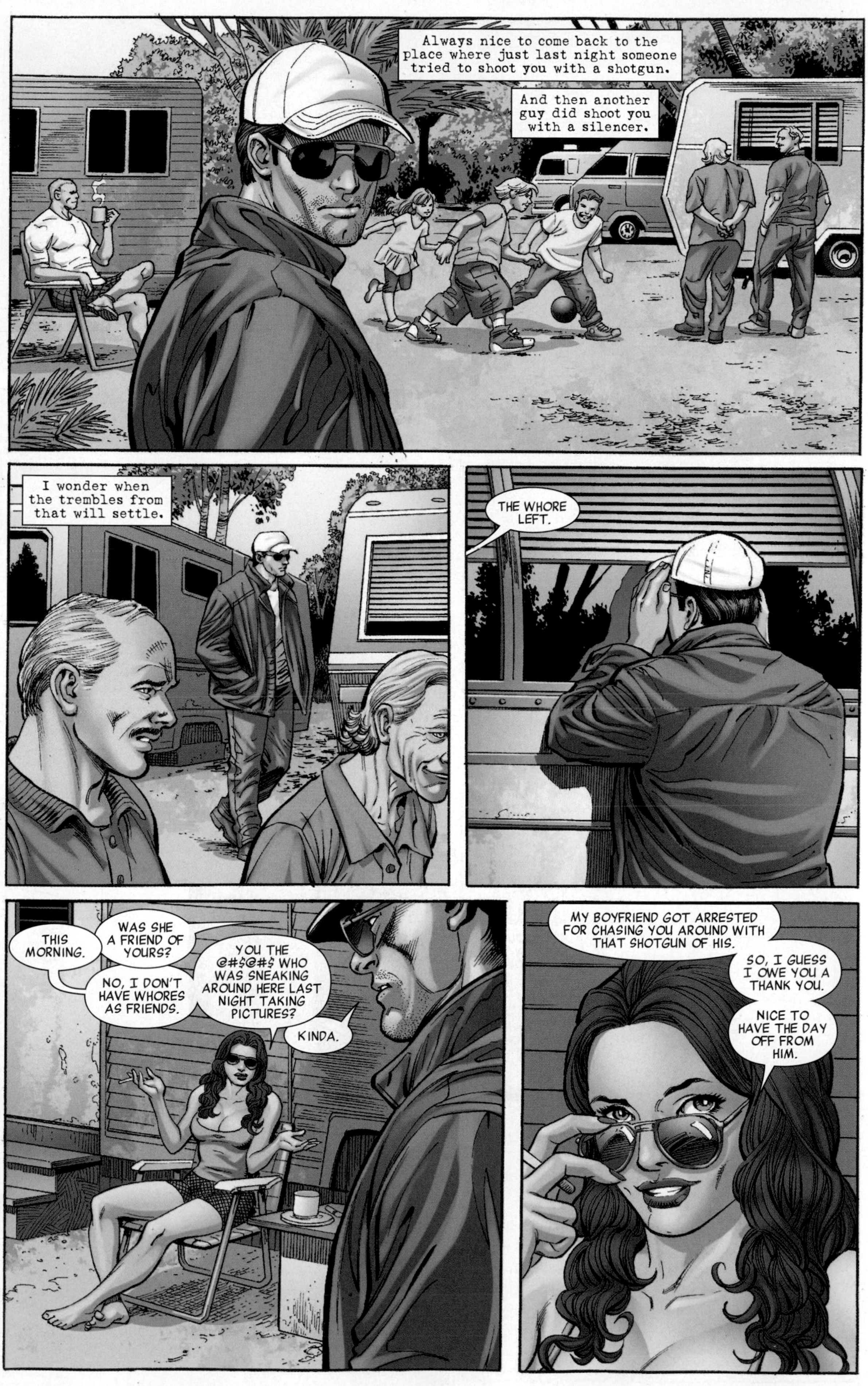
Always nice to come back to the place where just last night someone tried to shoot you with a shotgun.
And then another guy did shoot you with a silencer.
I wonder when the trembles from that will settle.
THE WHORE LEFT.
THIS MORNING.
WAS SHE A FRIEND OF YOURS?
NO, I DON'T HAVE WHORES AS FRIENDS.
YOU THE @#$@#$ WHO WAS SNEAKING AROUND HERE LAST NIGHT TAKING PICTURES?
KINDA.
MY BOYFRIEND GOT ARRESTED FOR CHASING YOU AROUND WITH THAT SHOTGUN OF HIS.
SO, I GUESS I OWE YOU A THANK YOU.
NICE TO HAVE THE DAY OFF FROM HIM.

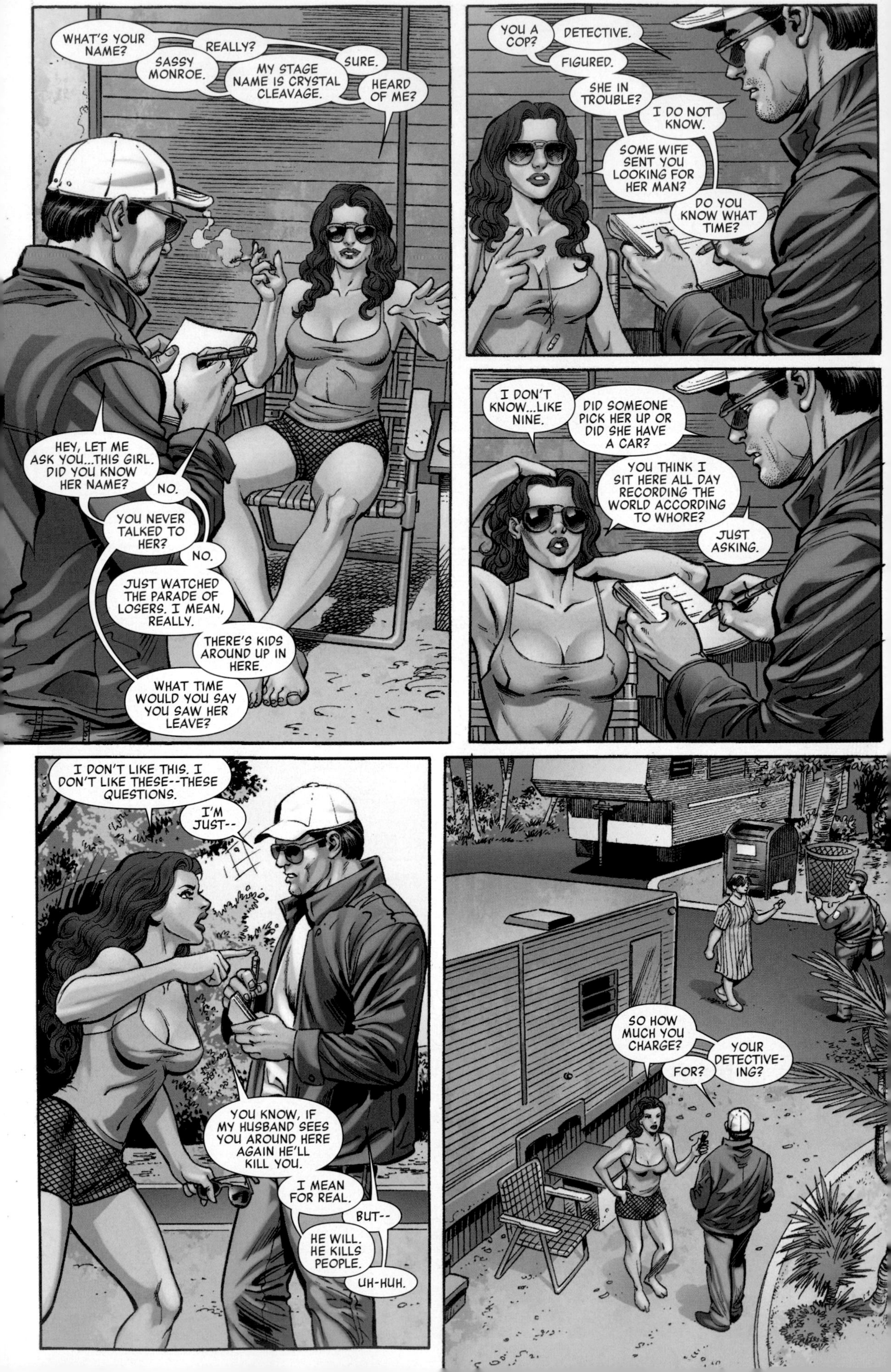
WHAT'S YOUR NAME?
REALLY?
SASSY MONROE.
MY STAGE NAME IS CRYSTAL CLEAVAGE.
SURE.
HEARD OF ME?
HEY, LET ME ASK YOU...THIS GIRL. DID YOU KNOW HER NAME?
NO.
YOU NEVER TALKED TO HER?
NO.
JUST WATCHED THE PARADE OF LOSERS. I MEAN, REALLY.
THERE'S KIDS AROUND UP IN HERE.
WHAT TIME WOULD YOU SAY YOU SAW HER LEAVE?
YOU A COP?
DETECTIVE.
FIGURED.
SHE IN TROUBLE?
I DO NOT KNOW.
SOME WIFE SENT YOU LOOKING FOR HER MAN?
DO YOU KNOW WHAT TIME?
I DON'T KNOW...LIKE NINE.
DID SOMEONE PICK HER UP OR DID SHE HAVE A CAR?
YOU THINK I SIT HERE ALL DAY RECORDING THE WORLD ACCORDING TO WHORE?
JUST ASKING.
I DON'T LIKE THIS. I DON'T LIKE THESE--THESE QUESTIONS.
I'M JUST--
YOU KNOW, IF MY HUSBAND SEES YOU AROUND HERE AGAIN HE'LL KILL YOU.
I MEAN FOR REAL.
BUT--
HE WILL. HE KILLS PEOPLE.
UH-HUH.
SO HOW MUCH YOU CHARGE?
FOR?
YOUR DETECTIVE-ING?

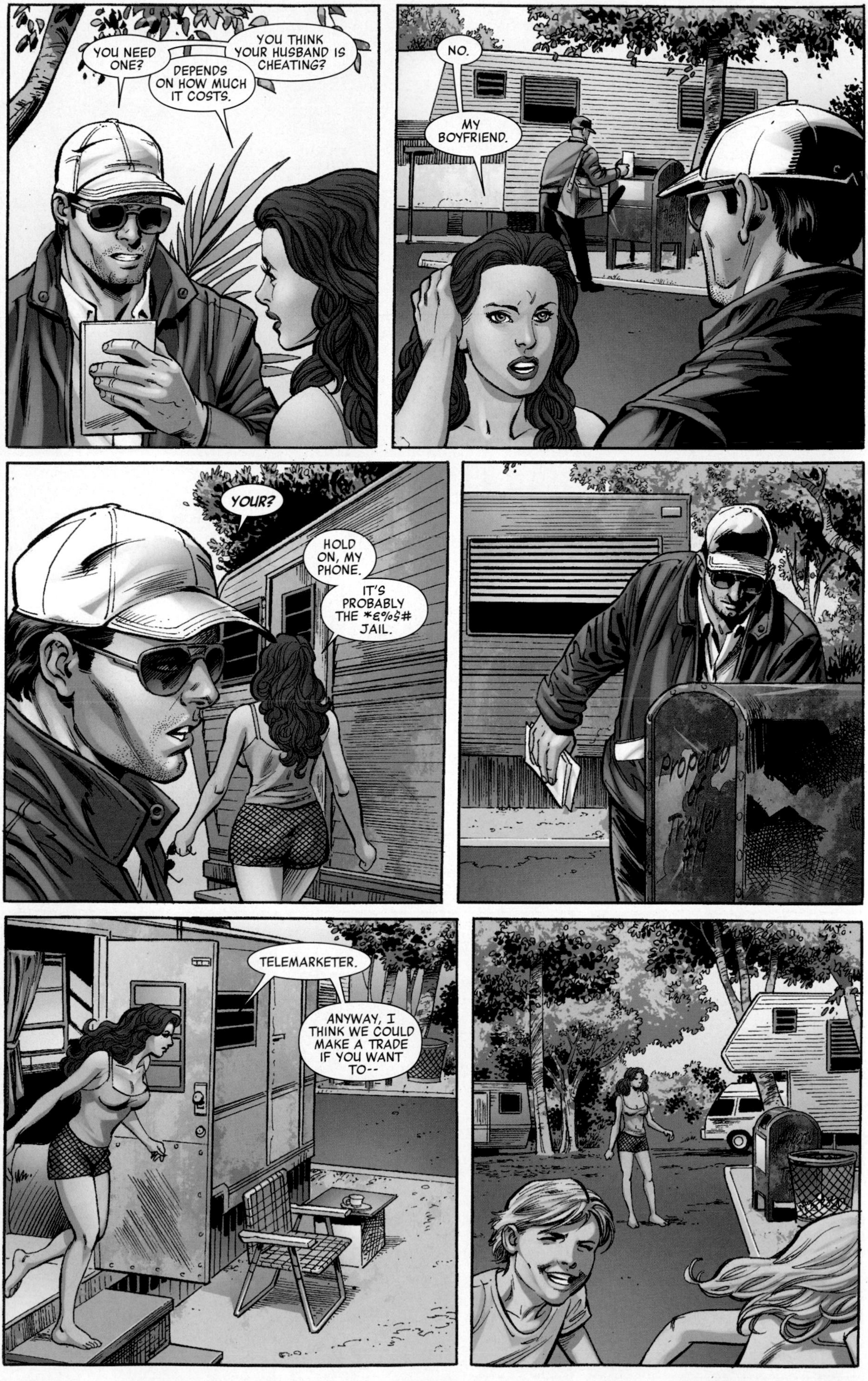
YOU NEED ONE?
YOU THINK YOUR HUSBAND IS CHEATING?
DEPENDS ON HOW MUCH IT COSTS.
NO.
MY BOYFRIEND.
YOUR?
HOLD ON, MY PHONE.
IT'S PROBABLY THE *£%$# JAIL.
Property of Trailer
TELEMARKETER.
ANYWAY, I THINK WE COULD MAKE A TRADE IF YOU WANT TO--

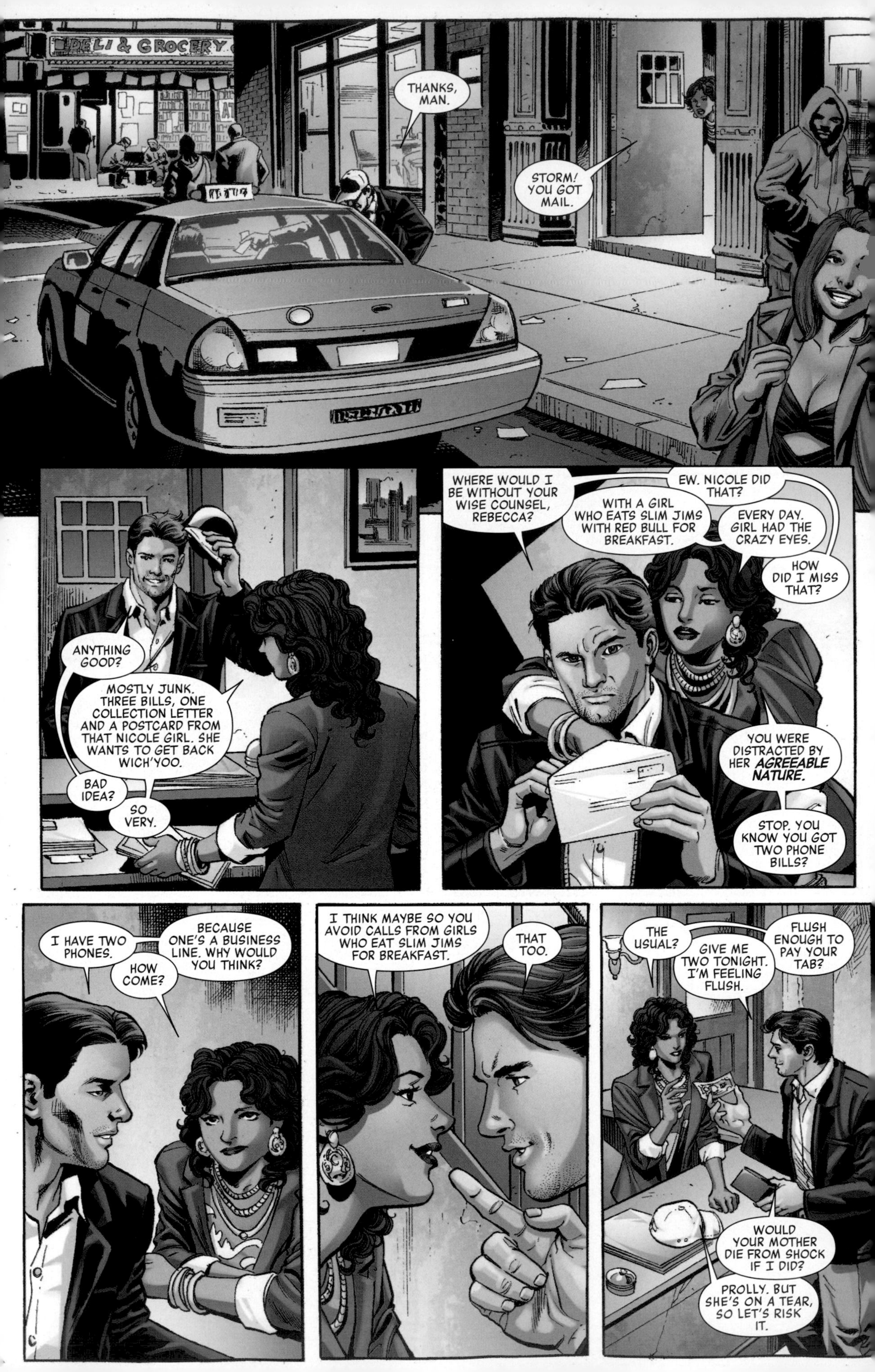
DELI & GROCERY
THANKS, MAN.
STORM! YOU GOT MAIL.
ANYTHING GOOD?
MOSTLY JUNK. THREE BILLS, ONE COLLECTION LETTER AND A POSTCARD FROM THAT NICOLE GIRL. SHE WANTS TO GET BACK WICH'YOO.
BAD IDEA?
SO VERY.
WHERE WOULD I BE WITHOUT YOUR WISE COUNSEL, REBECCA?
WITH A GIRL WHO EATS SLIM JIMS WITH RED BULL FOR BREAKFAST.
EW. NICOLE DID THAT?
EVERY DAY. GIRL HAD THE CRAZY EYES.
HOW DID I MISS THAT?
YOU WERE DISTRACTED BY HER AGREEABLE NATURE.
STOP. YOU KNOW YOU GOT TWO PHONE BILLS?
I HAVE TWO PHONES.
HOW COME?
BECAUSE ONE'S A BUSINESS LINE. WHY WOULD YOU THINK?
I THINK MAYBE SO YOU AVOID CALLS FROM GIRLS WHO EAT SLIM JIMS FOR BREAKFAST.
THAT TOO.
THE USUAL?
GIVE ME TWO TONIGHT. I'M FEELING FLUSH.
FLUSH ENOUGH TO PAY YOUR TAB?
WOULD YOUR MOTHER DIE FROM SHOCK IF I DID?
PROLLY. BUT SHE'S ON A TEAR, SO LET'S RISK IT.

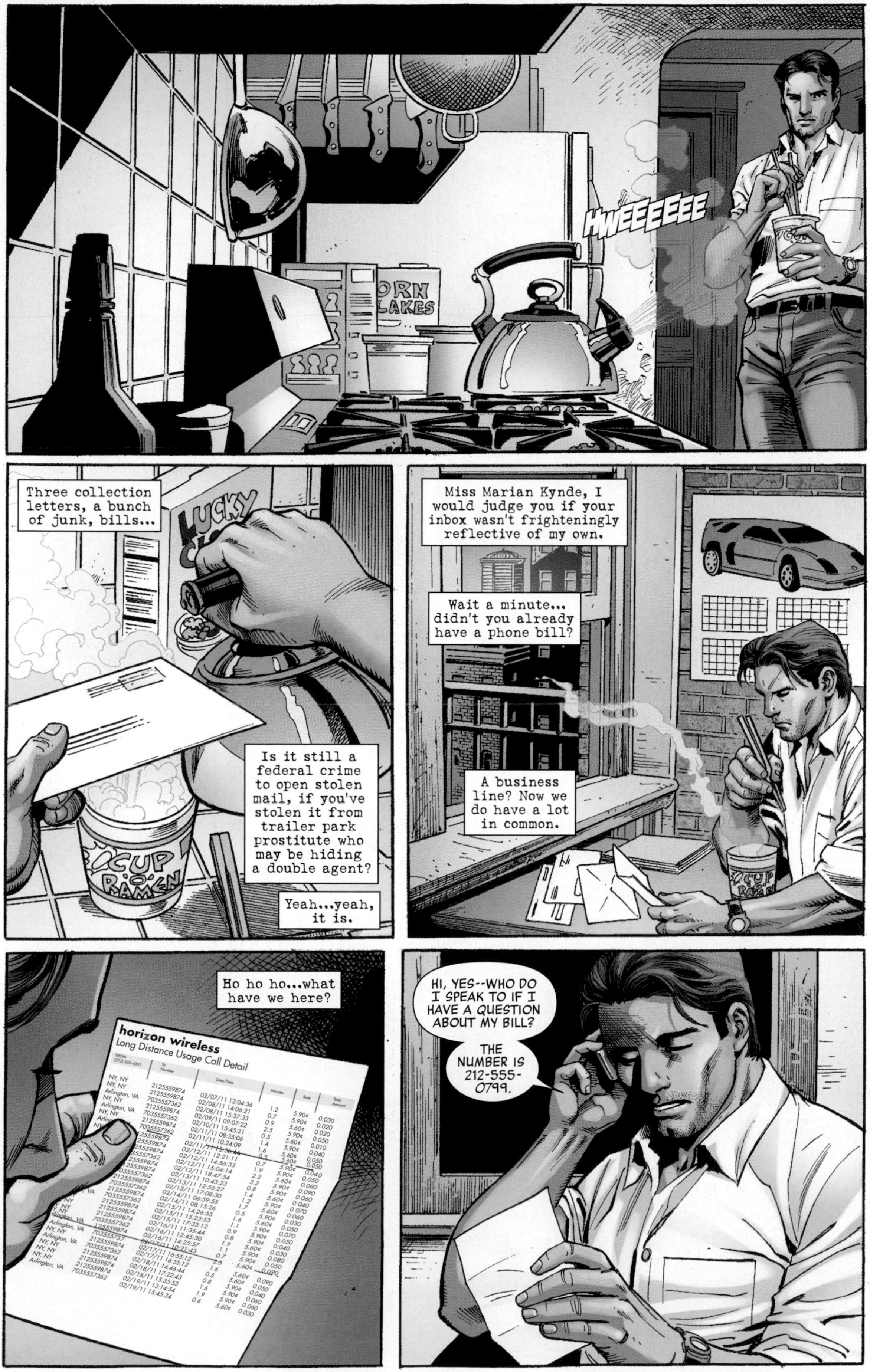
HWEEEEEE
CORN FLAKES
Three collection letters, a bunch of junk, bills...
Is it still a federal crime to open stolen mail, if you've stolen it from trailer park prostitute who may be hiding a double agent?
Yeah...yeah, it is.
CUP O' RAMEN
Miss Marian Kynde, I would judge you if your inbox wasn't frighteningly reflective of my own.
Wait a minute... didn't you already have a phone bill?
A business line? Now we do have a lot in common.
Ho ho ho...what have we here?
horizon wireless
Long Distance Usage Call Detail
HI, YES--WHO DO I SPEAK TO IF I HAVE A QUESTION ABOUT MY BILL?
THE NUMBER IS 212-555-0799.

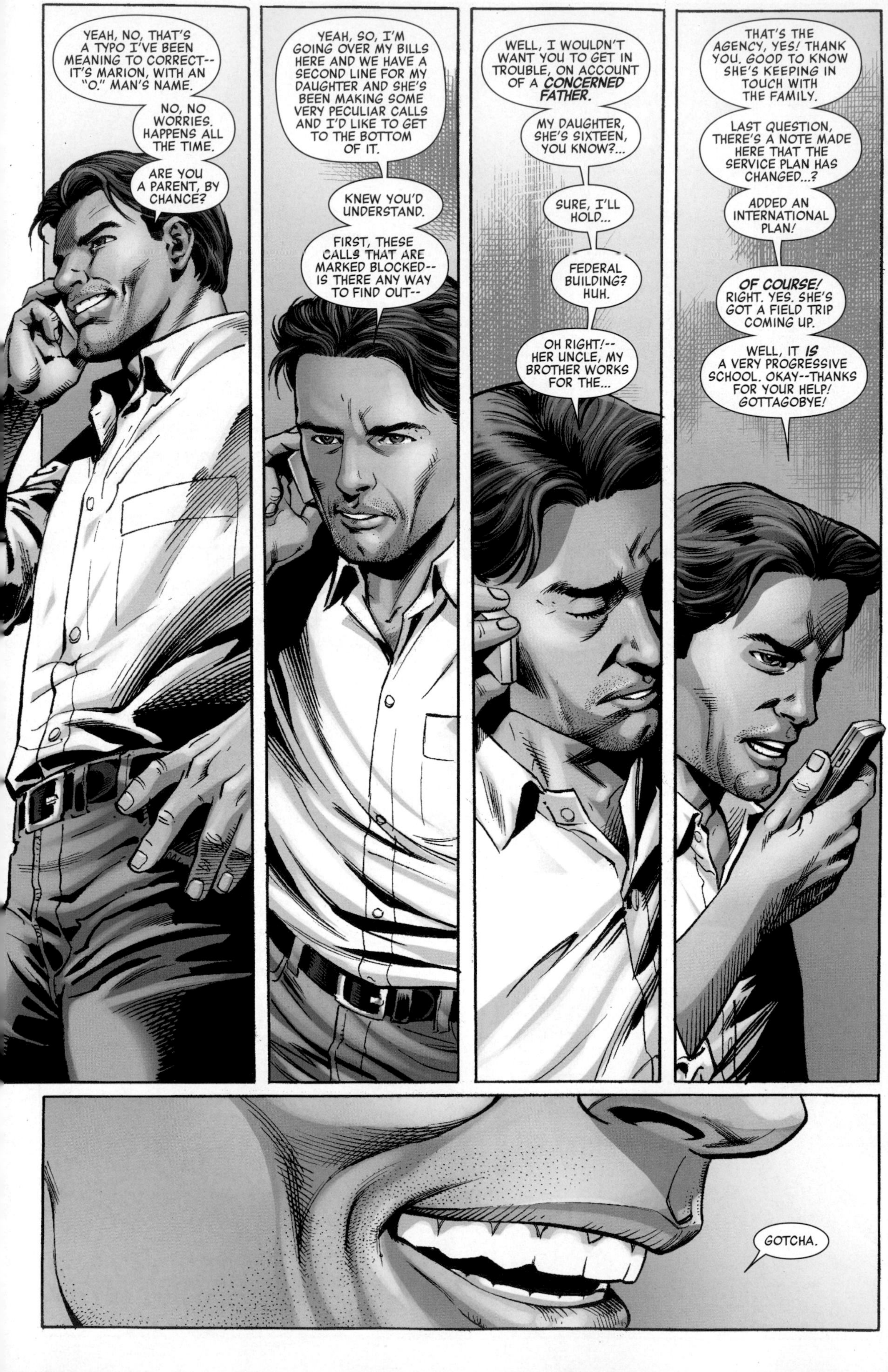
YEAH, NO, THAT'S A TYPO I'VE BEEN MEANING TO CORRECT-- IT'S MARION, WITH AN "O." MAN'S NAME.
NO, NO WORRIES. HAPPENS ALL THE TIME.
ARE YOU A PARENT, BY CHANCE?
YEAH, SO, I'M GOING OVER MY BILLS HERE AND WE HAVE A SECOND LINE FOR MY DAUGHTER AND SHE'S BEEN MAKING SOME VERY PECULIAR CALLS AND I'D LIKE TO GET TO THE BOTTOM OF IT.
KNEW YOU'D UNDERSTAND.
FIRST, THESE CALLS THAT ARE MARKED BLOCKED-- IS THERE ANY WAY TO FIND OUT--
WELL, I WOULDN'T WANT YOU TO GET IN TROUBLE, ON ACCOUNT OF A CONCERNED FATHER.
MY DAUGHTER, SHE'S SIXTEEN, YOU KNOW?...
SURE, I'LL HOLD...
FEDERAL BUILDING? HUH.
OH RIGHT!-- HER UNCLE, MY BROTHER WORKS FOR THE...
THAT'S THE AGENCY, YES! THANK YOU. GOOD TO KNOW SHE'S KEEPING IN TOUCH WITH THE FAMILY.
LAST QUESTION, THERE'S A NOTE MADE HERE THAT THE SERVICE PLAN HAS CHANGED...?
ADDED AN INTERNATIONAL PLAN!
OF COURSE! RIGHT. YES. SHE'S GOT A FIELD TRIP COMING UP.
WELL, IT IS A VERY PROGRESSIVE SCHOOL. OKAY--THANKS FOR YOUR HELP! GOTTAGOBYE!
GOTCHA.

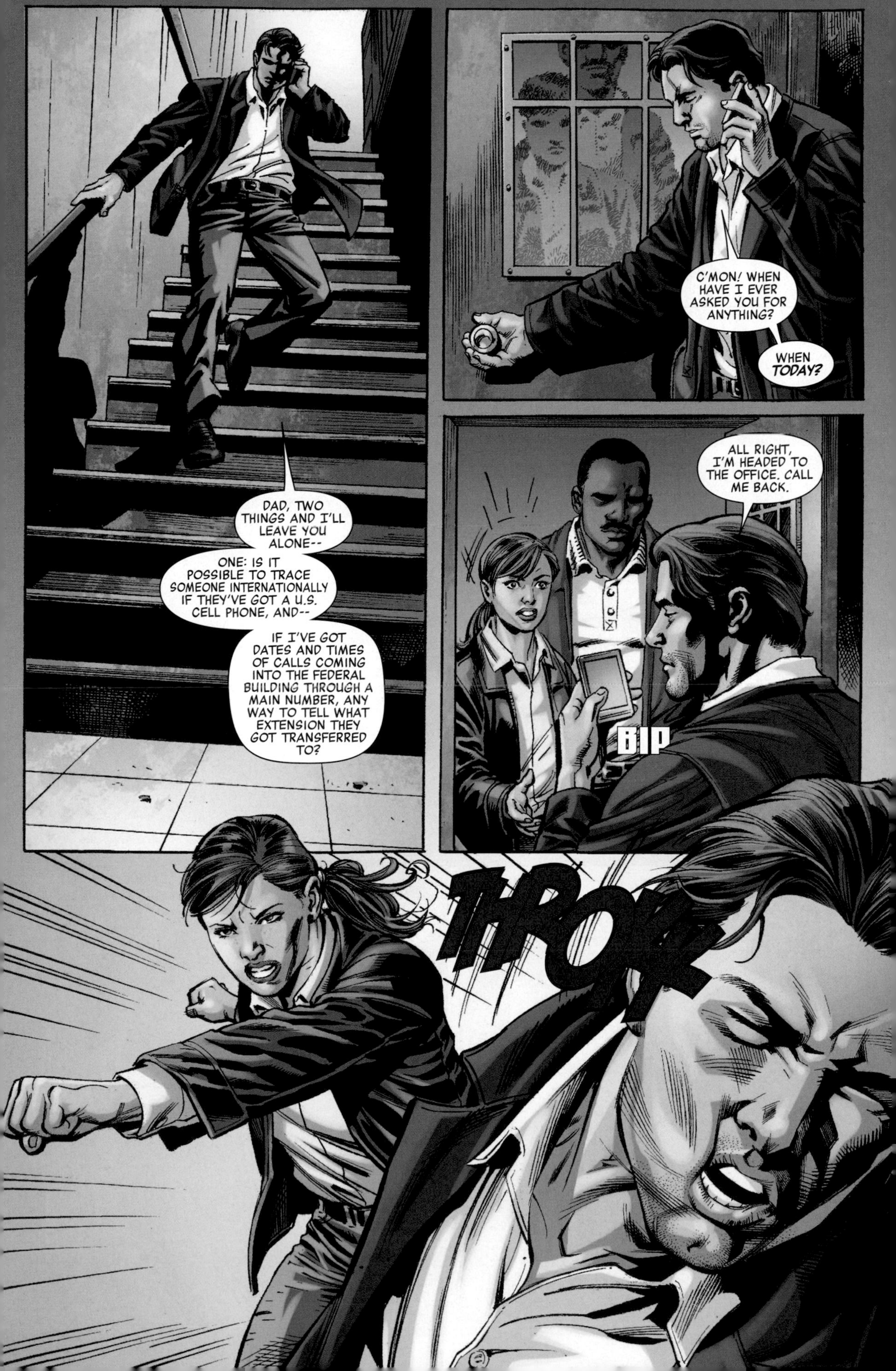
DAD, TWO THINGS AND I'LL LEAVE YOU ALONE--
ONE: IS IT POSSIBLE TO TRACE SOMEONE INTERNATIONALLY IF THEY'VE GOT A U.S. CELL PHONE, AND--
IF I'VE GOT DATES AND TIMES OF CALLS COMING INTO THE FEDERAL BUILDING THROUGH A MAIN NUMBER, ANY WAY TO TELL WHAT EXTENSION THEY GOT TRANSFERRED TO?
C'MON! WHEN HAVE I EVER ASKED YOU FOR ANYTHING?
WHEN *TODAY?*
ALL RIGHT, I'M HEADED TO THE OFFICE. CALL ME BACK.
BIP
THROK

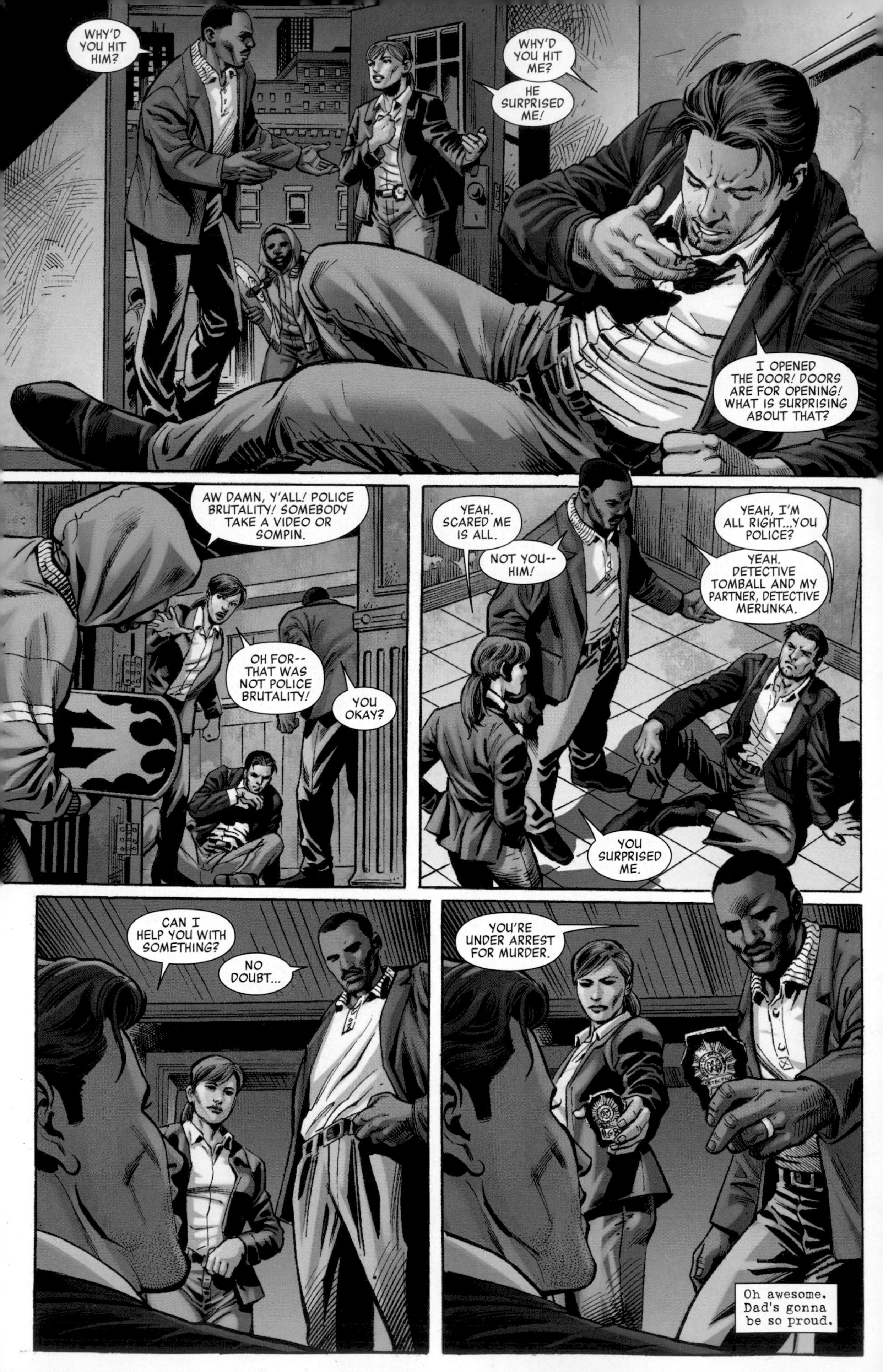
WHY'D YOU HIT HIM?
WHY'D YOU HIT ME?
HE SURPRISED ME!
I OPENED THE DOOR! DOORS ARE FOR OPENING! WHAT IS SURPRISING ABOUT THAT?
AW DAMN, Y'ALL! POLICE BRUTALITY! SOMEBODY TAKE A VIDEO OR SOMPIN.
OH FOR-- THAT WAS NOT POLICE BRUTALITY!
YOU OKAY?
YEAH. SCARED ME IS ALL.
NOT YOU-- HIM!
YEAH, I'M ALL RIGHT...YOU POLICE?
YEAH. DETECTIVE TOMBALL AND MY PARTNER, DETECTIVE MERUNKA.
YOU SURPRISED ME.
CAN I HELP YOU WITH SOMETHING?
NO DOUBT...
YOU'RE UNDER ARREST FOR MURDER.
Oh awesome. Dad's gonna be so proud.

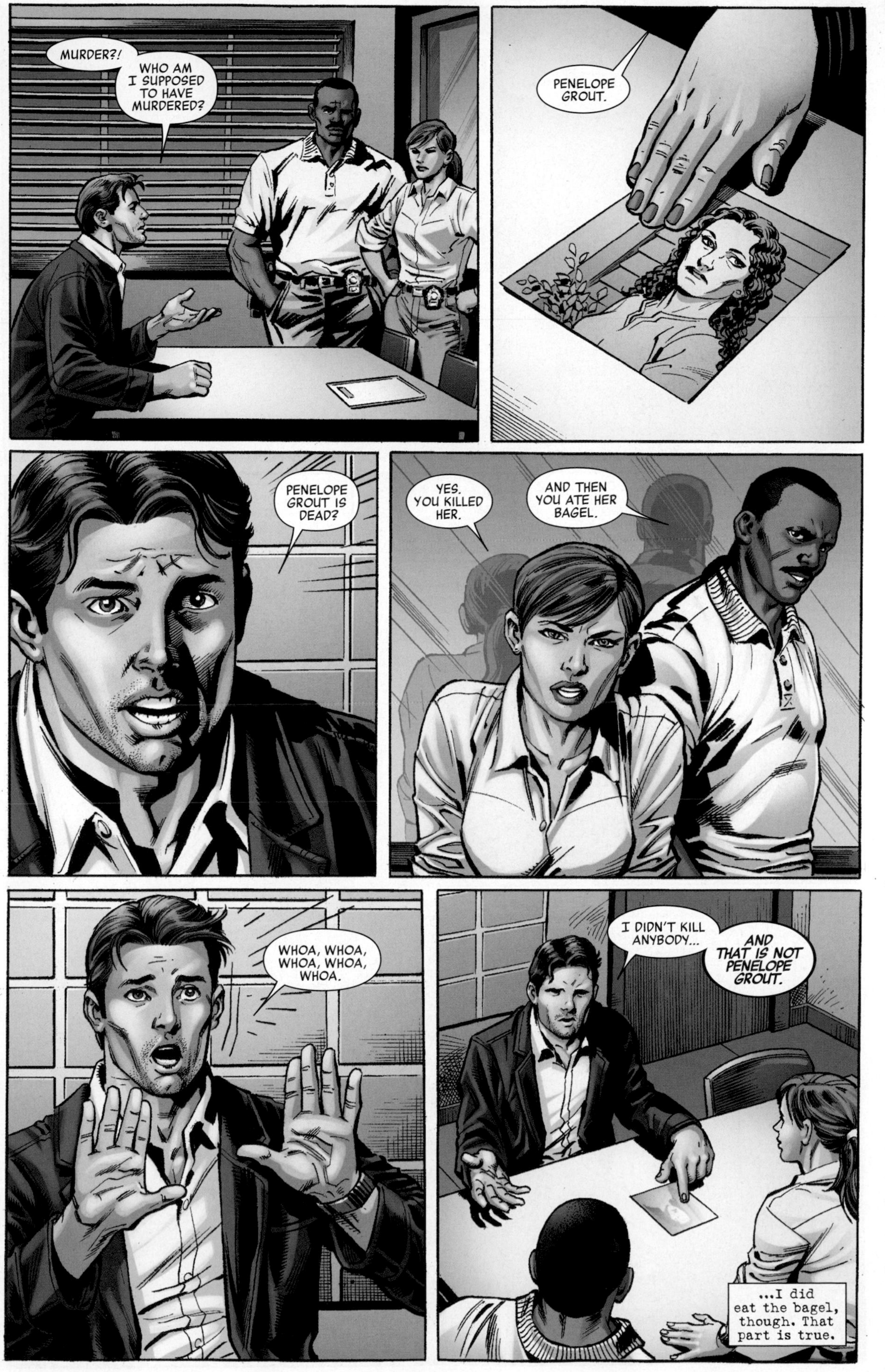
MURDER?!
WHO AM I SUPPOSED TO HAVE MURDERED?
PENELOPE GROUT.
PENELOPE GROUT IS DEAD?
YES. YOU KILLED HER.
AND THEN YOU ATE HER BAGEL.
WHOA, WHOA, WHOA, WHOA, WHOA.
I DIDN'T KILL ANYBODY...
AND THAT IS NOT PENELOPE GROUT.
...I did eat the bagel, though. That part is true.

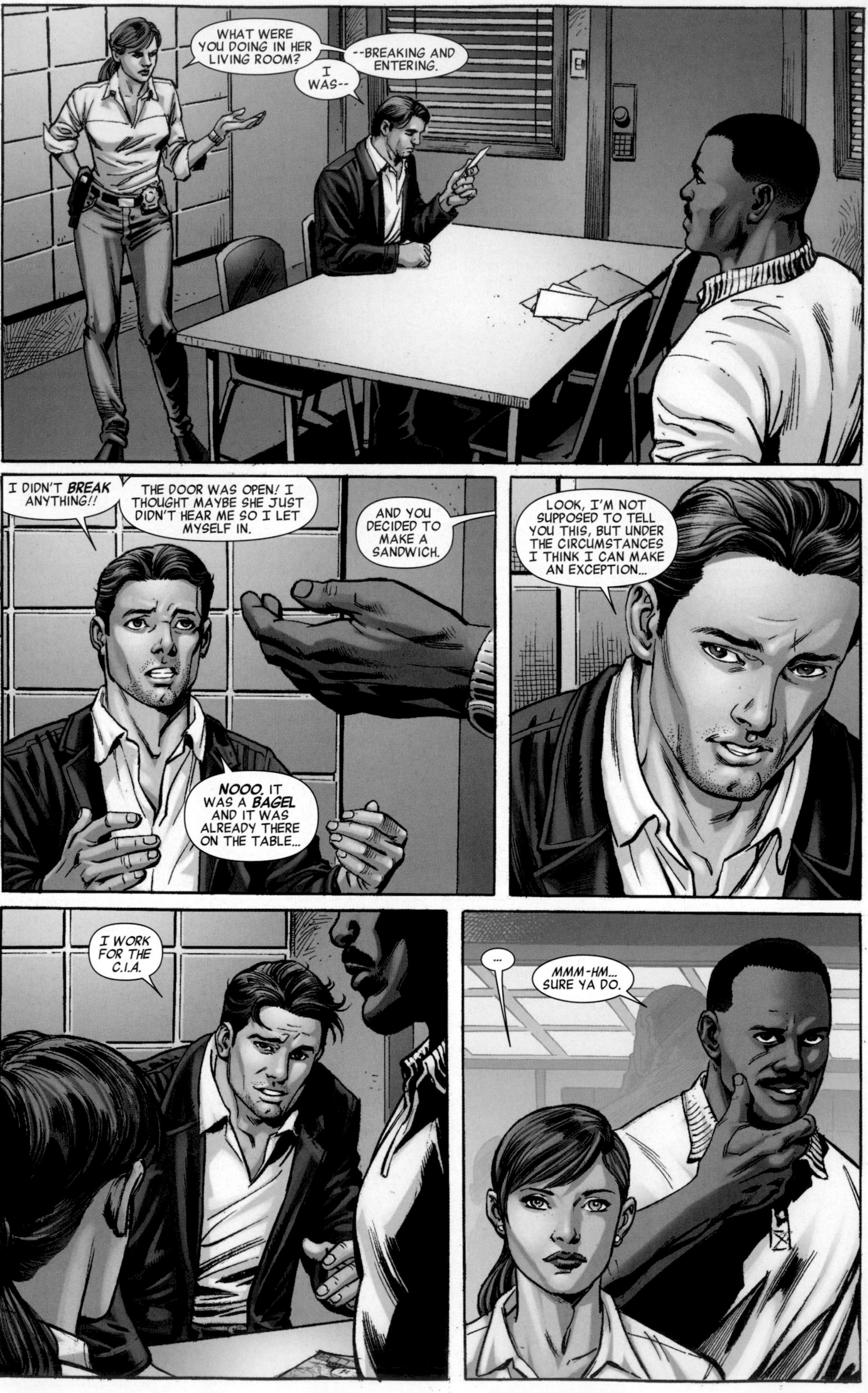
WHAT WERE YOU DOING IN HER LIVING ROOM?
I WAS--
--BREAKING AND ENTERING.
I DIDN'T **BREAK** ANYTHING!!
THE DOOR WAS OPEN! I THOUGHT MAYBE SHE JUST DIDN'T HEAR ME SO I LET MYSELF IN.
AND YOU DECIDED TO MAKE A SANDWICH.
NOOO. IT WAS A **BAGEL** AND IT WAS ALREADY THERE ON THE TABLE...
LOOK, I'M NOT SUPPOSED TO TELL YOU THIS, BUT UNDER THE CIRCUMSTANCES I THINK I CAN MAKE AN EXCEPTION...
I WORK FOR THE C.I.A.
...
MMM-HM... SURE YA DO.

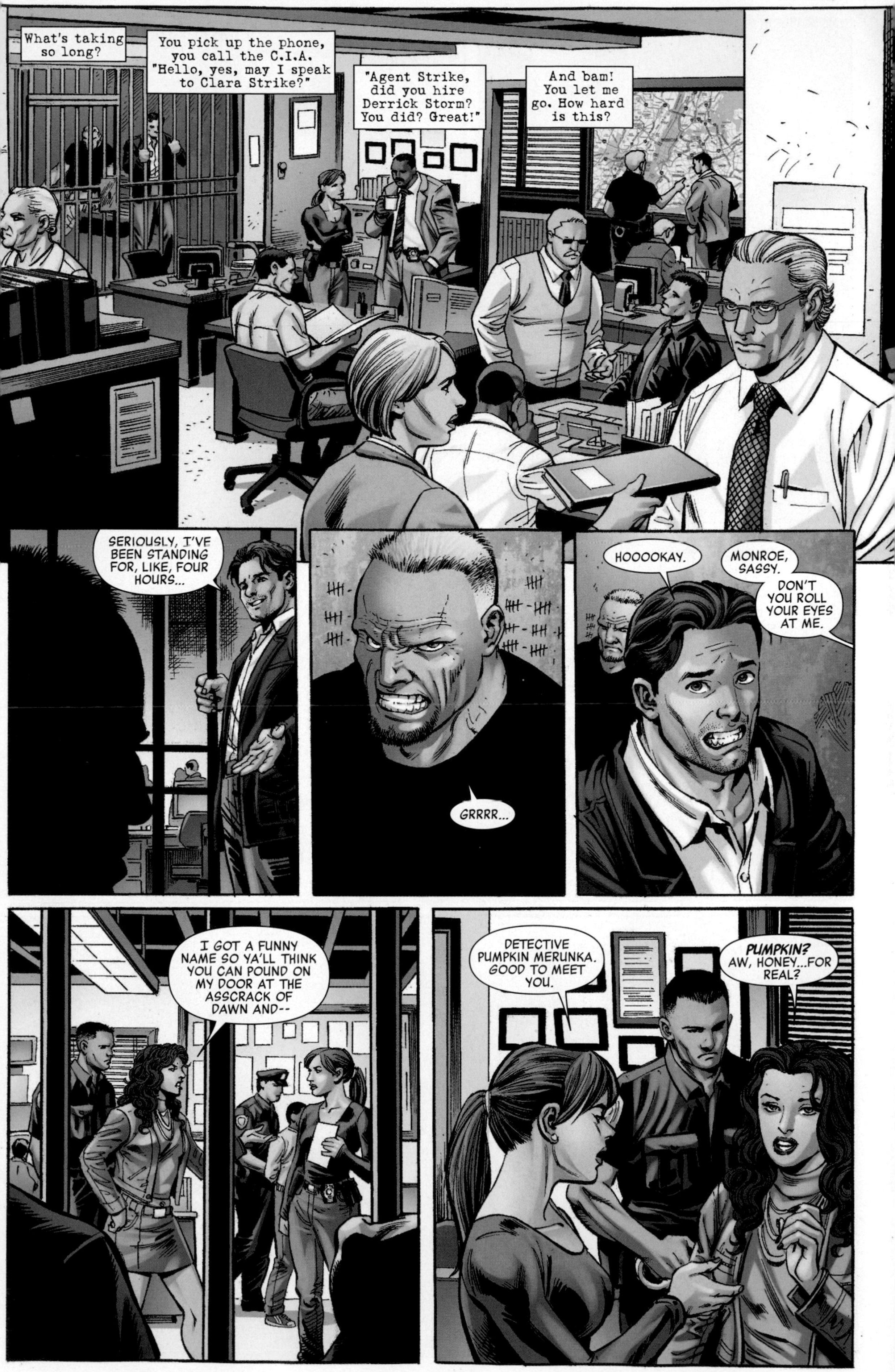
What's taking so long?
You pick up the phone, you call the C.I.A. "Hello, yes, may I speak to Clara Strike?"
"Agent Strike, did you hire Derrick Storm? You did? Great!"
And bam! You let me go. How hard is this?
SERIOUSLY, I'VE BEEN STANDING FOR, LIKE, FOUR HOURS...
GRRRR...
HOOOOKAY.
MONROE, SASSY.
DON'T YOU ROLL YOUR EYES AT ME.
I GOT A FUNNY NAME SO YA'LL THINK YOU CAN POUND ON MY DOOR AT THE ASSCRACK OF DAWN AND--
DETECTIVE PUMPKIN MERUNKA. GOOD TO MEET YOU.
PUMPKIN? AW, HONEY...FOR REAL?

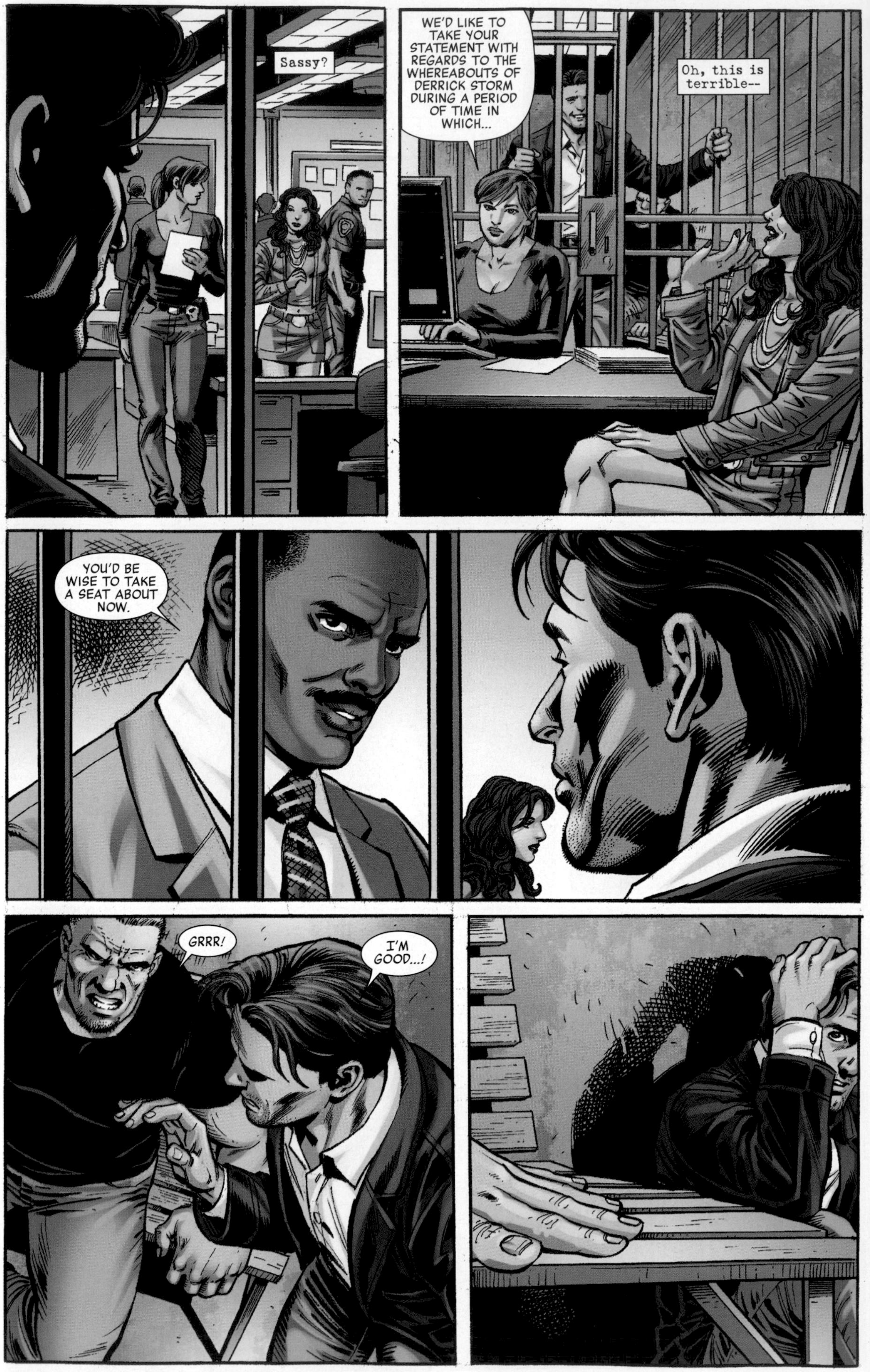
Sassy?
WE'D LIKE TO TAKE YOUR STATEMENT WITH REGARDS TO THE WHEREABOUTS OF DERRICK STORM DURING A PERIOD OF TIME IN WHICH...
Oh, this is terrible--
YOU'D BE WISE TO TAKE A SEAT ABOUT NOW.
GRRR!
I'M GOOD...!

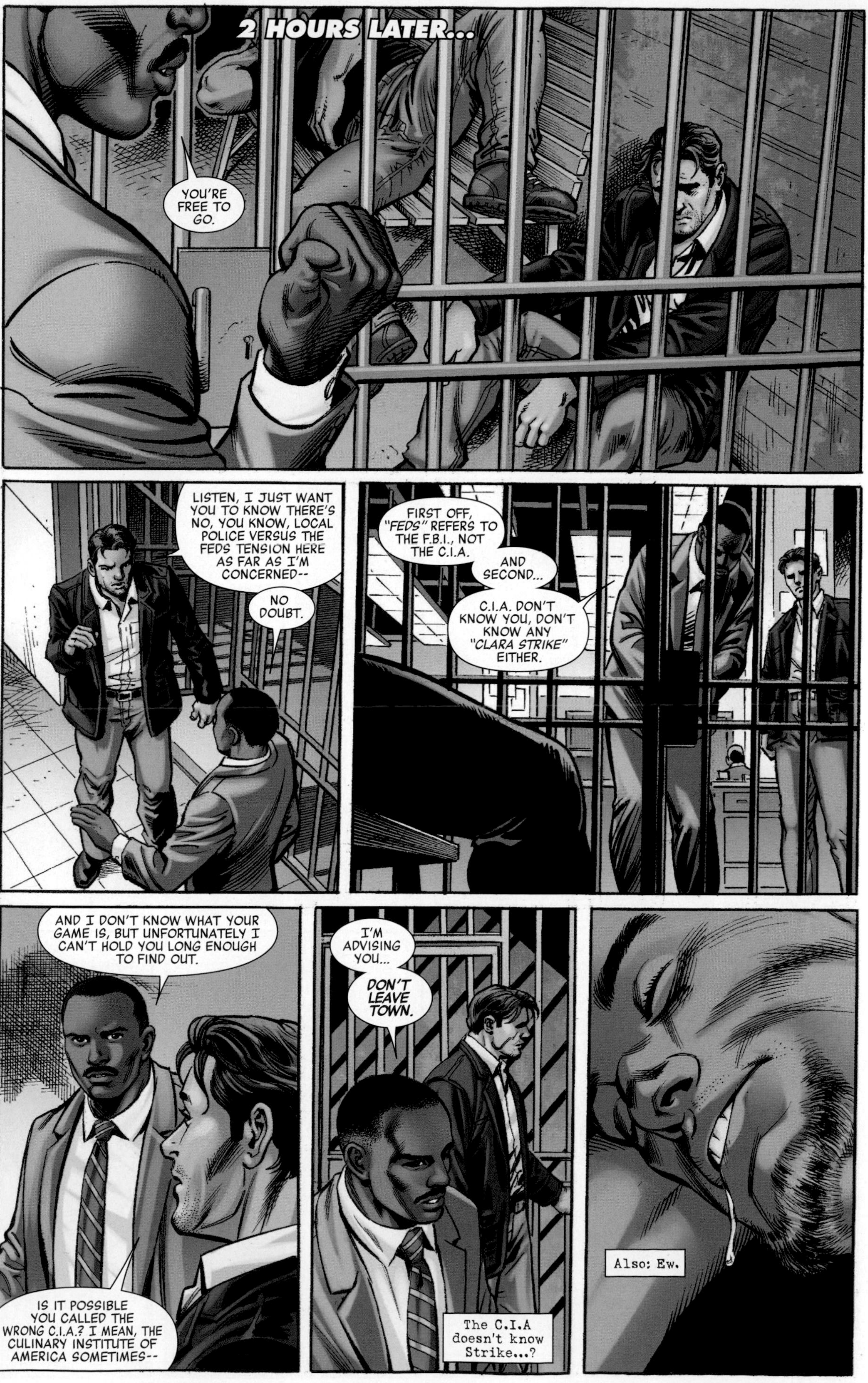
2 HOURS LATER...
YOU'RE FREE TO GO.
LISTEN, I JUST WANT YOU TO KNOW THERE'S NO, YOU KNOW, LOCAL POLICE VERSUS THE FEDS TENSION HERE AS FAR AS I'M CONCERNED--
NO DOUBT.
FIRST OFF, "FEDS" REFERS TO THE F.B.I., NOT THE C.I.A.
AND SECOND...
C.I.A. DON'T KNOW YOU, DON'T KNOW ANY "CLARA STRIKE" EITHER.
AND I DON'T KNOW WHAT YOUR GAME IS, BUT UNFORTUNATELY I CAN'T HOLD YOU LONG ENOUGH TO FIND OUT.
IS IT POSSIBLE YOU CALLED THE WRONG C.I.A.? I MEAN, THE CULINARY INSTITUTE OF AMERICA SOMETIMES--
I'M ADVISING YOU... DON'T LEAVE TOWN.
The C.I.A doesn't know Strike...?
Also: Ew.

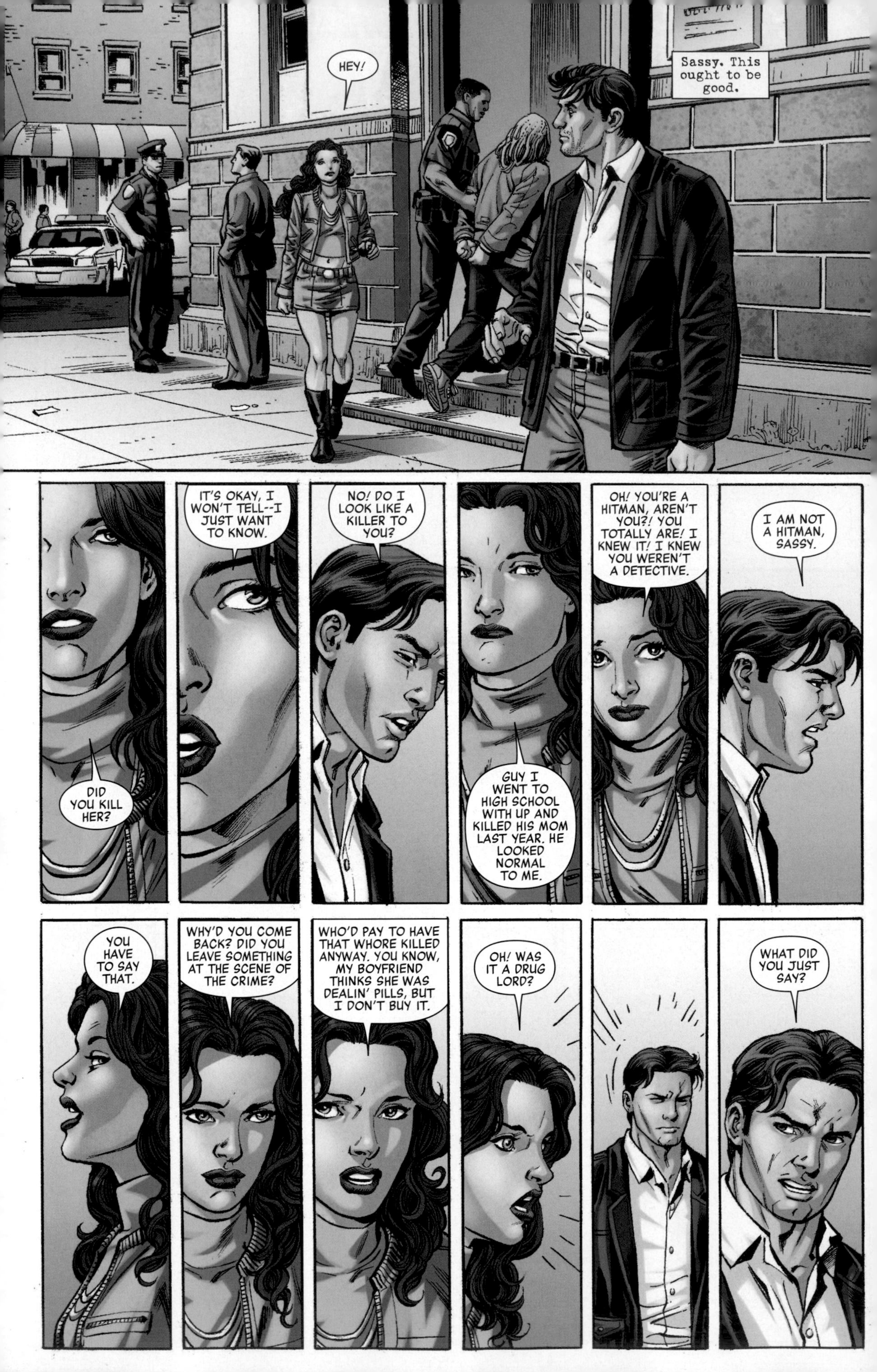
HEY!
Sassy. This ought to be good.
DID YOU KILL HER?
IT'S OKAY, I WON'T TELL--I JUST WANT TO KNOW.
NO! DO I LOOK LIKE A KILLER TO YOU?
GUY I WENT TO HIGH SCHOOL WITH UP AND KILLED HIS MOM LAST YEAR. HE LOOKED NORMAL TO ME.
OH! YOU'RE A HITMAN, AREN'T YOU?! YOU TOTALLY ARE! I KNEW IT! I KNEW YOU WEREN'T A DETECTIVE.
I AM NOT A HITMAN, SASSY.
YOU HAVE TO SAY THAT.
WHY'D YOU COME BACK? DID YOU LEAVE SOMETHING AT THE SCENE OF THE CRIME?
WHO'D PAY TO HAVE THAT WHORE KILLED ANYWAY. YOU KNOW, MY BOYFRIEND THINKS SHE WAS DEALIN' PILLS, BUT I DON'T BUY IT.
OH! WAS IT A DRUG LORD?
WHAT DID YOU JUST SAY?

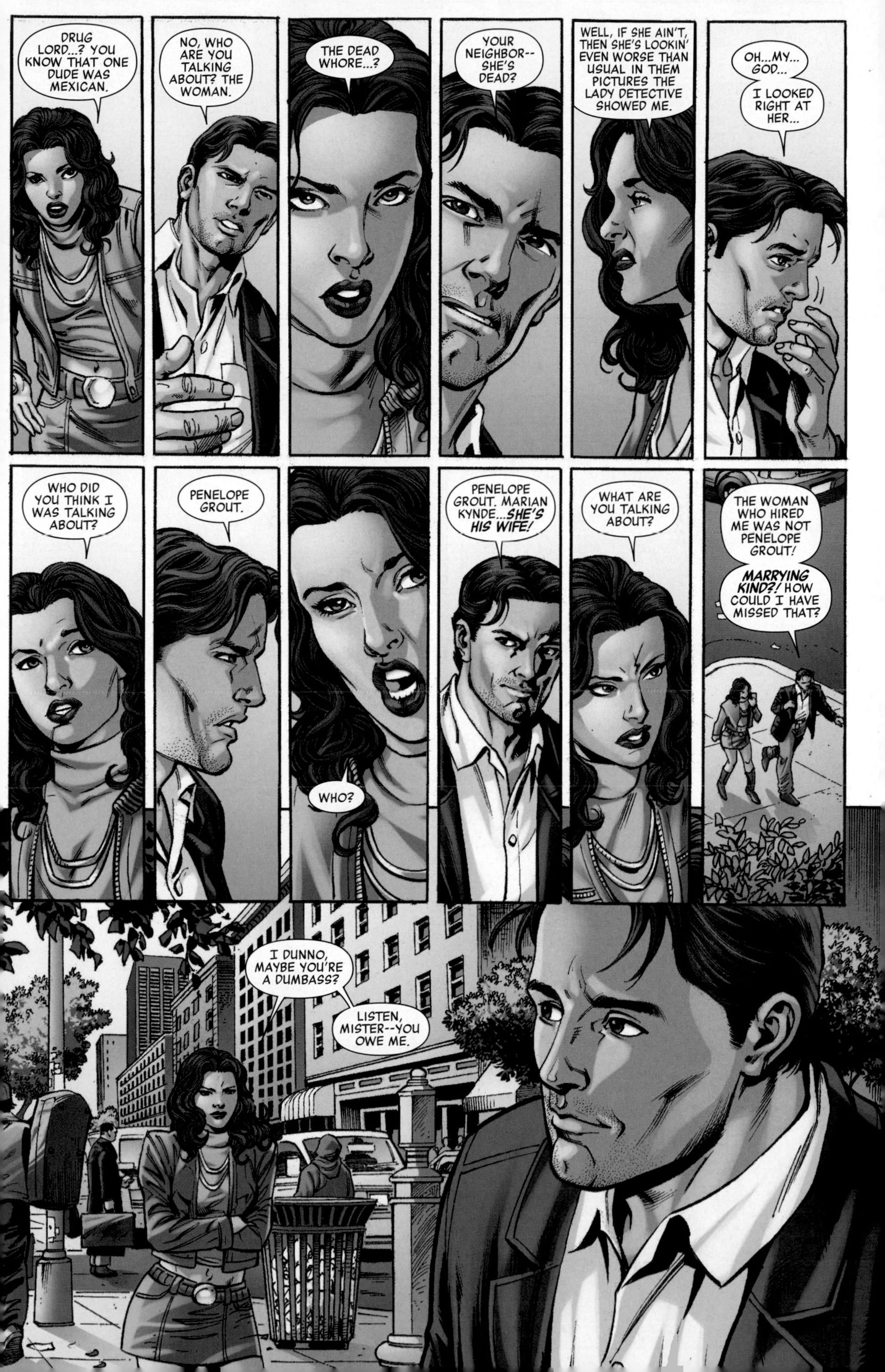
DRUG LORD...? YOU KNOW THAT ONE DUDE WAS MEXICAN.
NO, WHO ARE YOU TALKING ABOUT? THE WOMAN.
THE DEAD WHORE...?
YOUR NEIGHBOR-- SHE'S DEAD?
WELL, IF SHE AIN'T, THEN SHE'S LOOKIN' EVEN WORSE THAN USUAL IN THEM PICTURES THE LADY DETECTIVE SHOWED ME.
OH...MY... GOD...
I LOOKED RIGHT AT HER...
WHO DID YOU THINK I WAS TALKING ABOUT?
PENELOPE GROUT.
WHO?
PENELOPE GROUT. MARIAN KYNDE...SHE'S HIS WIFE!
WHAT ARE YOU TALKING ABOUT?
THE WOMAN WHO HIRED ME WAS NOT PENELOPE GROUT!
MARRYING KIND?! HOW COULD I HAVE MISSED THAT?
I DUNNO, MAYBE YOU'RE A DUMBASS?
LISTEN, MISTER--YOU OWE ME.

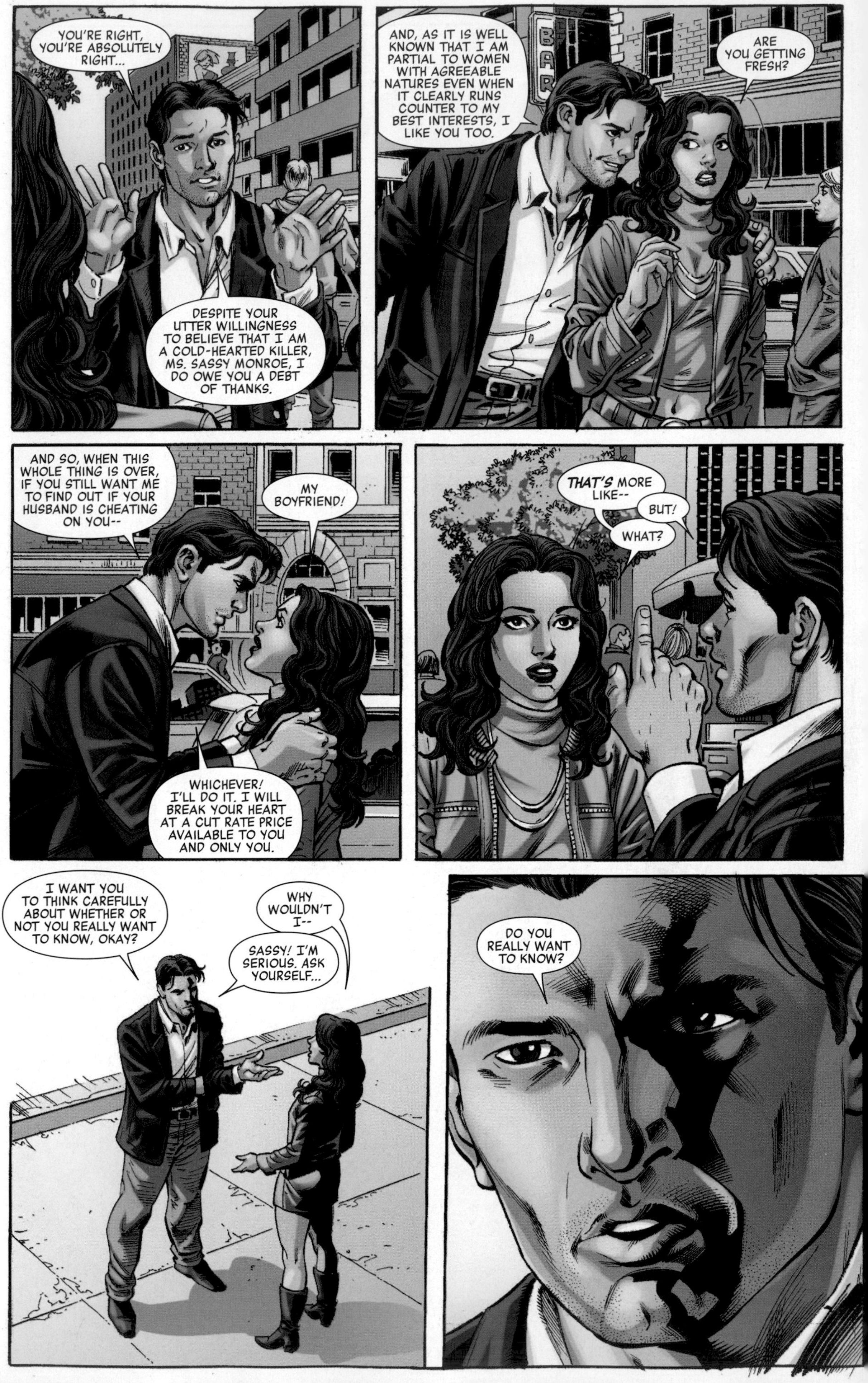
YOU'RE RIGHT, YOU'RE ABSOLUTELY RIGHT...
DESPITE YOUR UTTER WILLINGNESS TO BELIEVE THAT I AM A COLD-HEARTED KILLER, MS. SASSY MONROE, I DO OWE YOU A DEBT OF THANKS.
AND, AS IT IS WELL KNOWN THAT I AM PARTIAL TO WOMEN WITH AGREEABLE NATURES EVEN WHEN IT CLEARLY RUNS COUNTER TO MY BEST INTERESTS, I LIKE YOU TOO.
ARE YOU GETTING FRESH?
AND SO, WHEN THIS WHOLE THING IS OVER, IF YOU STILL WANT ME TO FIND OUT IF YOUR HUSBAND IS CHEATING ON YOU--
MY BOYFRIEND!
WHICHEVER! I'LL DO IT. I WILL BREAK YOUR HEART AT A CUT RATE PRICE AVAILABLE TO YOU AND ONLY YOU.
THAT'S MORE LIKE--
BUT!
WHAT?
I WANT YOU TO THINK CAREFULLY ABOUT WHETHER OR NOT YOU REALLY WANT TO KNOW, OKAY?
WHY WOULDN'T I--
SASSY! I'M SERIOUS. ASK YOURSELF...
DO YOU REALLY WANT TO KNOW?

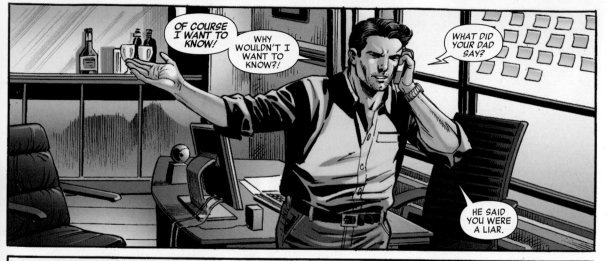

OF COURSE I WANT TO KNOW!

WHY WOULDN'T I WANT TO KNOW?!

WHAT DID YOUR DAD SAY?

HE SAID YOU WERE A LIAR.

NICE.

YOU'RE BEING EVASIVE.

THAT'S MY JOB.

WHO DO YOU WORK FOR, CLARA STRIKE--IF THAT IS YOUR REAL NAME?

I TOLD YOU. I'M C.I.A.

THE C.I.A. DOESN'T SEEM TO KNOW THAT.

DO YOU REALLY THINK THAT THE C.I.A. GOES AROUND IDENTIFYING AGENTS TO ANYONE WHO CALLS?

WELL...

LET ME HELP YOU WITH THAT-- WE DO NOT.

DO YOU REALLY THINK YOU WERE RELEASED AS A MURDER SUSPECT ON THE WORD OF CHESTY MCSPARKLES?

CRYSTAL CLEAVAGE.

WHATEVER.

...

I HADN'T REALLY CONSIDERED THAT.

ARE YOU SAYING--

I'M SAYING THAT THE U.S. GOVERNMENT THANKS YOU FOR YOUR ASSISTANCE IN THIS MATTER AND IF WE HAVE FURTHER--

WHOA, WHOA, WHOA--

YOU'RE FIRING ME?!

FIRING YOU WOULD IMPLY AN OFFICIAL RELATIONSHIP, WHICH--

I WAS JUST GETTING STARTED!

WELL, I'M **SORRY** BUT I THINK WE'VE GOT IT FROM HERE.

GROUT'S WIFE IS **DEAD.**

YES, I KNOW. AND YOU ATE HER BAGEL. I KNOW THAT BECAUSE YOU WENT AND TOLD TWO OFFICERS OF THE NYPD THAT--

--ARE YOU GOING TO LET ME FINISH?

PROBABLY NOT. BUT GIVE IT A SHOT.

I'M PUTTING YOU ON SPEAKER.

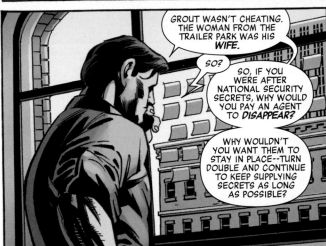

GROUT WASN'T CHEATING. THE WOMAN FROM THE TRAILER PARK WAS HIS **WIFE.**

SO?

SO, IF YOU WERE AFTER NATIONAL SECURITY SECRETS, WHY WOULD YOU PAY AN AGENT TO **DISAPPEAR?**

WHY WOULDN'T YOU WANT THEM TO STAY IN PLACE--TURN DOUBLE AND CONTINUE TO KEEP SUPPLYING SECRETS AS LONG AS POSSIBLE?

WHAT ARE YOU GETTING AT?

WHOEVER'S BEHIND THIS, THEY DON'T NEED **INTEL...**

THEY'RE AFTER A PARTICULAR SKILL SET. THEY WANT **THE AGENTS THEMSELVES.**

FOR WHAT?

I DON'T KNOW! I HAVEN'T GOTTEN THAT FAR.

GROUT/ SANCHEZ

IF PENELOPE IS DEAD, WHO WAS PENELOPE?

SILENCER

HE KILL ME?

INT'L PLAN

WHY NOT DOUBLE

WHATEVER THEY WERE DOING, IT WORKED UNTIL THEY GOT TO GROUT. HE WOULDN'T BITE, SO THEY THREATENED HIS WIFE.

HE TOOK HER OFF THE TABLE--HID HER AWAY IN A CRAPPY LITTLE MOBILE HOME AND TRIED TO FIND OUT WHO WAS BEHIND IT.

OR MAYBE HE ALREADY KNEW.

...MAYBE.

HE WAS TRYING TO SAVE HER.

He ran so I'd run after him. But as soon as he got a good look at me, he knew.

I was just a distraction.

One look at me, and he knew he'd made a mistake.

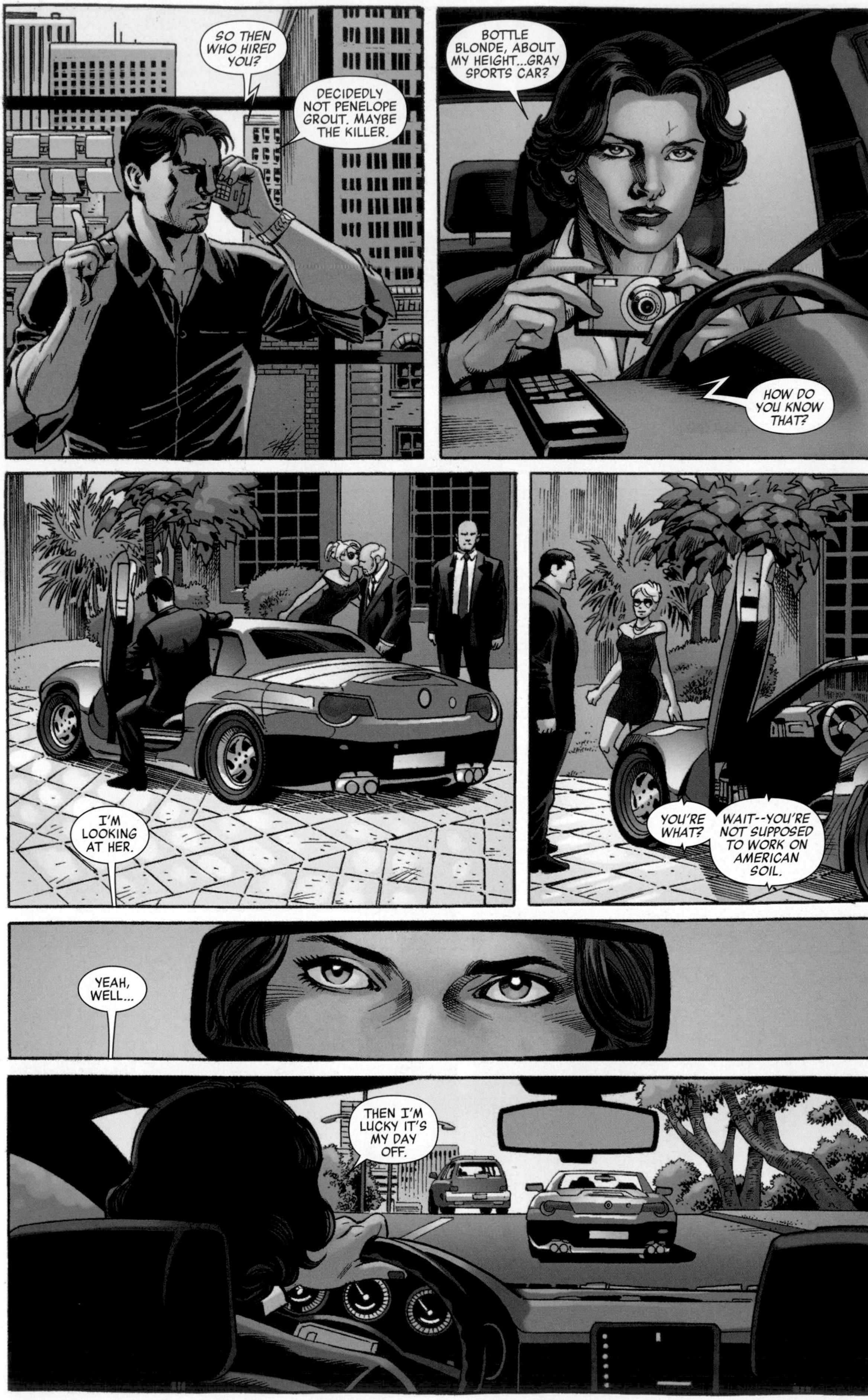
SO THEN WHO HIRED YOU?
DECIDEDLY NOT PENELOPE GROUT. MAYBE THE KILLER.
BOTTLE BLONDE, ABOUT MY HEIGHT...GRAY SPORTS CAR?
HOW DO YOU KNOW THAT?
I'M LOOKING AT HER.
YOU'RE WHAT?
WAIT--YOU'RE NOT SUPPOSED TO WORK ON AMERICAN SOIL.
YEAH, WELL...
THEN I'M LUCKY IT'S MY DAY OFF.

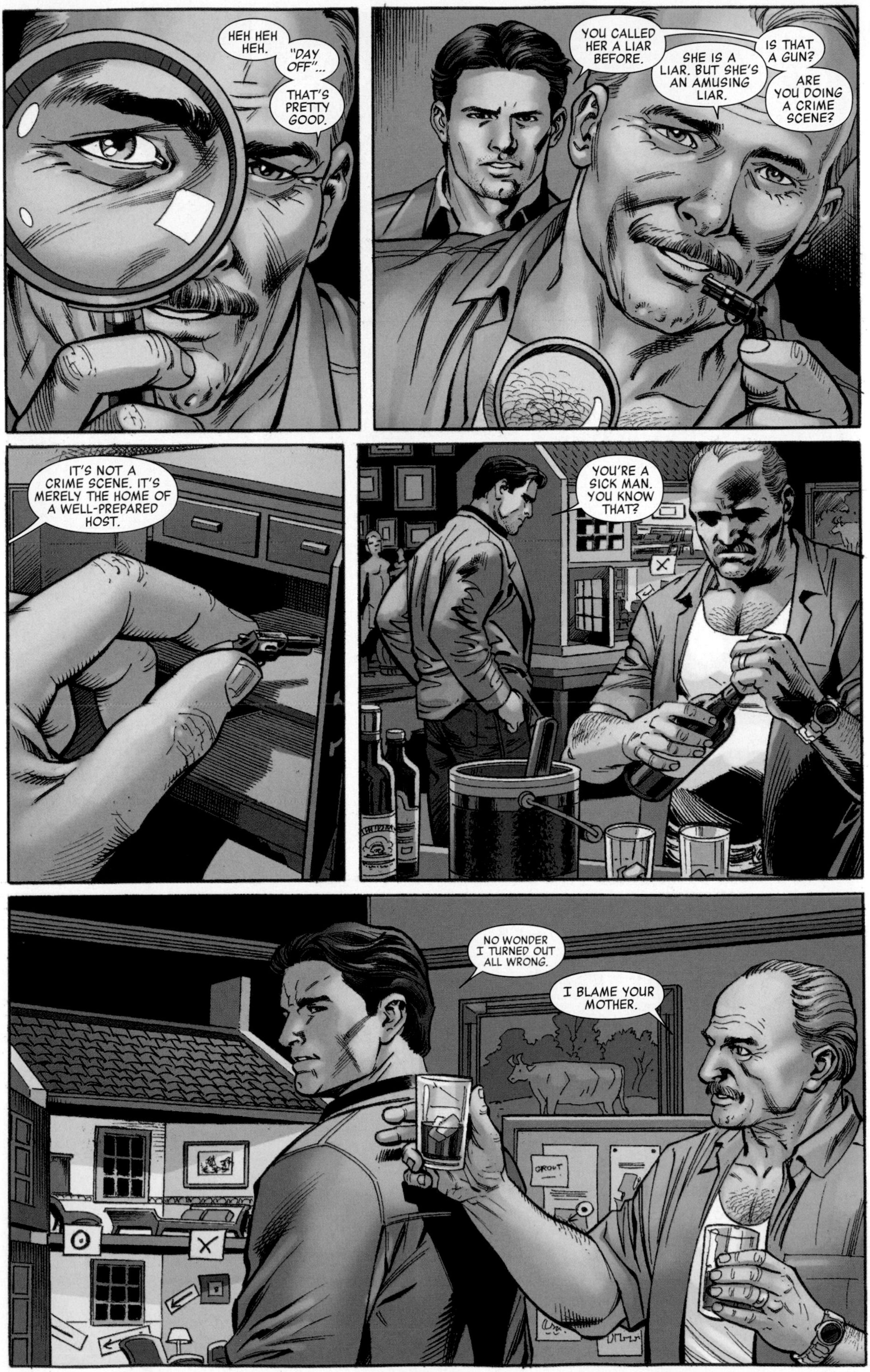
HEH HEH HEH.
"DAY OFF"...
THAT'S PRETTY GOOD.
YOU CALLED HER A LIAR BEFORE.
SHE IS A LIAR. BUT SHE'S AN AMUSING LIAR.
IS THAT A GUN?
ARE YOU DOING A CRIME SCENE?
IT'S NOT A CRIME SCENE. IT'S MERELY THE HOME OF A WELL-PREPARED HOST.
YOU'RE A SICK MAN. YOU KNOW THAT?
NO WONDER I TURNED OUT ALL WRONG.
I BLAME YOUR MOTHER.
GROUT

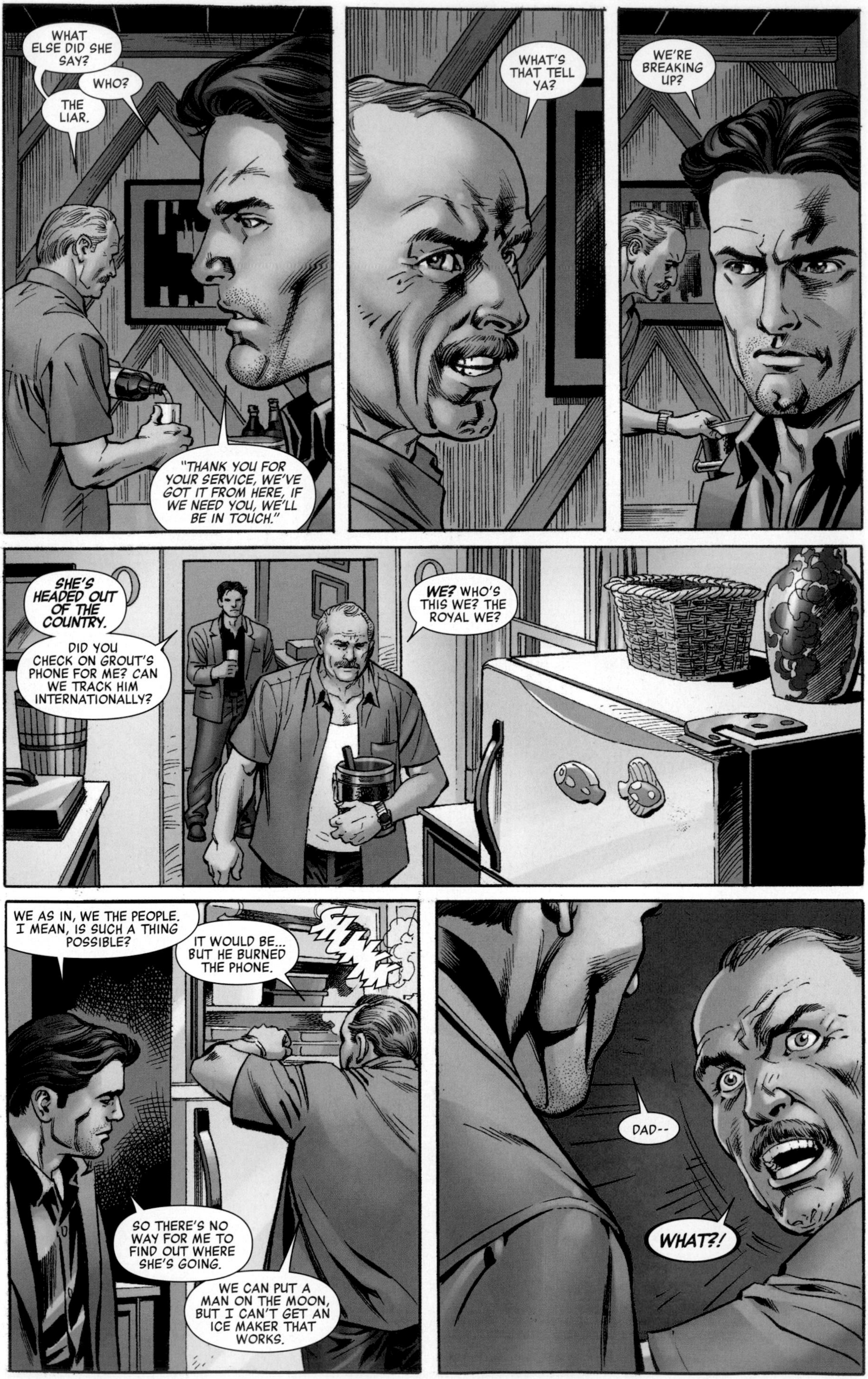
WHAT ELSE DID SHE SAY?
WHO?
THE LIAR.
"THANK YOU FOR YOUR SERVICE, WE'VE GOT IT FROM HERE, IF WE NEED YOU, WE'LL BE IN TOUCH."
WHAT'S THAT TELL YA?
WE'RE BREAKING UP?
SHE'S HEADED OUT OF THE COUNTRY.
DID YOU CHECK ON GROUT'S PHONE FOR ME? CAN WE TRACK HIM INTERNATIONALLY?
WE? WHO'S THIS WE? THE ROYAL WE?
WE AS IN, WE THE PEOPLE. I MEAN, IS SUCH A THING POSSIBLE?
IT WOULD BE... BUT HE BURNED THE PHONE.
SHUNK
SO THERE'S NO WAY FOR ME TO FIND OUT WHERE SHE'S GOING.
WE CAN PUT A MAN ON THE MOON, BUT I CAN'T GET AN ICE MAKER THAT WORKS.
DAD--
WHAT?!

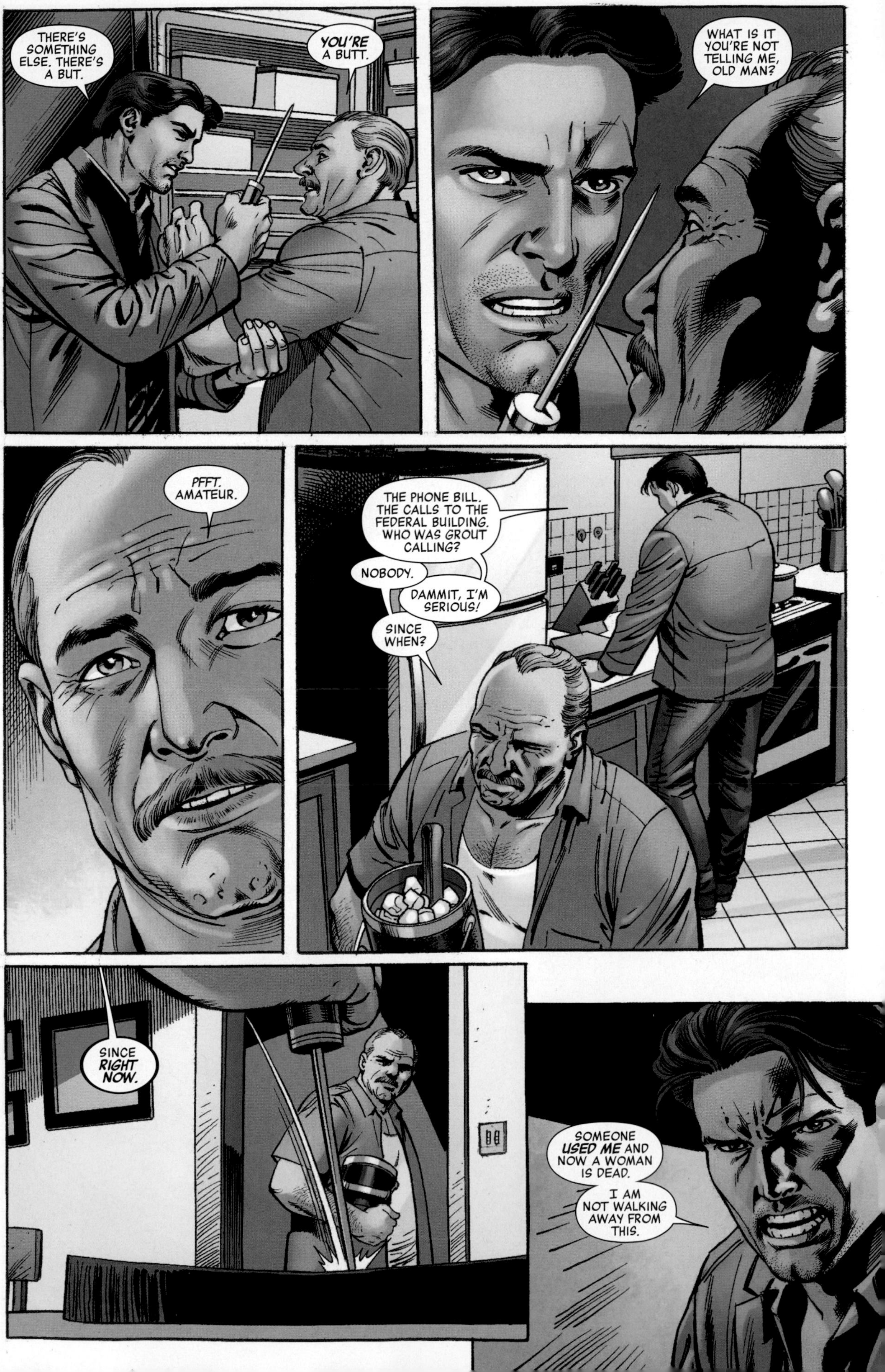
THERE'S SOMETHING ELSE. THERE'S A BUT.
YOU'RE A BUTT.
WHAT IS IT YOU'RE NOT TELLING ME, OLD MAN?
PFFT. AMATEUR.
THE PHONE BILL. THE CALLS TO THE FEDERAL BUILDING. WHO WAS GROUT CALLING?
NOBODY.
DAMMIT, I'M SERIOUS!
SINCE WHEN?
SINCE RIGHT NOW.
SOMEONE USED ME AND NOW A WOMAN IS DEAD.
I AM NOT WALKING AWAY FROM THIS.

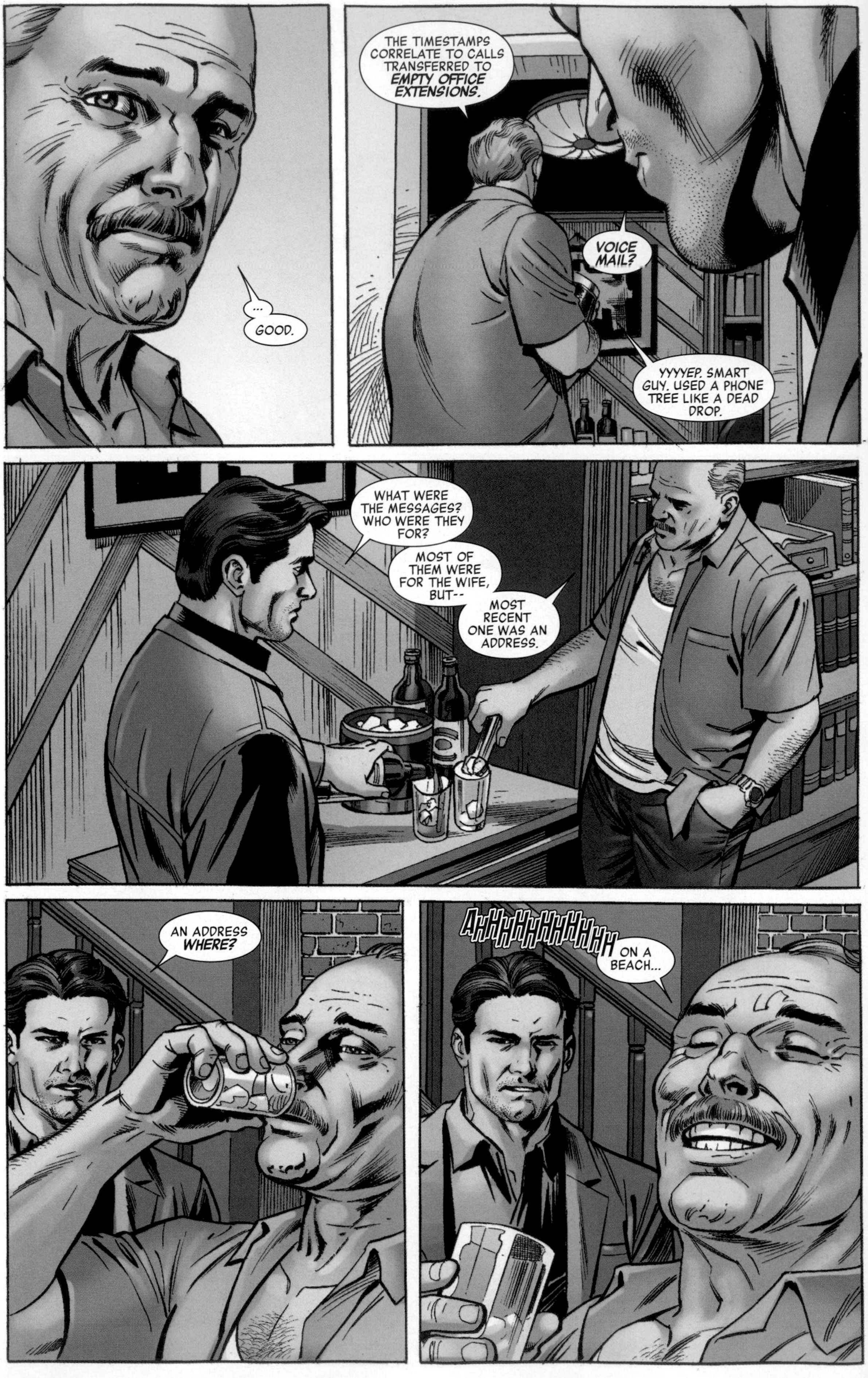
...
GOOD.
THE TIMESTAMPS CORRELATE TO CALLS TRANSFERRED TO EMPTY OFFICE EXTENSIONS.
VOICE MAIL?
YYYYEP. SMART GUY. USED A PHONE TREE LIKE A DEAD DROP.
WHAT WERE THE MESSAGES? WHO WERE THEY FOR?
MOST OF THEM WERE FOR THE WIFE, BUT--
MOST RECENT ONE WAS AN ADDRESS.
AN ADDRESS WHERE?
AHHHHHHHHHHH
ON A BEACH...

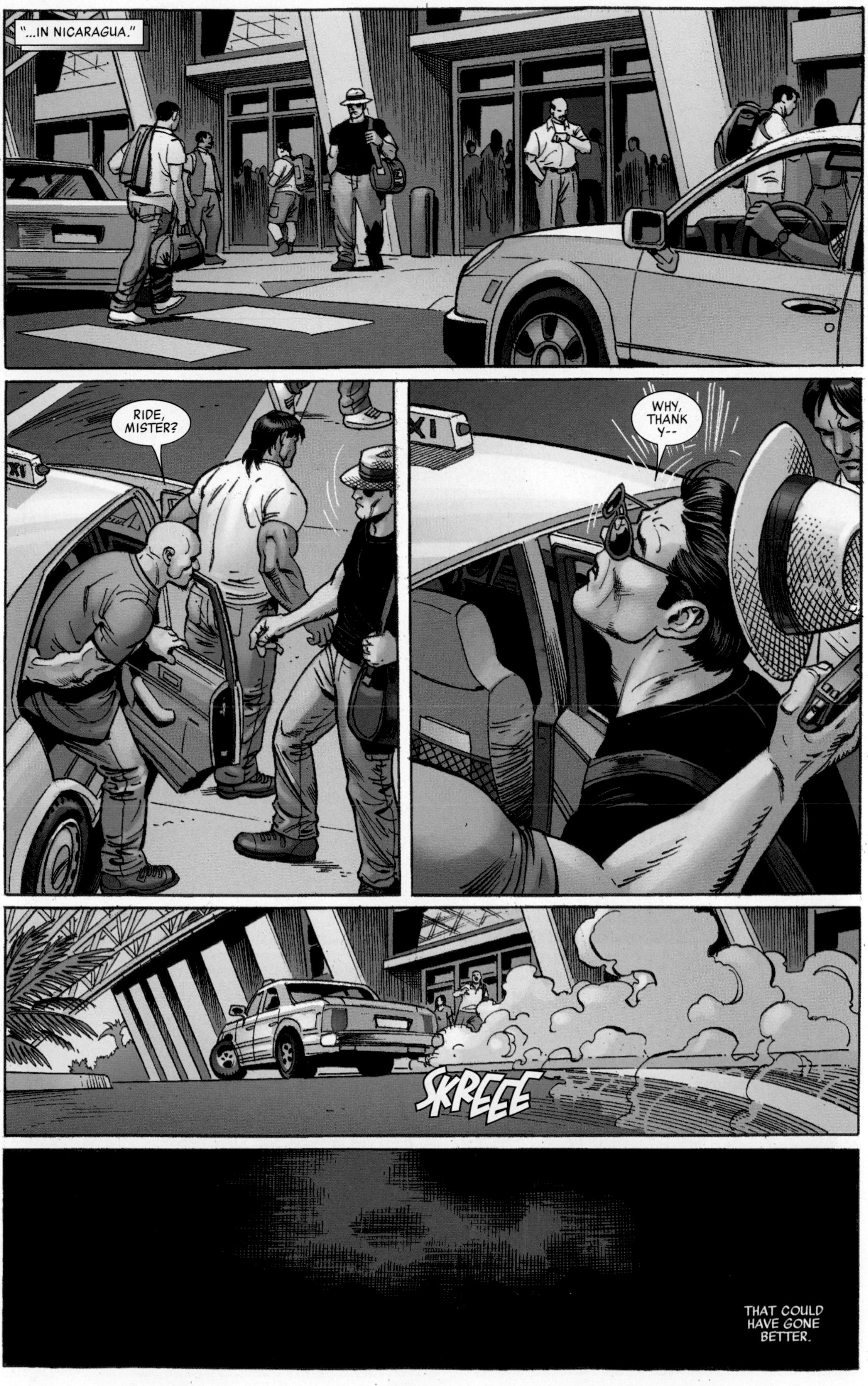
"...IN NICARAGUA."
RIDE, MISTER?
WHY, THANK Y--
SKREEEE
THAT COULD HAVE GONE BETTER.

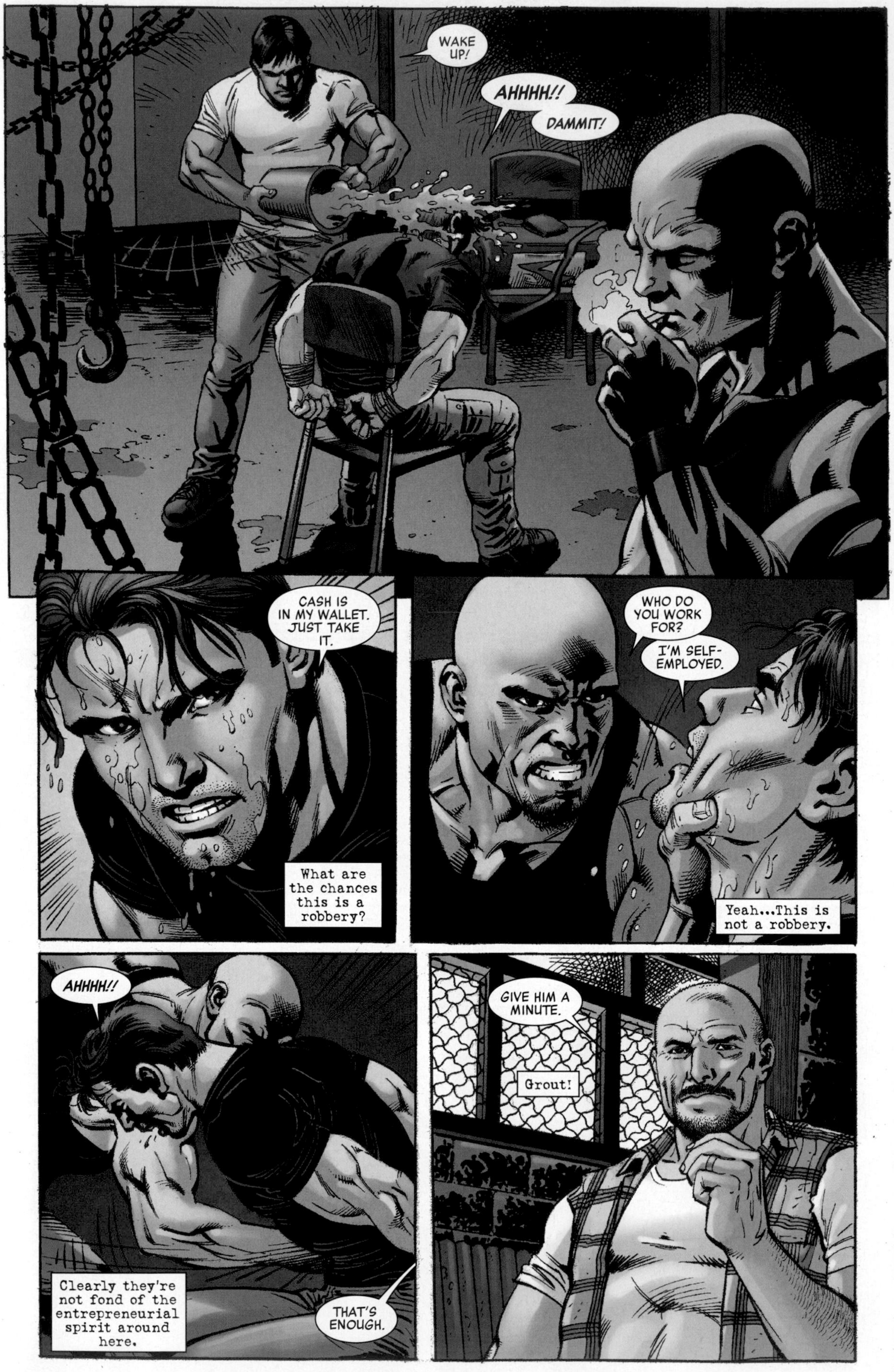
WAKE UP!
AHHHH!!
DAMMIT!
CASH IS IN MY WALLET. JUST TAKE IT.
What are the chances this is a robbery?
WHO DO YOU WORK FOR?
I'M SELF-EMPLOYED.
Yeah...This is not a robbery.
AHHHH!!
Clearly they're not fond of the entrepreneurial spirit around here.
THAT'S ENOUGH.
GIVE HIM A MINUTE.
Grout!

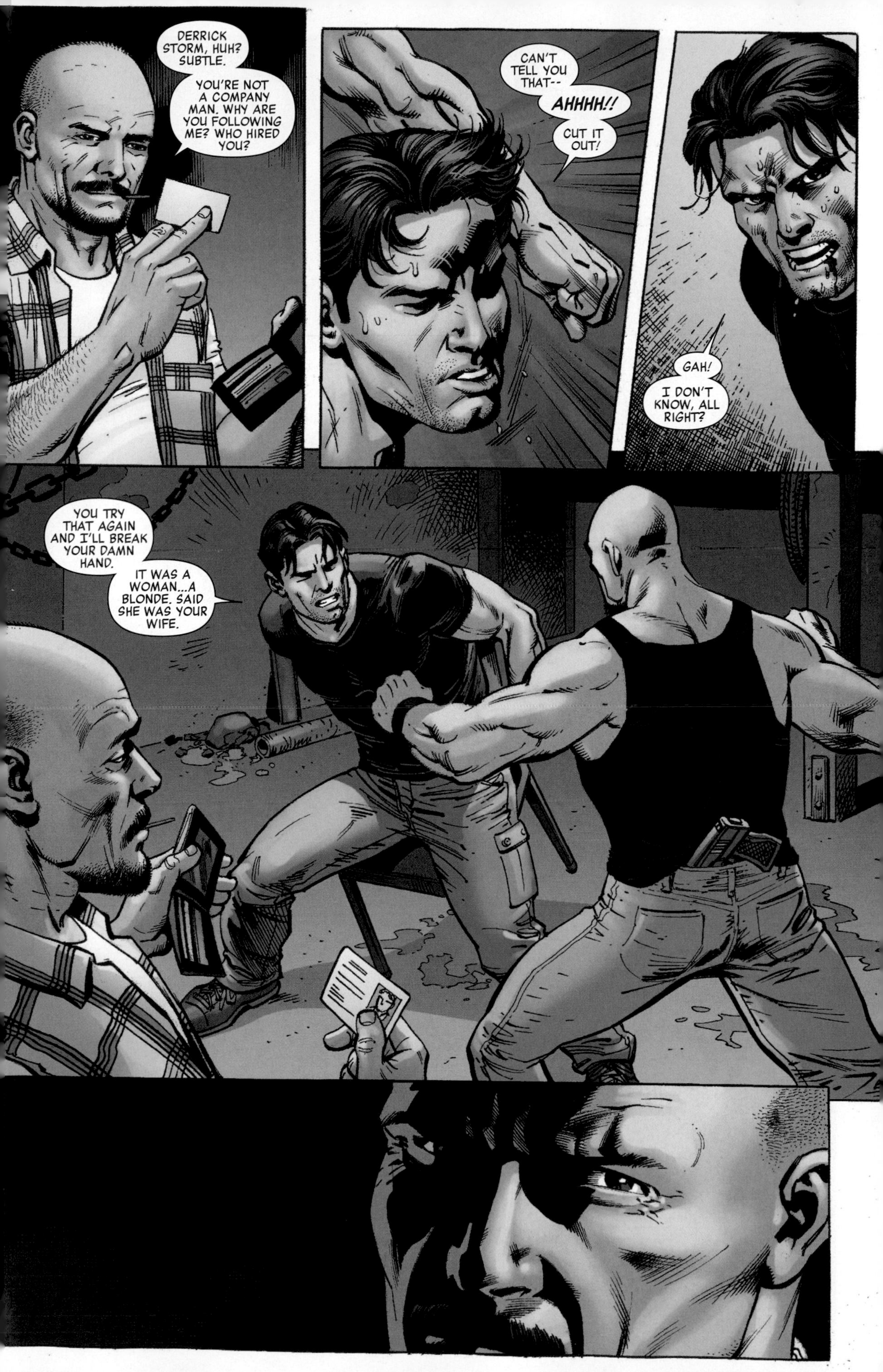
DERRICK STORM, HUH? SUBTLE.
YOU'RE NOT A COMPANY MAN. WHY ARE YOU FOLLOWING ME? WHO HIRED YOU?
CAN'T TELL YOU THAT--
AHHHH!!
CUT IT OUT!
GAH!
I DON'T KNOW, ALL RIGHT?
YOU TRY THAT AGAIN AND I'LL BREAK YOUR DAMN HAND.
IT WAS A WOMAN...A BLONDE. SAID SHE WAS YOUR WIFE.

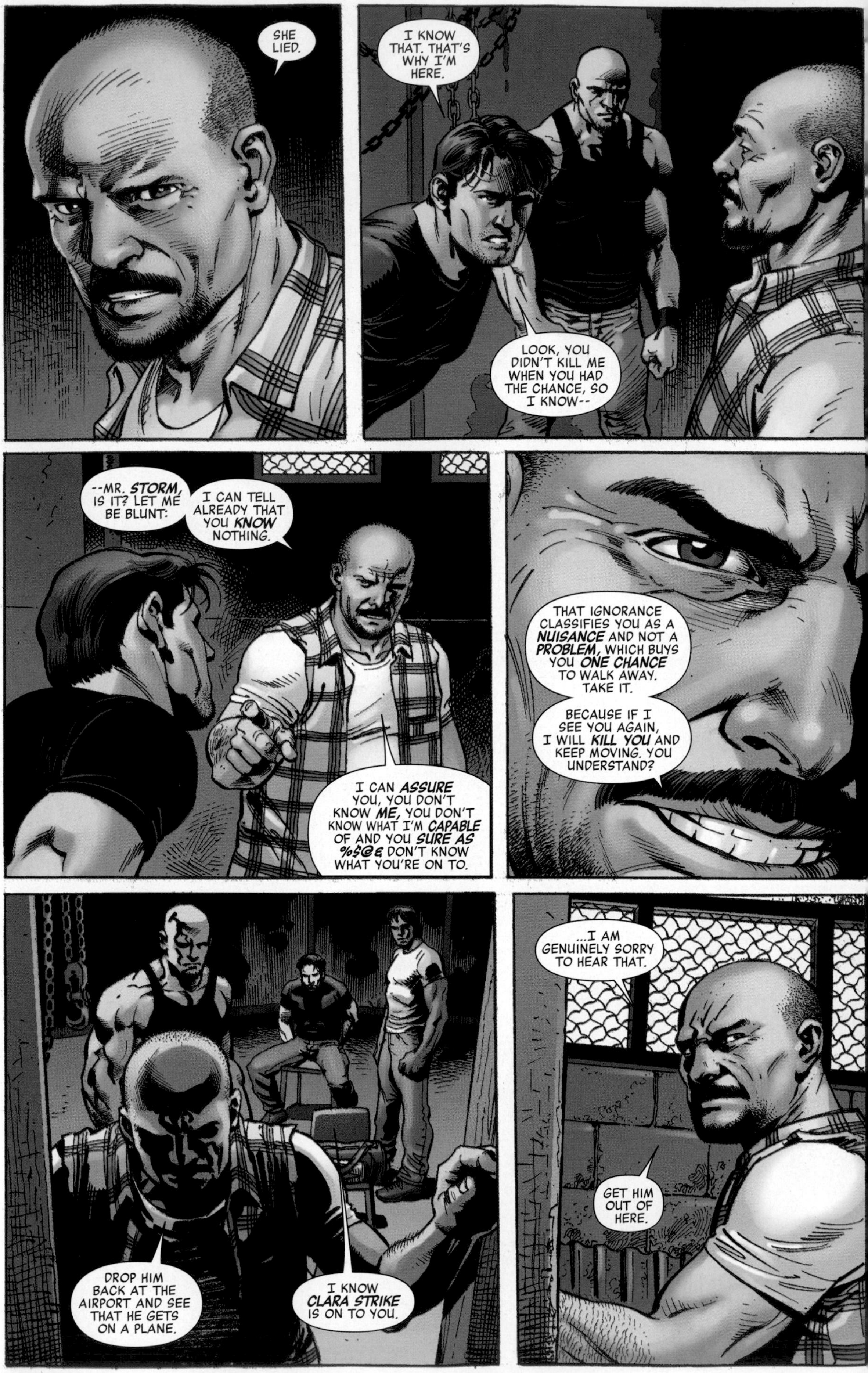
SHE LIED.
I KNOW THAT. THAT'S WHY I'M HERE.
LOOK, YOU DIDN'T KILL ME WHEN YOU HAD THE CHANCE, SO I KNOW--
--MR. STORM, IS IT? LET ME BE BLUNT:
I CAN TELL ALREADY THAT YOU KNOW NOTHING.
I CAN ASSURE YOU, YOU DON'T KNOW ME, YOU DON'T KNOW WHAT I'M CAPABLE OF AND YOU SURE AS %$@& DON'T KNOW WHAT YOU'RE ON TO.
THAT IGNORANCE CLASSIFIES YOU AS A NUISANCE AND NOT A PROBLEM, WHICH BUYS YOU ONE CHANCE TO WALK AWAY. TAKE IT.
BECAUSE IF I SEE YOU AGAIN, I WILL KILL YOU AND KEEP MOVING. YOU UNDERSTAND?
I KNOW CLARA STRIKE IS ON TO YOU.
DROP HIM BACK AT THE AIRPORT AND SEE THAT HE GETS ON A PLANE.
...I AM GENUINELY SORRY TO HEAR THAT.
GET HIM OUT OF HERE.

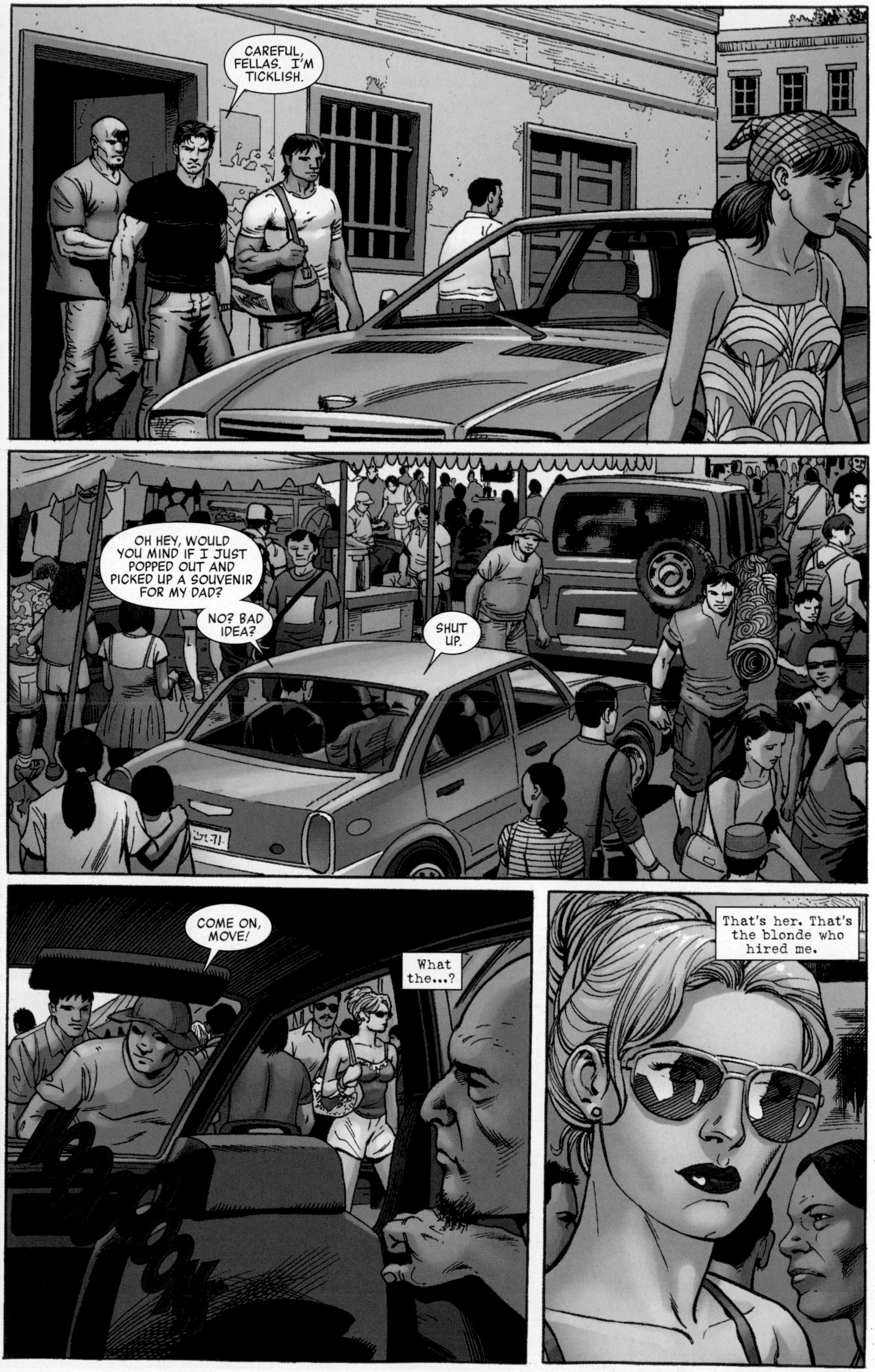
CAREFUL, FELLAS. I'M TICKLISH.
OH HEY, WOULD YOU MIND IF I JUST POPPED OUT AND PICKED UP A SOUVENIR FOR MY DAD?
NO? BAD IDEA?
SHUT UP.
COME ON, MOVE!
What the...?
That's her. That's the blonde who hired me.

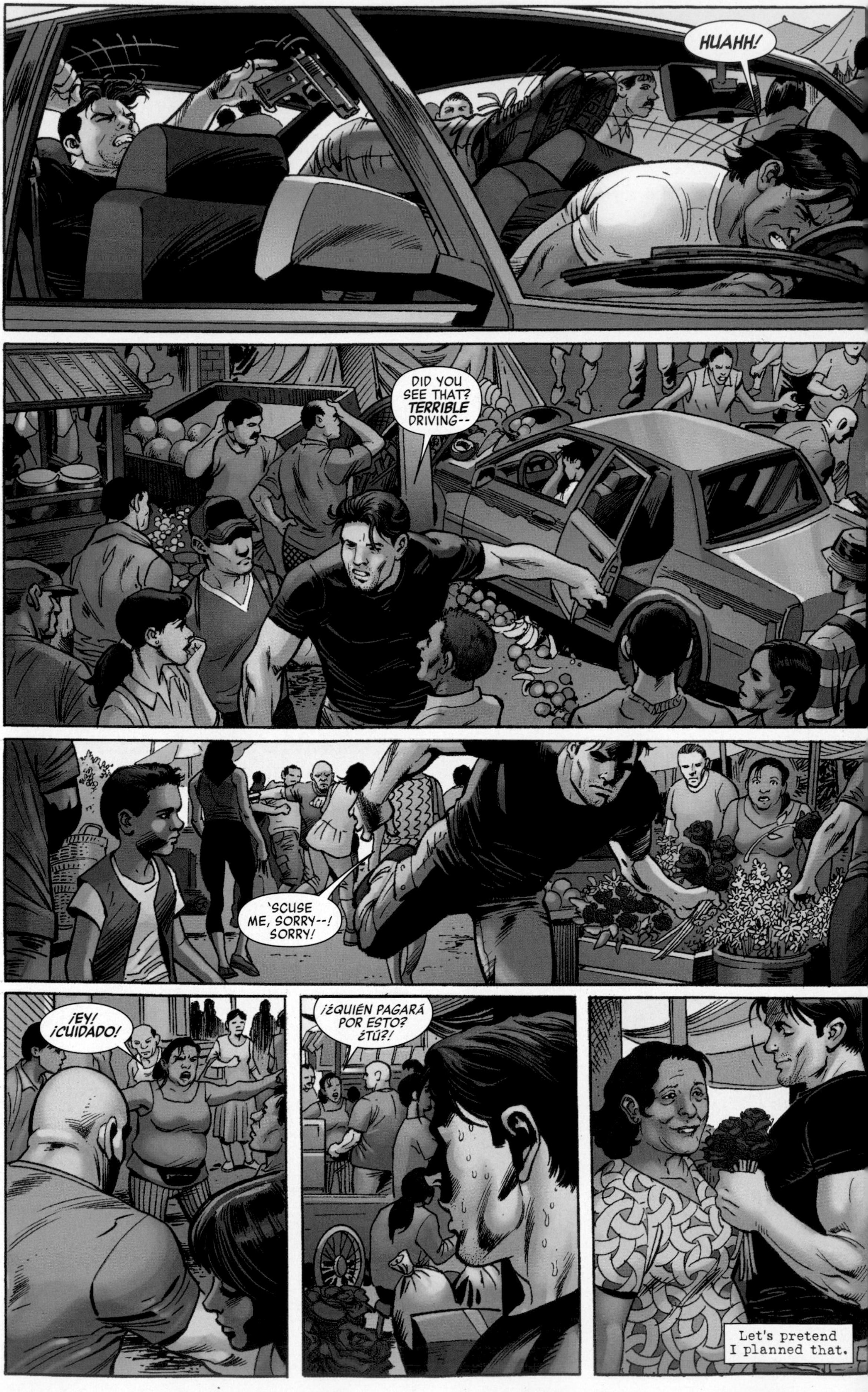
HUAHH!
DID YOU SEE THAT? TERRIBLE DRIVING--
'SCUSE ME, SORRY--! SORRY!
¡EY! ¡CUIDADO!
¡¿QUIÉN PAGARÁ POR ESTO? ¿TÚ?!
Let's pretend I planned that.

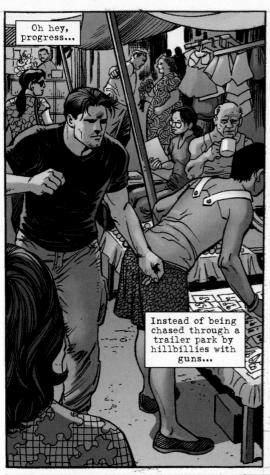

Oh hey, progress...

Instead of being chased through a trailer park by hillbillies with guns...

Here I am in an exotic locale...

Trying to make my way back to where I may or may not have seen an unnamed blonde who is my one and only lead.

Did I mention the part about how I lost my wallet and passport and ugly James Bond just promised to shoot me if he ever lays eyes on me again?

Really? I left that part out?

Kill me.

DON'T MOVE.

...I didn't mean that.

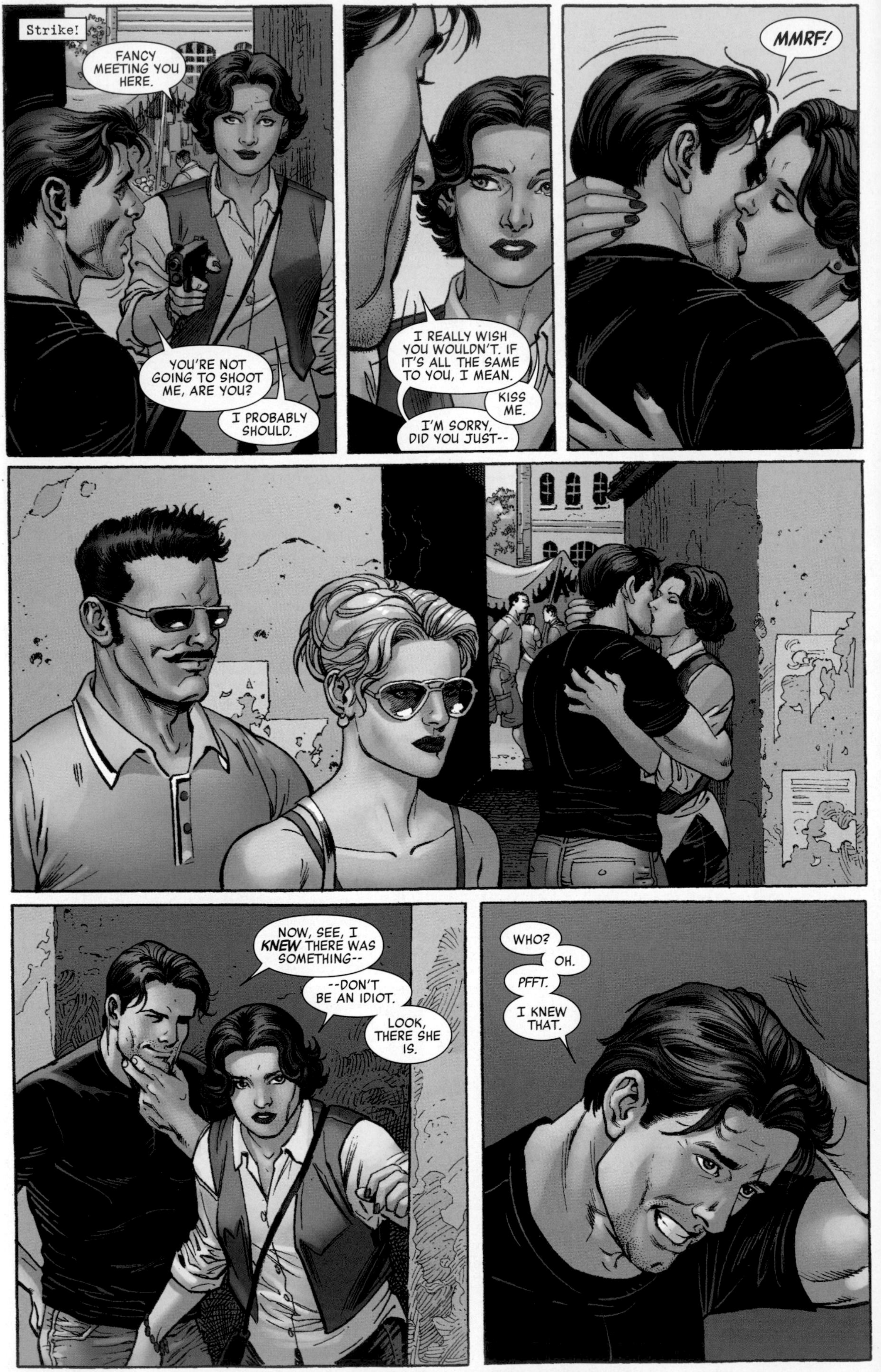
Strike!
FANCY MEETING YOU HERE.
YOU'RE NOT GOING TO SHOOT ME, ARE YOU?
I PROBABLY SHOULD.
I REALLY WISH YOU WOULDN'T. IF IT'S ALL THE SAME TO YOU, I MEAN.
KISS ME.
I'M SORRY, DID YOU JUST--
MMRF!
NOW, SEE, I KNEW THERE WAS SOMETHING--
--DON'T BE AN IDIOT.
LOOK, THERE SHE IS.
WHO?
OH.
PFFT.
I KNEW THAT.

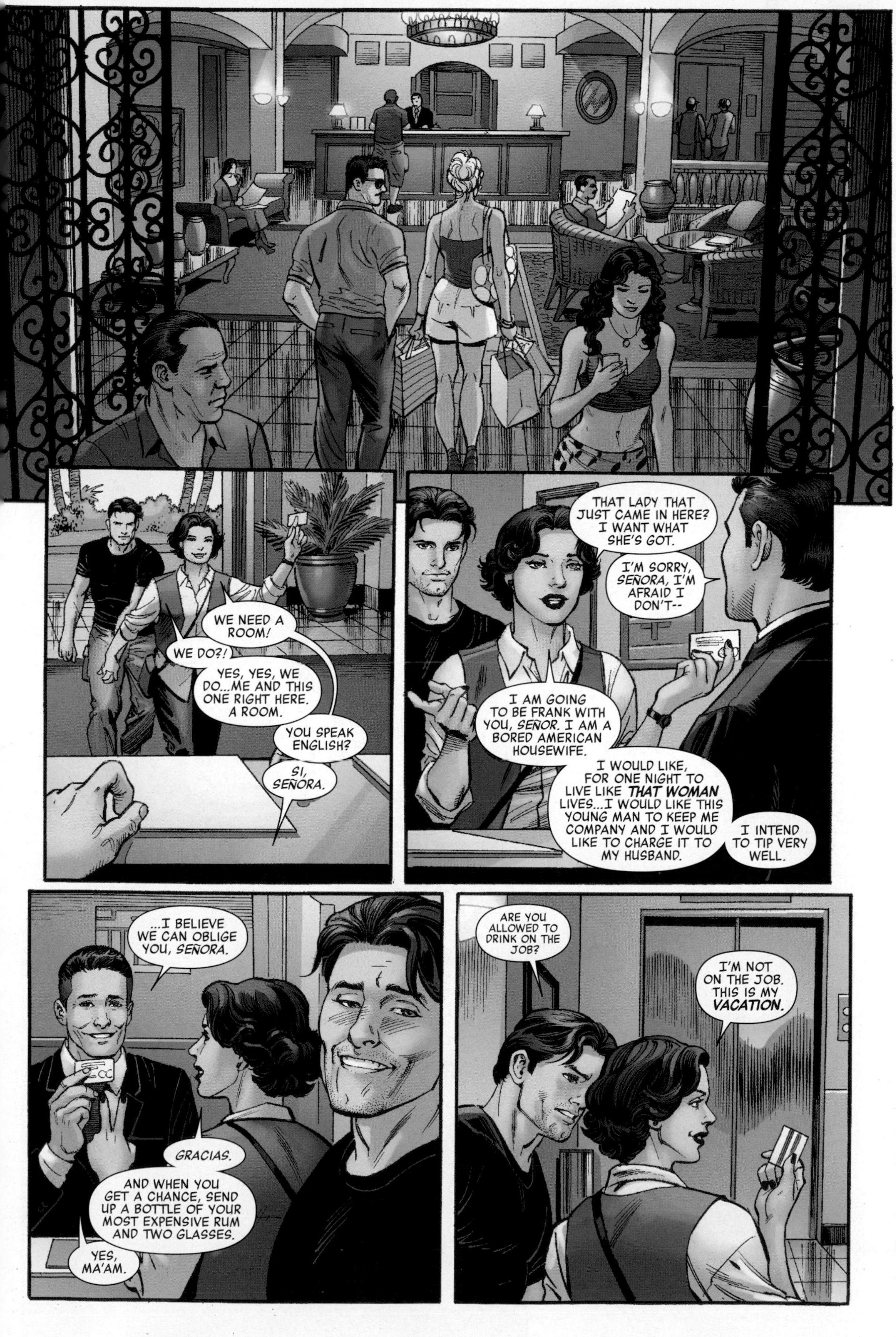
WE NEED A ROOM!
WE DO?!
YES, YES, WE DO...ME AND THIS ONE RIGHT HERE. A ROOM.
YOU SPEAK ENGLISH?
SI, SEÑORA.
THAT LADY THAT JUST CAME IN HERE? I WANT WHAT SHE'S GOT.
I'M SORRY, SEÑORA, I'M AFRAID I DON'T--
I AM GOING TO BE FRANK WITH YOU, SEÑOR. I AM A BORED AMERICAN HOUSEWIFE.
I WOULD LIKE, FOR ONE NIGHT TO LIVE LIKE THAT WOMAN LIVES...I WOULD LIKE THIS YOUNG MAN TO KEEP ME COMPANY AND I WOULD LIKE TO CHARGE IT TO MY HUSBAND.
I INTEND TO TIP VERY WELL.
...I BELIEVE WE CAN OBLIGE YOU, SEÑORA.
GRACIAS.
AND WHEN YOU GET A CHANCE, SEND UP A BOTTLE OF YOUR MOST EXPENSIVE RUM AND TWO GLASSES.
YES, MA'AM.
ARE YOU ALLOWED TO DRINK ON THE JOB?
I'M NOT ON THE JOB. THIS IS MY VACATION.

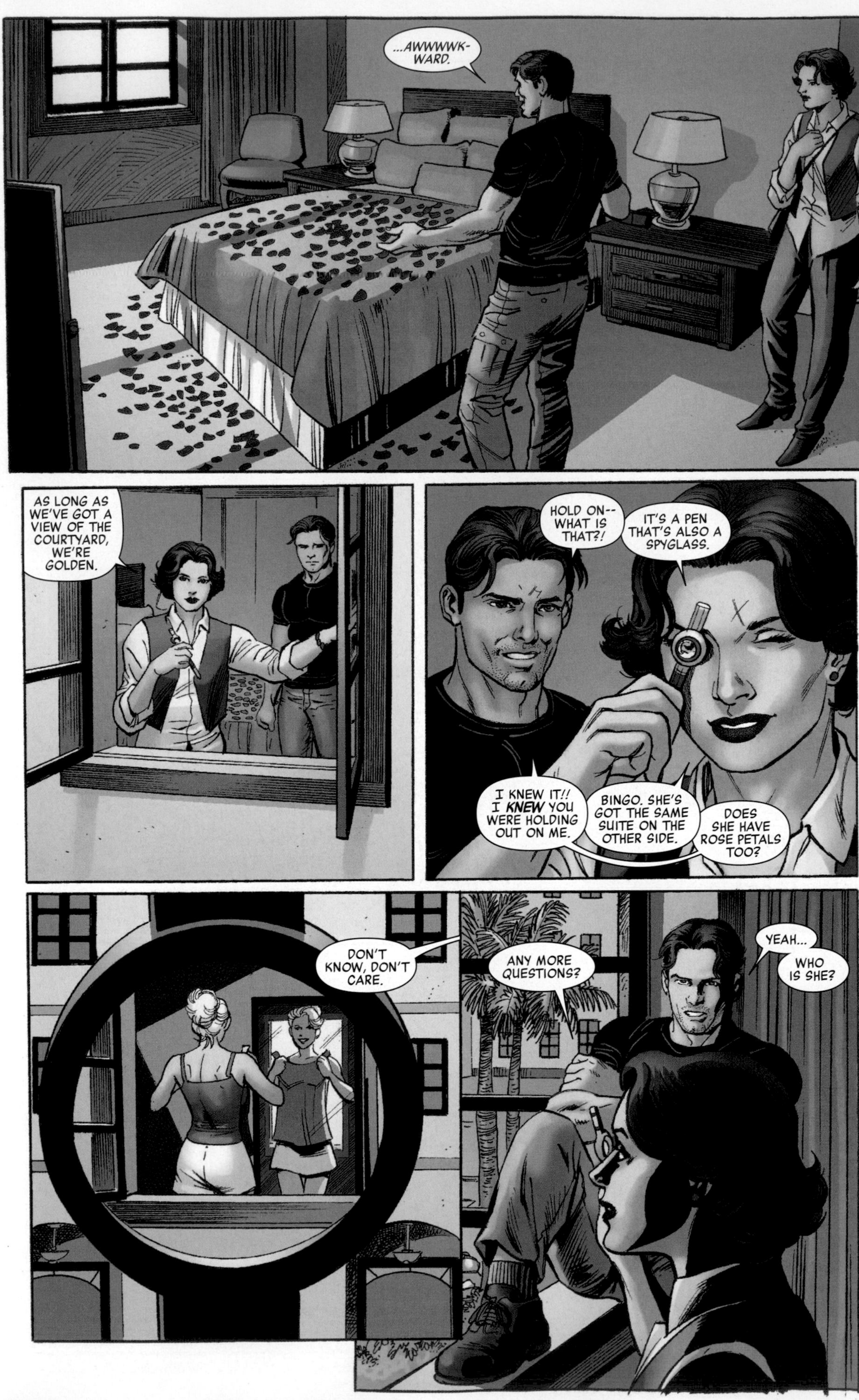
...AWWWWK-WARD.
AS LONG AS WE'VE GOT A VIEW OF THE COURTYARD, WE'RE GOLDEN.
HOLD ON-- WHAT IS THAT?!
IT'S A PEN THAT'S ALSO A SPYGLASS.
I KNEW IT!! I *KNEW* YOU WERE HOLDING OUT ON ME.
BINGO. SHE'S GOT THE SAME SUITE ON THE OTHER SIDE.
DOES SHE HAVE ROSE PETALS TOO?
DON'T KNOW, DON'T CARE.
ANY MORE QUESTIONS?
YEAH...
WHO IS SHE?

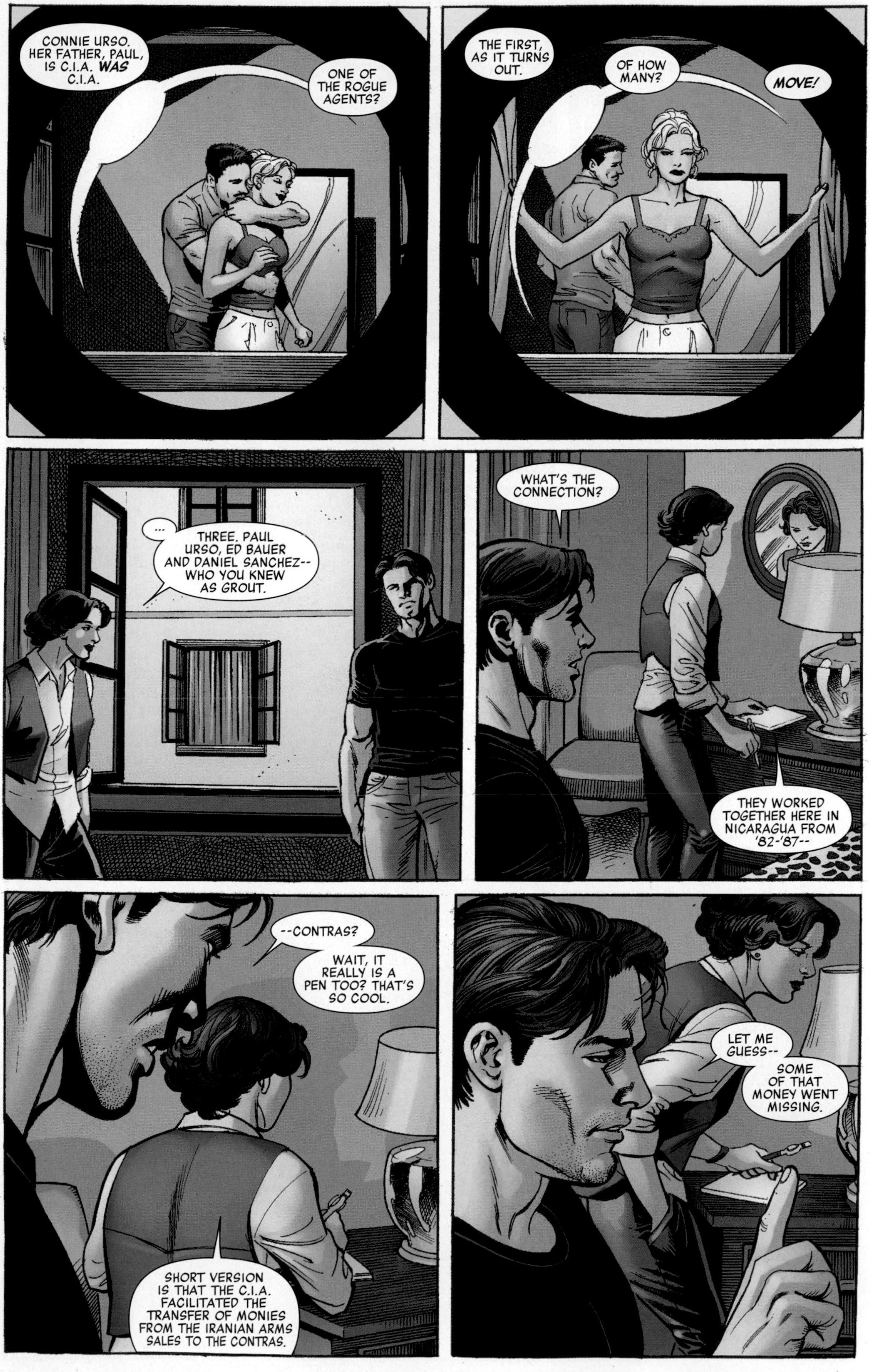
CONNIE URSO. HER FATHER, PAUL, IS C.I.A. WAS C.I.A.
ONE OF THE ROGUE AGENTS?
THE FIRST, AS IT TURNS OUT.
OF HOW MANY?
MOVE!
...THREE. PAUL URSO, ED BAUER AND DANIEL SANCHEZ-- WHO YOU KNEW AS GROUT.
WHAT'S THE CONNECTION?
THEY WORKED TOGETHER HERE IN NICARAGUA FROM '82-'87--
--CONTRAS?
WAIT, IT REALLY IS A PEN TOO? THAT'S SO COOL.
SHORT VERSION IS THAT THE C.I.A. FACILITATED THE TRANSFER OF MONIES FROM THE IRANIAN ARMS SALES TO THE CONTRAS.
LET ME GUESS--
SOME OF THAT MONEY WENT MISSING.

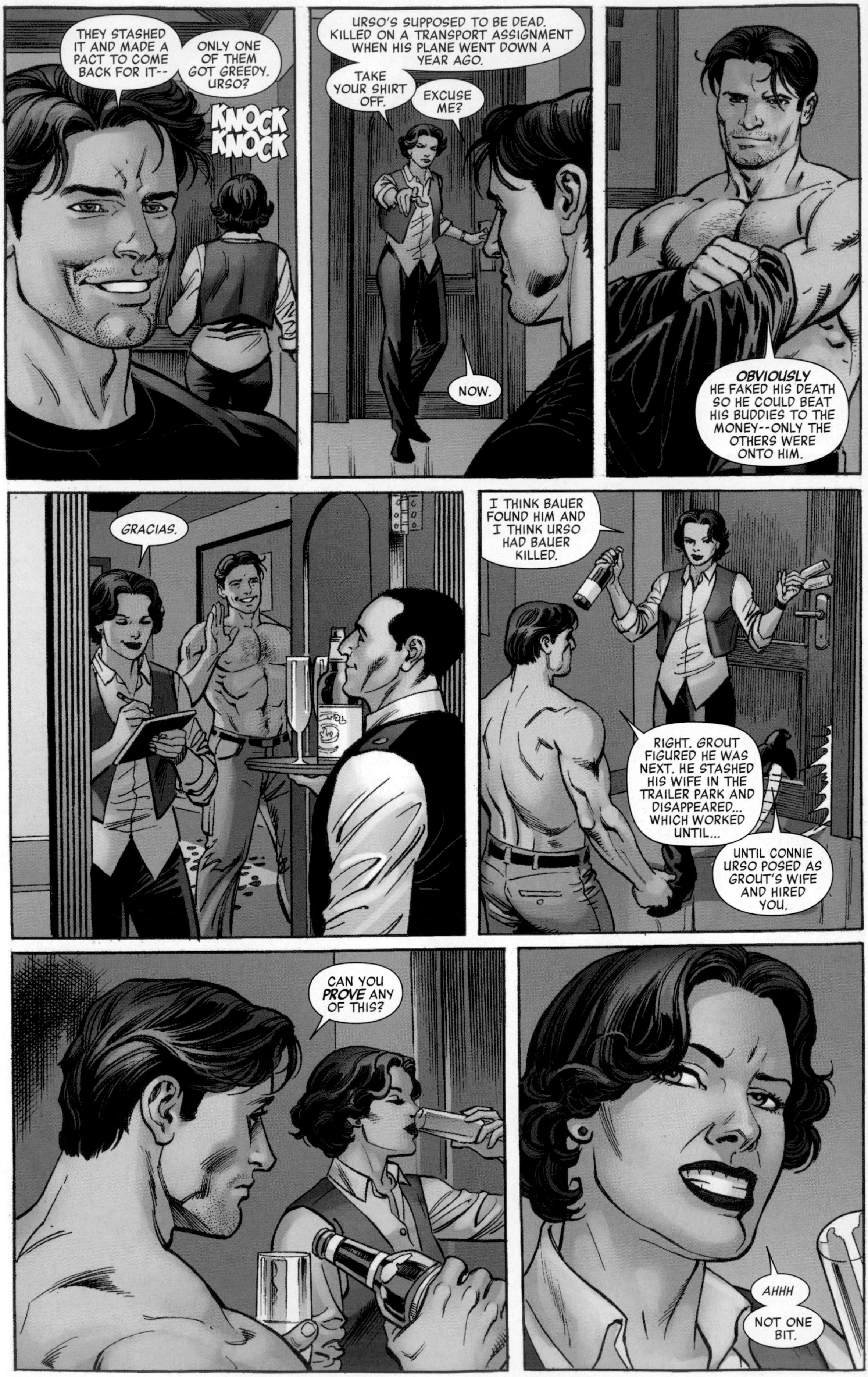
THEY STASHED IT AND MADE A PACT TO COME BACK FOR IT--
ONLY ONE OF THEM GOT GREEDY. URSO?
KNOCK KNOCK
URSO'S SUPPOSED TO BE DEAD. KILLED ON A TRANSPORT ASSIGNMENT WHEN HIS PLANE WENT DOWN A YEAR AGO.
TAKE YOUR SHIRT OFF.
EXCUSE ME?
NOW.
OBVIOUSLY HE FAKED HIS DEATH SO HE COULD BEAT HIS BUDDIES TO THE MONEY--ONLY THE OTHERS WERE ONTO HIM.
GRACIAS.
I THINK BAUER FOUND HIM AND I THINK URSO HAD BAUER KILLED.
RIGHT. GROUT FIGURED HE WAS NEXT. HE STASHED HIS WIFE IN THE TRAILER PARK AND DISAPPEARED... WHICH WORKED UNTIL...
UNTIL CONNIE URSO POSED AS GROUT'S WIFE AND HIRED YOU.
CAN YOU PROVE ANY OF THIS?
AHHH
NOT ONE BIT.

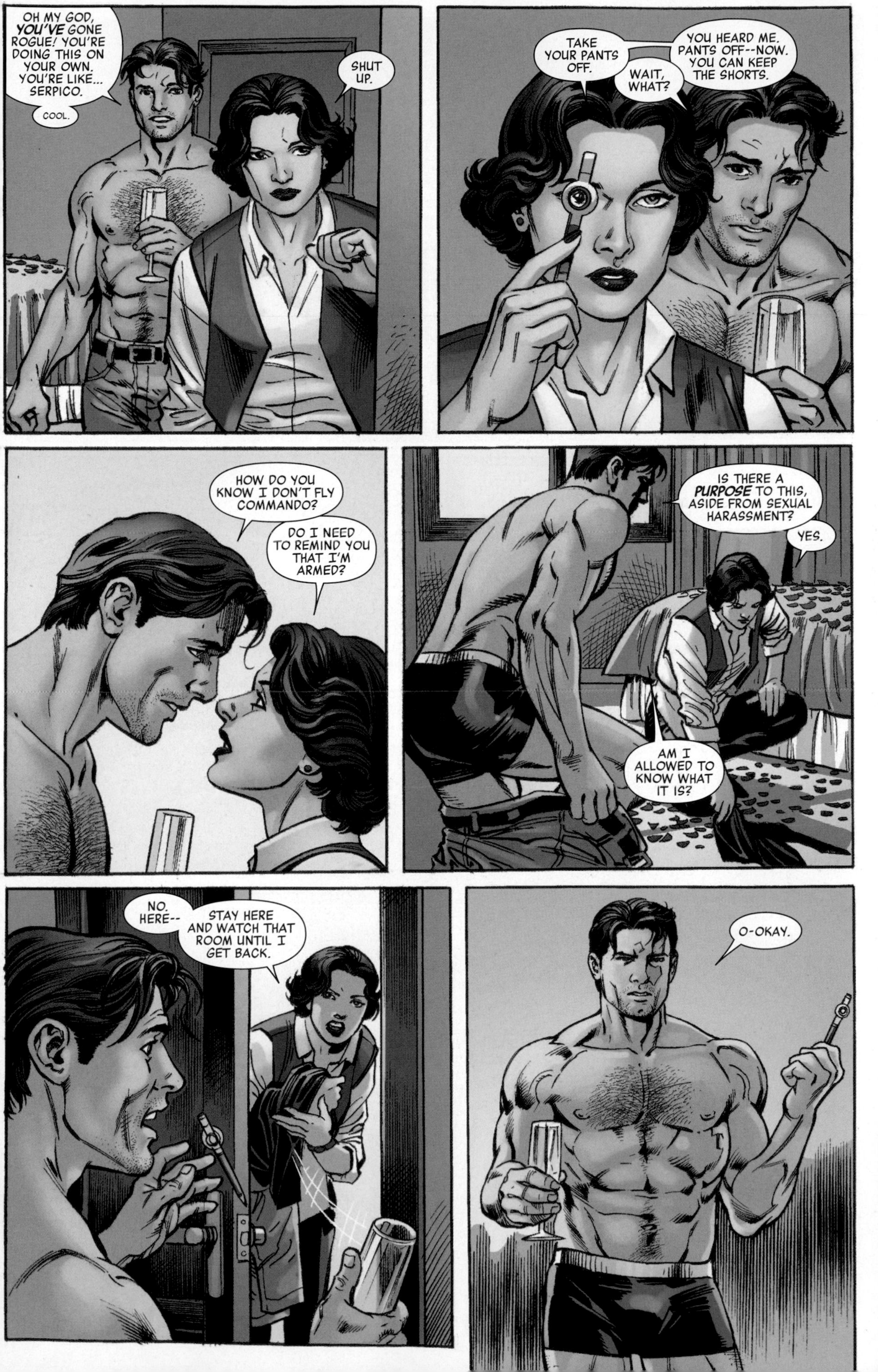
OH MY GOD, YOU'VE GONE ROGUE! YOU'RE DOING THIS ON YOUR OWN. YOU'RE LIKE... SERPICO.
COOL.
SHUT UP.
TAKE YOUR PANTS OFF.
WAIT, WHAT?
YOU HEARD ME. PANTS OFF--NOW. YOU CAN KEEP THE SHORTS.
HOW DO YOU KNOW I DON'T FLY COMMANDO?
DO I NEED TO REMIND YOU THAT I'M ARMED?
IS THERE A PURPOSE TO THIS, ASIDE FROM SEXUAL HARASSMENT?
YES.
AM I ALLOWED TO KNOW WHAT IT IS?
NO. HERE--
STAY HERE AND WATCH THAT ROOM UNTIL I GET BACK.
O-OKAY.

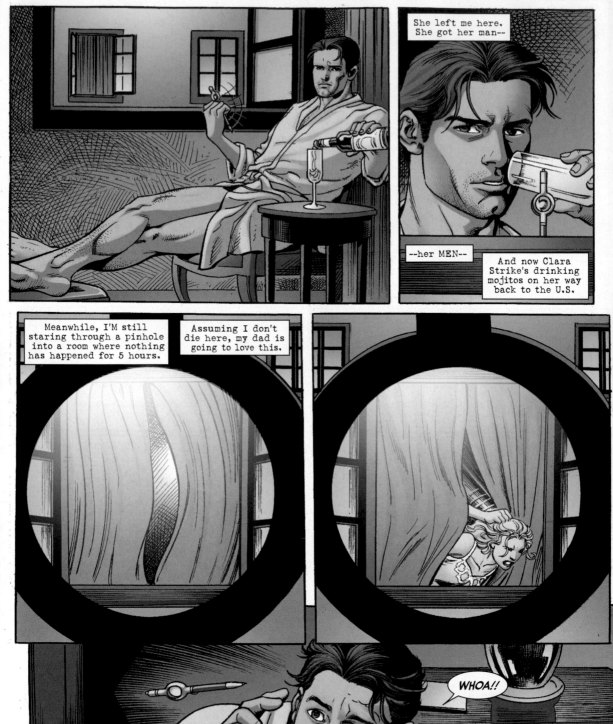

She left me here. She got her man—

—her MEN—

And now Clara Strike's drinking mojitos on her way back to the U.S.

Meanwhile, I'M still staring through a pinhole into a room where nothing has happened for 5 hours.

Assuming I don't die here, my dad is going to love this.

WHOA!!

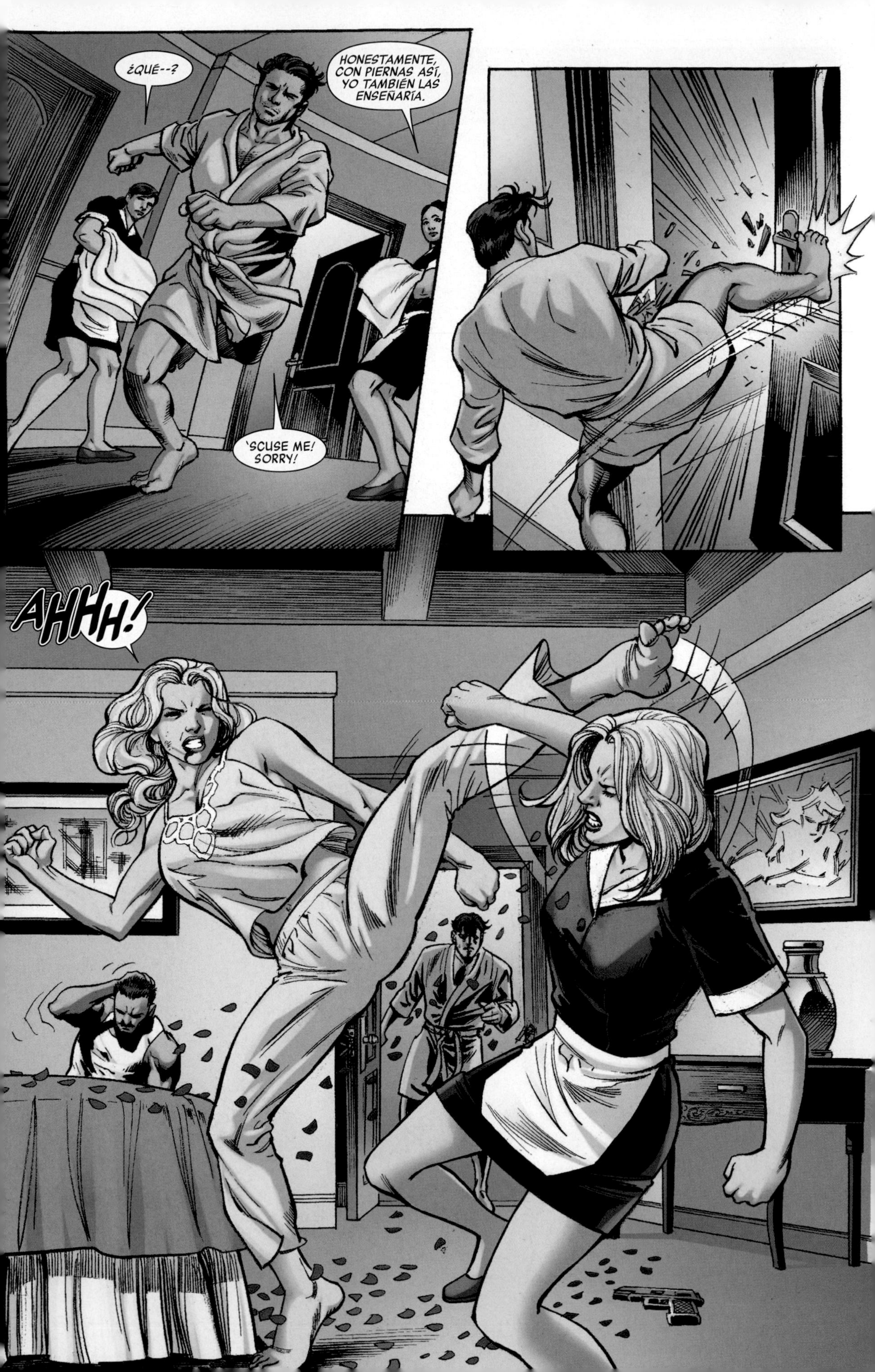
¿QUÉ--?
HONESTAMENTE, CON PIERNAS ASÍ, YO TAMBIÉN LAS ENSEÑARÍA.
'SCUSE ME! SORRY!
AHHH!

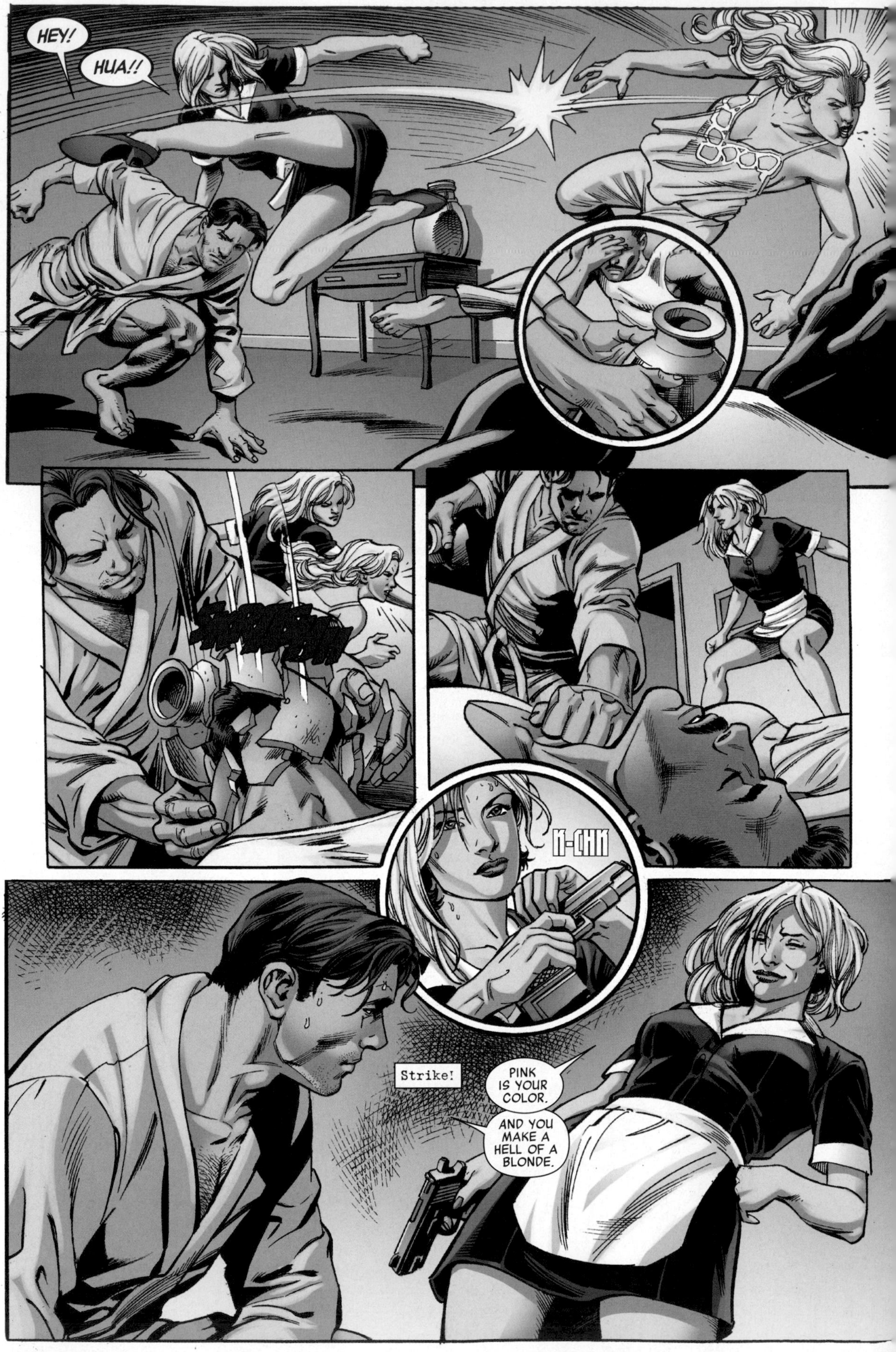
HEY!
HUA!!
K-CHK
Strike!
PINK IS YOUR COLOR.
AND YOU MAKE A HELL OF A BLONDE.

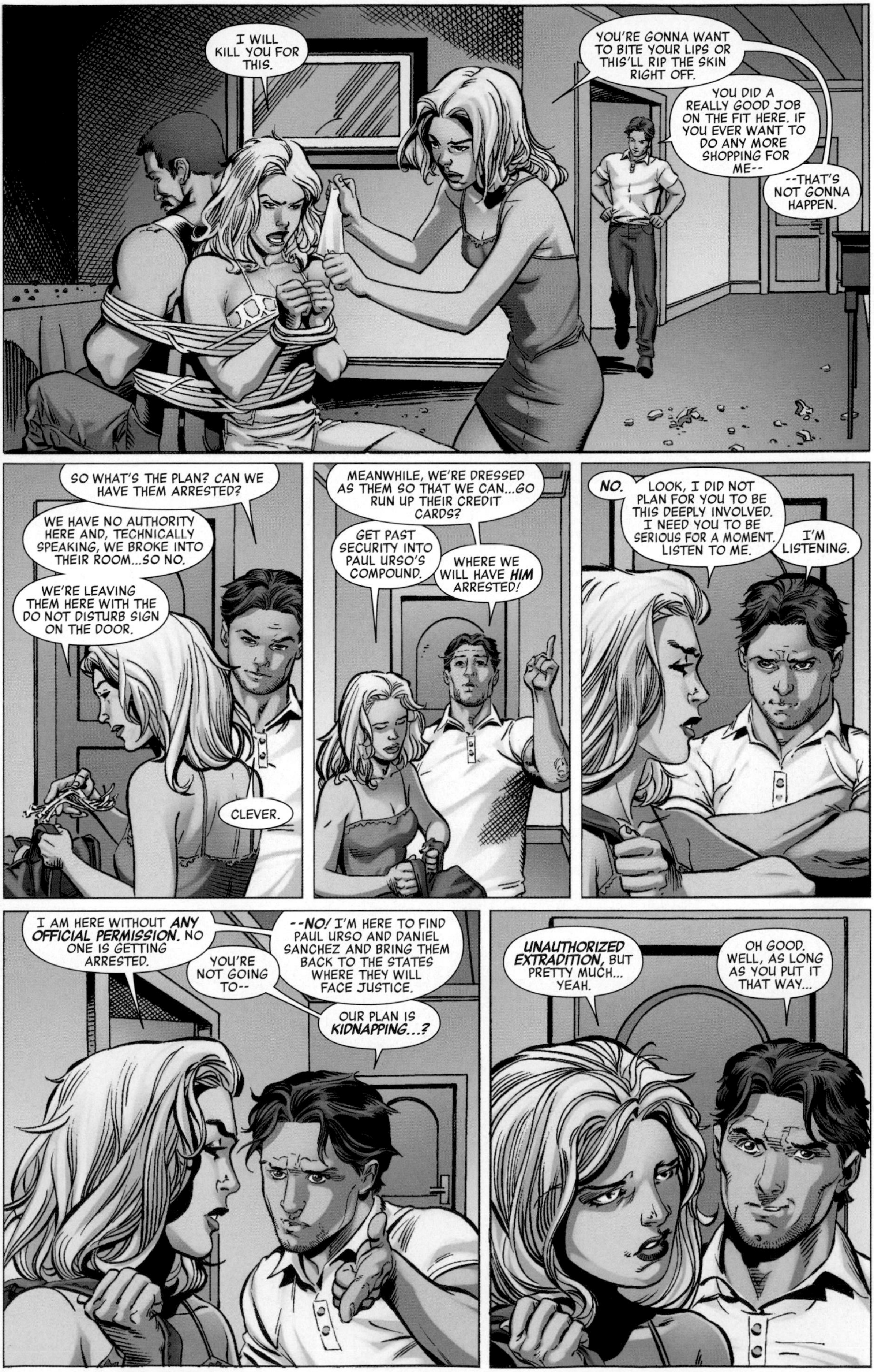
I WILL KILL YOU FOR THIS.
YOU'RE GONNA WANT TO BITE YOUR LIPS OR THIS'LL RIP THE SKIN RIGHT OFF.
YOU DID A REALLY GOOD JOB ON THE FIT HERE. IF YOU EVER WANT TO DO ANY MORE SHOPPING FOR ME--
--THAT'S NOT GONNA HAPPEN.
SO WHAT'S THE PLAN? CAN WE HAVE THEM ARRESTED?
WE HAVE NO AUTHORITY HERE AND, TECHNICALLY SPEAKING, WE BROKE INTO THEIR ROOM...SO NO.
WE'RE LEAVING THEM HERE WITH THE DO NOT DISTURB SIGN ON THE DOOR.
CLEVER.
MEANWHILE, WE'RE DRESSED AS THEM SO THAT WE CAN...GO RUN UP THEIR CREDIT CARDS?
GET PAST SECURITY INTO PAUL URSO'S COMPOUND.
WHERE WE WILL HAVE HIM ARRESTED!
NO.
LOOK, I DID NOT PLAN FOR YOU TO BE THIS DEEPLY INVOLVED. I NEED YOU TO BE SERIOUS FOR A MOMENT. LISTEN TO ME.
I'M LISTENING.
I AM HERE WITHOUT ANY OFFICIAL PERMISSION. NO ONE IS GETTING ARRESTED.
YOU'RE NOT GOING TO--
--NO! I'M HERE TO FIND PAUL URSO AND DANIEL SANCHEZ AND BRING THEM BACK TO THE STATES WHERE THEY WILL FACE JUSTICE.
OUR PLAN IS KIDNAPPING...?
UNAUTHORIZED EXTRADITION, BUT PRETTY MUCH... YEAH.
OH GOOD. WELL, AS LONG AS YOU PUT IT THAT WAY...

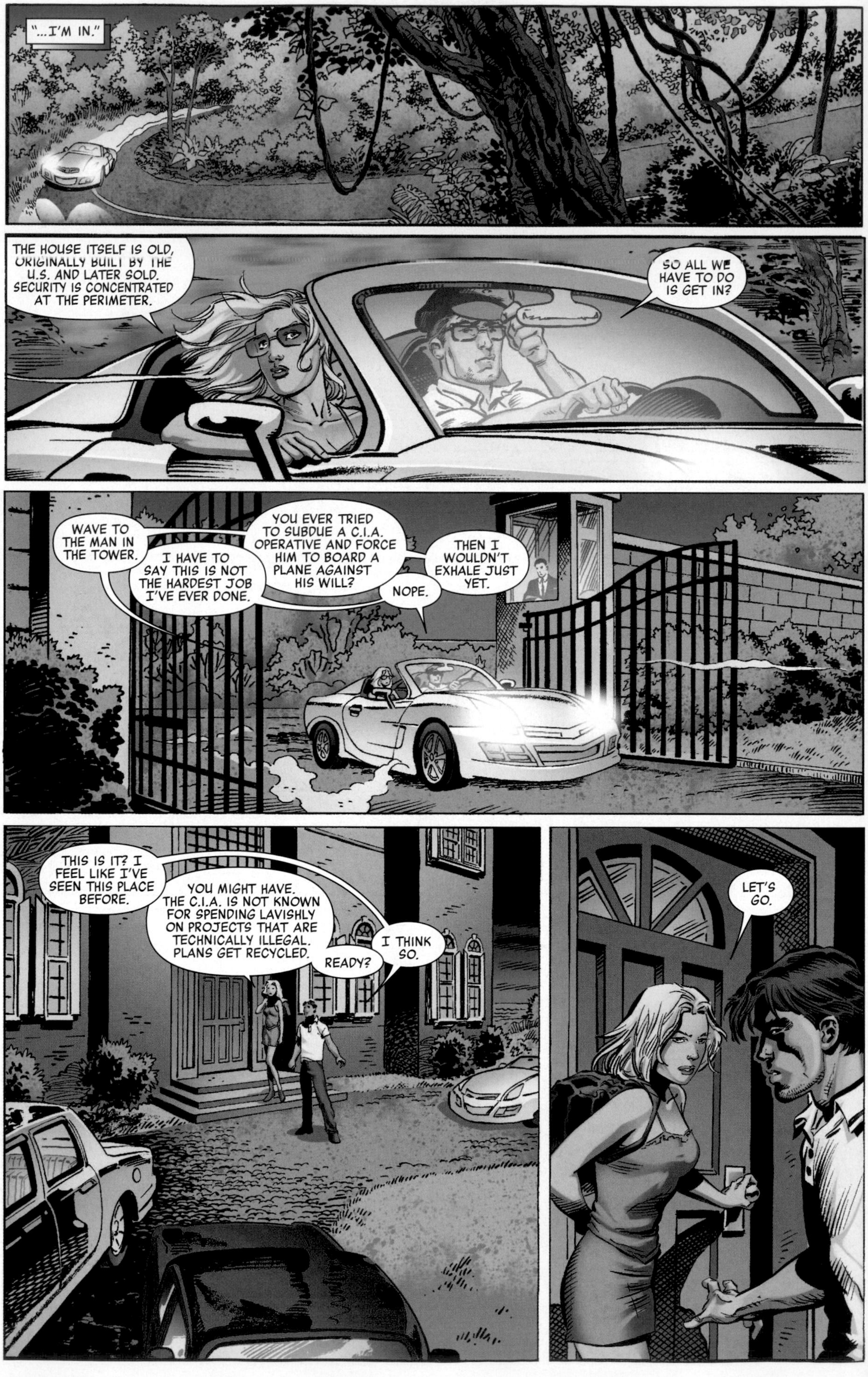
"...I'M IN."
THE HOUSE ITSELF IS OLD, ORIGINALLY BUILT BY THE U.S. AND LATER SOLD. SECURITY IS CONCENTRATED AT THE PERIMETER.
SO ALL WE HAVE TO DO IS GET IN?
WAVE TO THE MAN IN THE TOWER.
I HAVE TO SAY THIS IS NOT THE HARDEST JOB I'VE EVER DONE.
YOU EVER TRIED TO SUBDUE A C.I.A. OPERATIVE AND FORCE HIM TO BOARD A PLANE AGAINST HIS WILL?
NOPE.
THEN I WOULDN'T EXHALE JUST YET.
THIS IS IT? I FEEL LIKE I'VE SEEN THIS PLACE BEFORE.
YOU MIGHT HAVE. THE C.I.A. IS NOT KNOWN FOR SPENDING LAVISHLY ON PROJECTS THAT ARE TECHNICALLY ILLEGAL. PLANS GET RECYCLED.
READY?
I THINK SO.
LET'S GO.

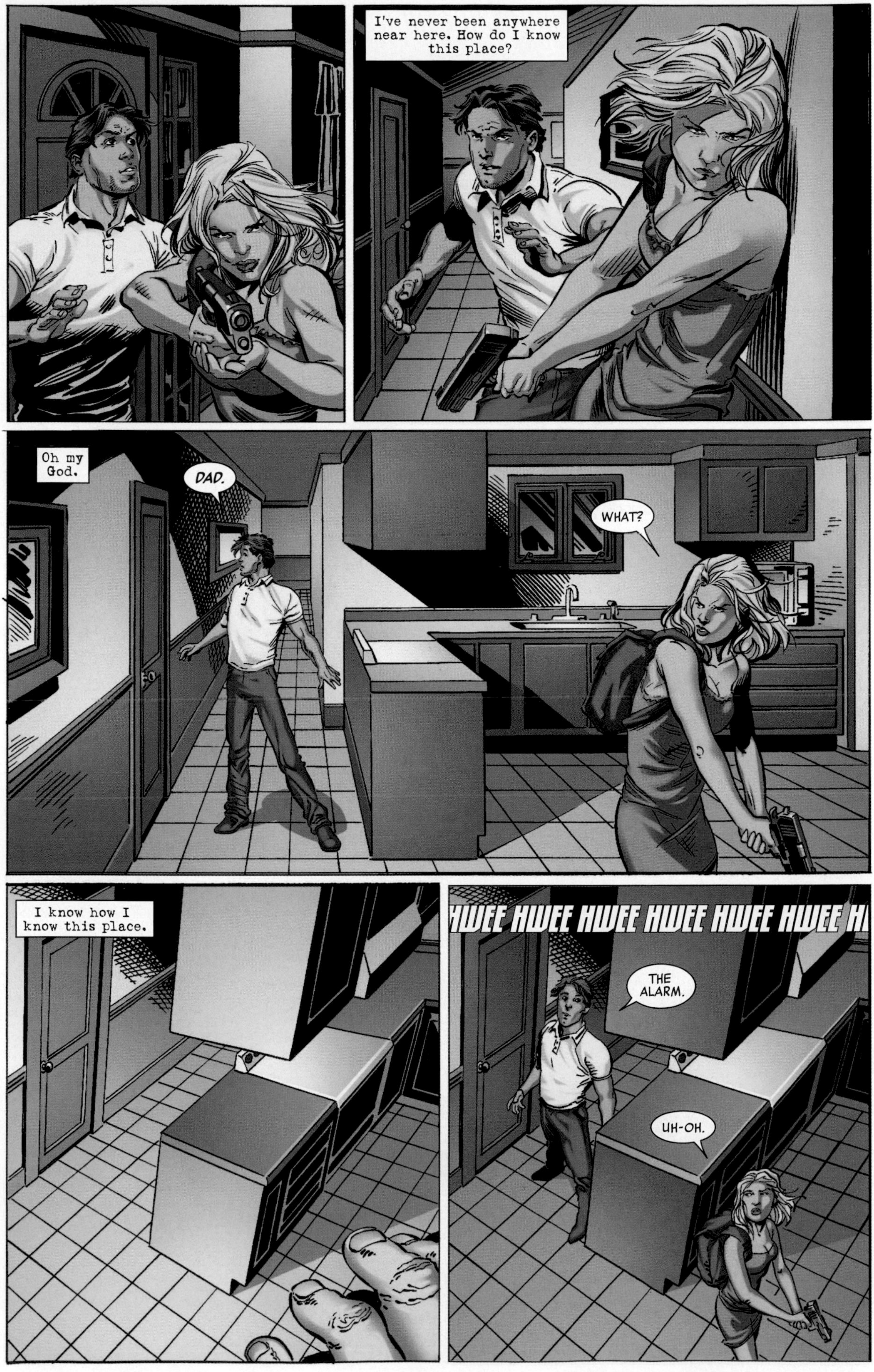

I've never been anywhere near here. How do I know this place?
Oh my God.
DAD.
WHAT?
I know how I know this place.
HWEE HWEE HWEE HWEE HWEE HWEE
THE ALARM.
UH-OH.

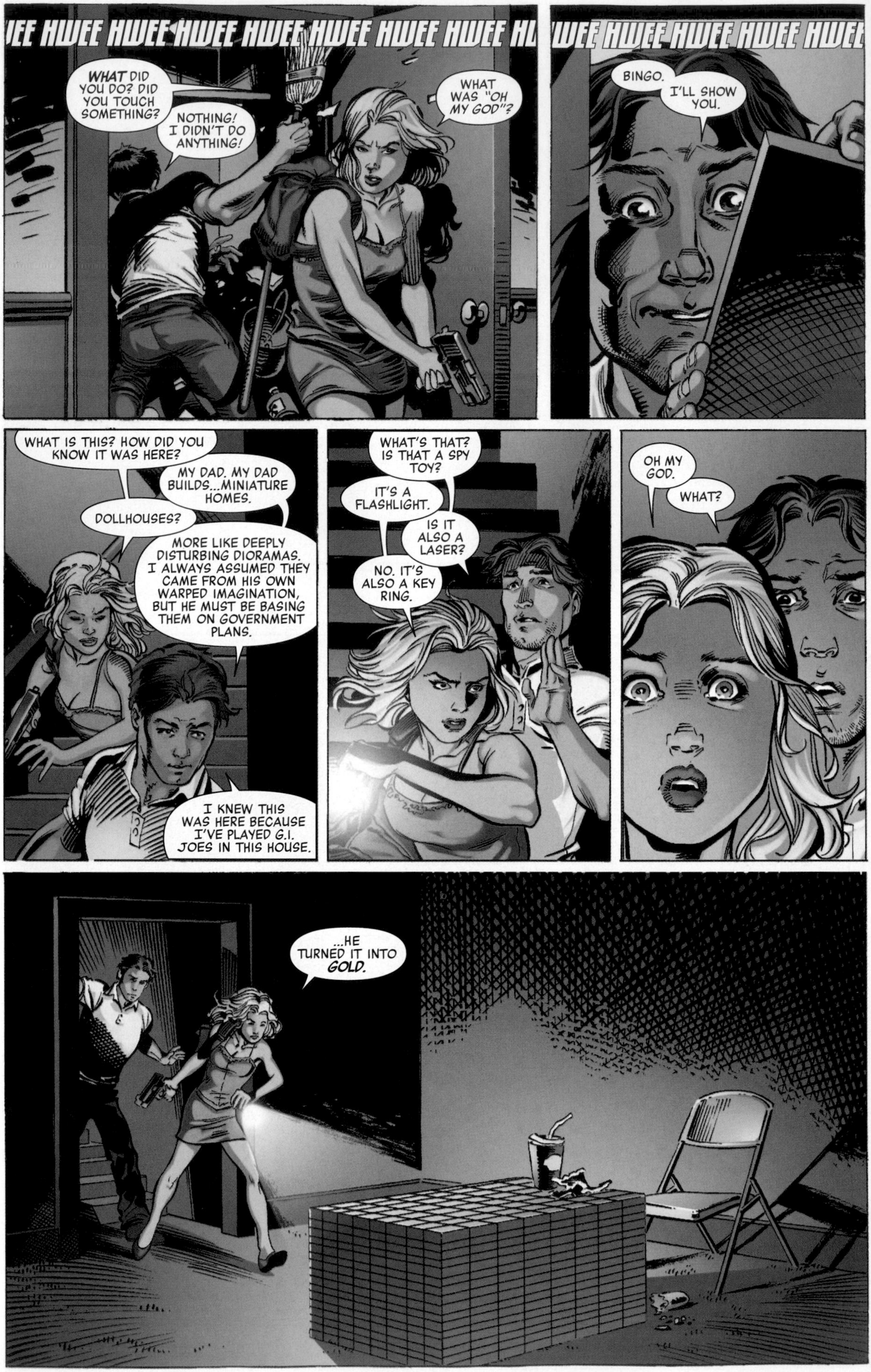

HWEE HWEE HWEE HWEE HWEE HWEE HWEE HWEE HWEE HWEE HWEE
WHAT DID YOU DO? DID YOU TOUCH SOMETHING?
NOTHING! I DIDN'T DO ANYTHING!
WHAT WAS "OH MY GOD"?
BINGO.
I'LL SHOW YOU.
WHAT IS THIS? HOW DID YOU KNOW IT WAS HERE?
MY DAD. MY DAD BUILDS...MINIATURE HOMES.
DOLLHOUSES?
MORE LIKE DEEPLY DISTURBING DIORAMAS. I ALWAYS ASSUMED THEY CAME FROM HIS OWN WARPED IMAGINATION, BUT HE MUST BE BASING THEM ON GOVERNMENT PLANS.
I KNEW THIS WAS HERE BECAUSE I'VE PLAYED G.I. JOES IN THIS HOUSE.
WHAT'S THAT? IS THAT A SPY TOY?
IT'S A FLASHLIGHT.
IS IT ALSO A LASER?
NO. IT'S ALSO A KEY RING.
OH MY GOD.
WHAT?
...HE TURNED IT INTO GOLD.

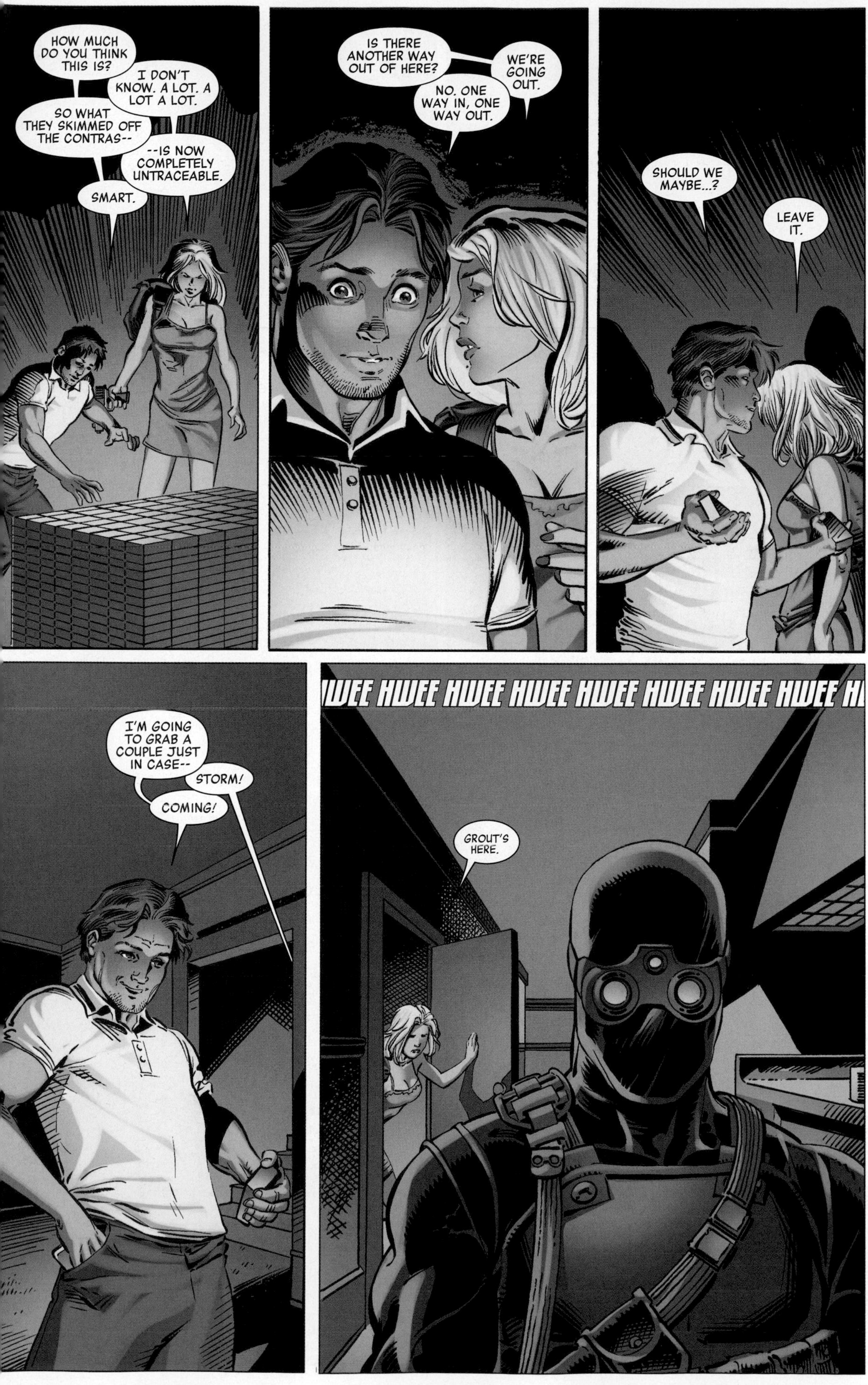
HOW MUCH DO YOU THINK THIS IS?
I DON'T KNOW. A LOT. A LOT A LOT.
SO WHAT THEY SKIMMED OFF THE CONTRAS--
--IS NOW COMPLETELY UNTRACEABLE.
SMART.
IS THERE ANOTHER WAY OUT OF HERE?
NO. ONE WAY IN, ONE WAY OUT.
WE'RE GOING OUT.
SHOULD WE MAYBE...?
LEAVE IT.
I'M GOING TO GRAB A COUPLE JUST IN CASE--
STORM!
COMING!
HWEE HWEE HWEE HWEE HWEE HWEE HWEE HWEE
GROUT'S HERE.

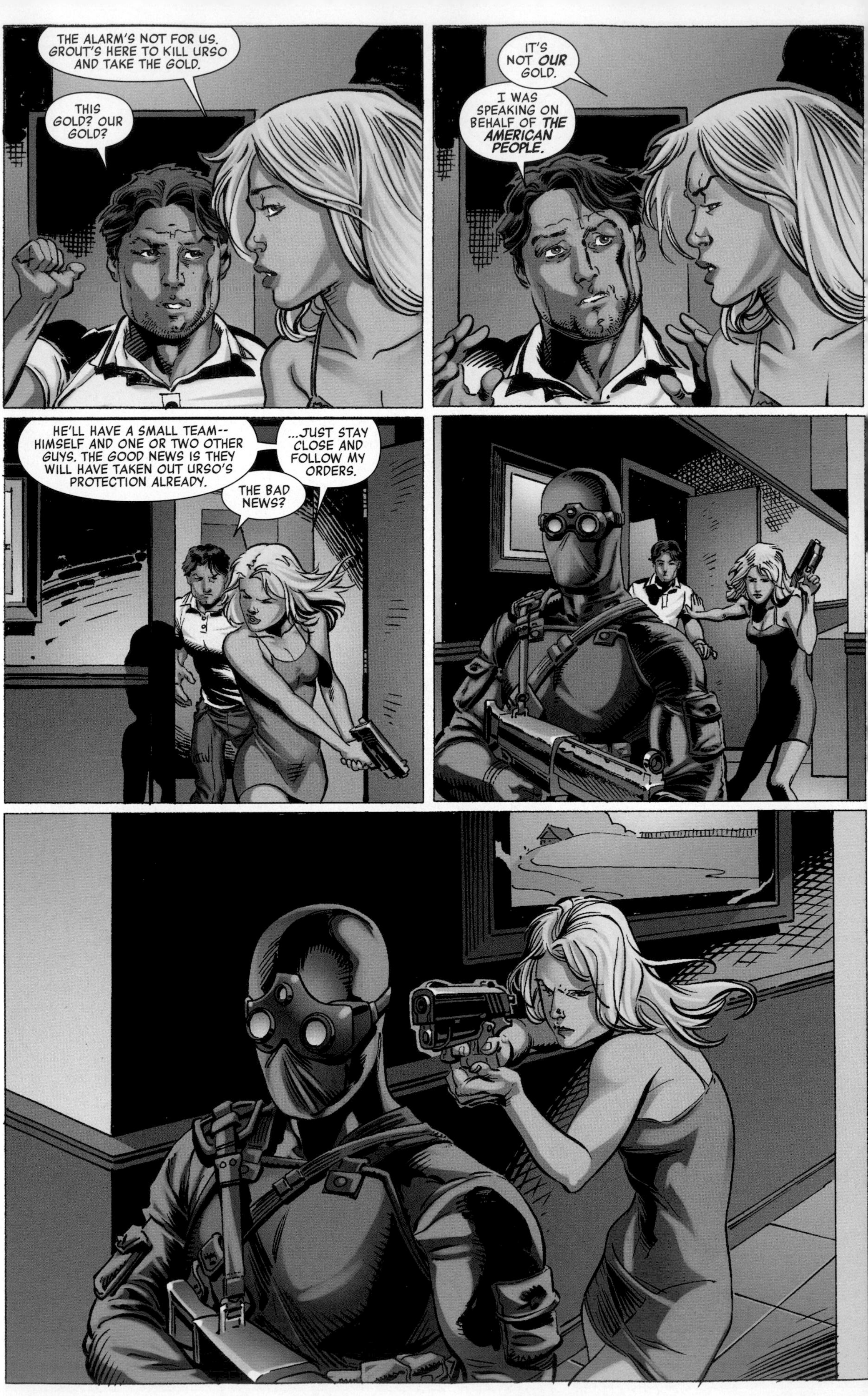
THE ALARM'S NOT FOR US. GROUT'S HERE TO KILL URSO AND TAKE THE GOLD.
THIS GOLD? OUR GOLD?
IT'S NOT OUR GOLD.
I WAS SPEAKING ON BEHALF OF THE AMERICAN PEOPLE.
HE'LL HAVE A SMALL TEAM-- HIMSELF AND ONE OR TWO OTHER GUYS. THE GOOD NEWS IS THEY WILL HAVE TAKEN OUT URSO'S PROTECTION ALREADY.
THE BAD NEWS?
...JUST STAY CLOSE AND FOLLOW MY ORDERS.

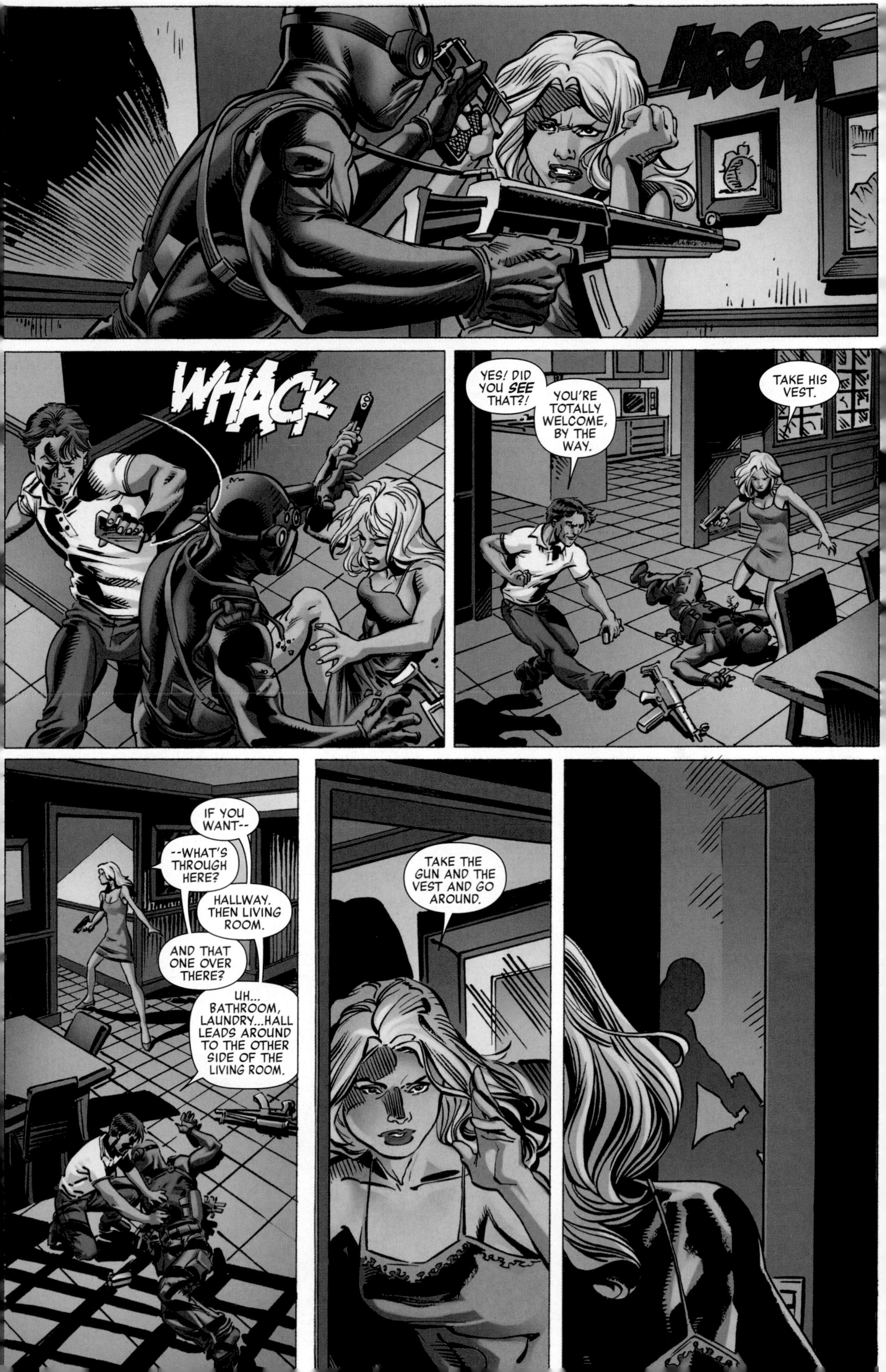
HROKK
WHACK
YES! DID YOU SEE THAT?!
YOU'RE TOTALLY WELCOME, BY THE WAY.
TAKE HIS VEST.
IF YOU WANT--
--WHAT'S THROUGH HERE?
HALLWAY. THEN LIVING ROOM.
AND THAT ONE OVER THERE?
UH... BATHROOM, LAUNDRY...HALL LEADS AROUND TO THE OTHER SIDE OF THE LIVING ROOM.
TAKE THE GUN AND THE VEST AND GO AROUND.

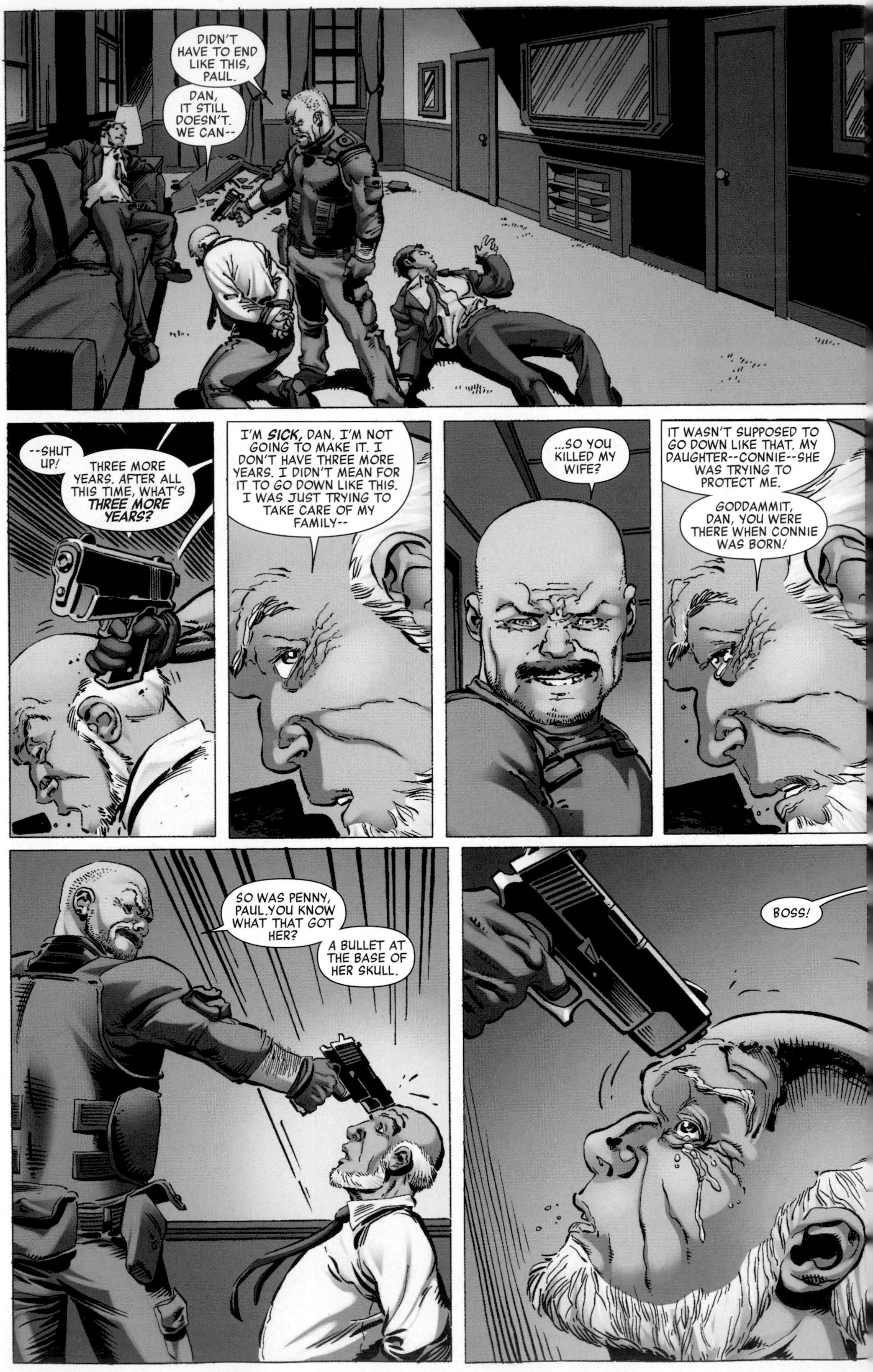
DIDN'T HAVE TO END LIKE THIS, PAUL.
DAN, IT STILL DOESN'T. WE CAN--
--SHUT UP!
THREE MORE YEARS. AFTER ALL THIS TIME, WHAT'S THREE MORE YEARS?
I'M SICK, DAN. I'M NOT GOING TO MAKE IT. I DON'T HAVE THREE MORE YEARS. I DIDN'T MEAN FOR IT TO GO DOWN LIKE THIS. I WAS JUST TRYING TO TAKE CARE OF MY FAMILY--
...SO YOU KILLED MY WIFE?
IT WASN'T SUPPOSED TO GO DOWN LIKE THAT. MY DAUGHTER--CONNIE--SHE WAS TRYING TO PROTECT ME.
GODDAMMIT, DAN, YOU WERE THERE WHEN CONNIE WAS BORN!
SO WAS PENNY, PAUL. YOU KNOW WHAT THAT GOT HER?
A BULLET AT THE BASE OF HER SKULL.
BOSS!

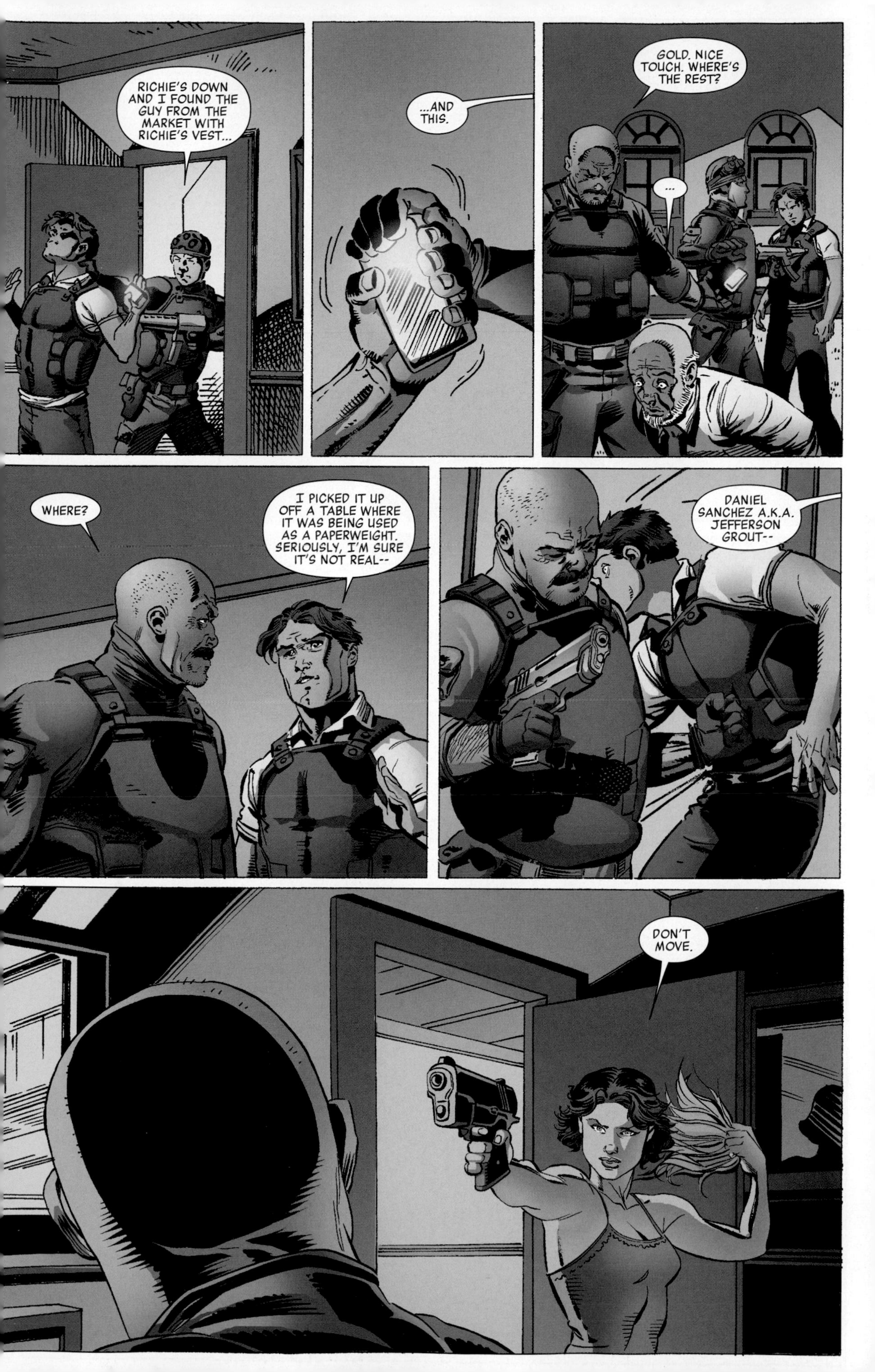
RICHIE'S DOWN AND I FOUND THE GUY FROM THE MARKET WITH RICHIE'S VEST...
...AND THIS.
GOLD. NICE TOUCH. WHERE'S THE REST?
...
WHERE?
I PICKED IT UP OFF A TABLE WHERE IT WAS BEING USED AS A PAPERWEIGHT. SERIOUSLY, I'M SURE IT'S NOT REAL--
DANIEL SANCHEZ A.K.A. JEFFERSON GROUT--
DON'T MOVE.

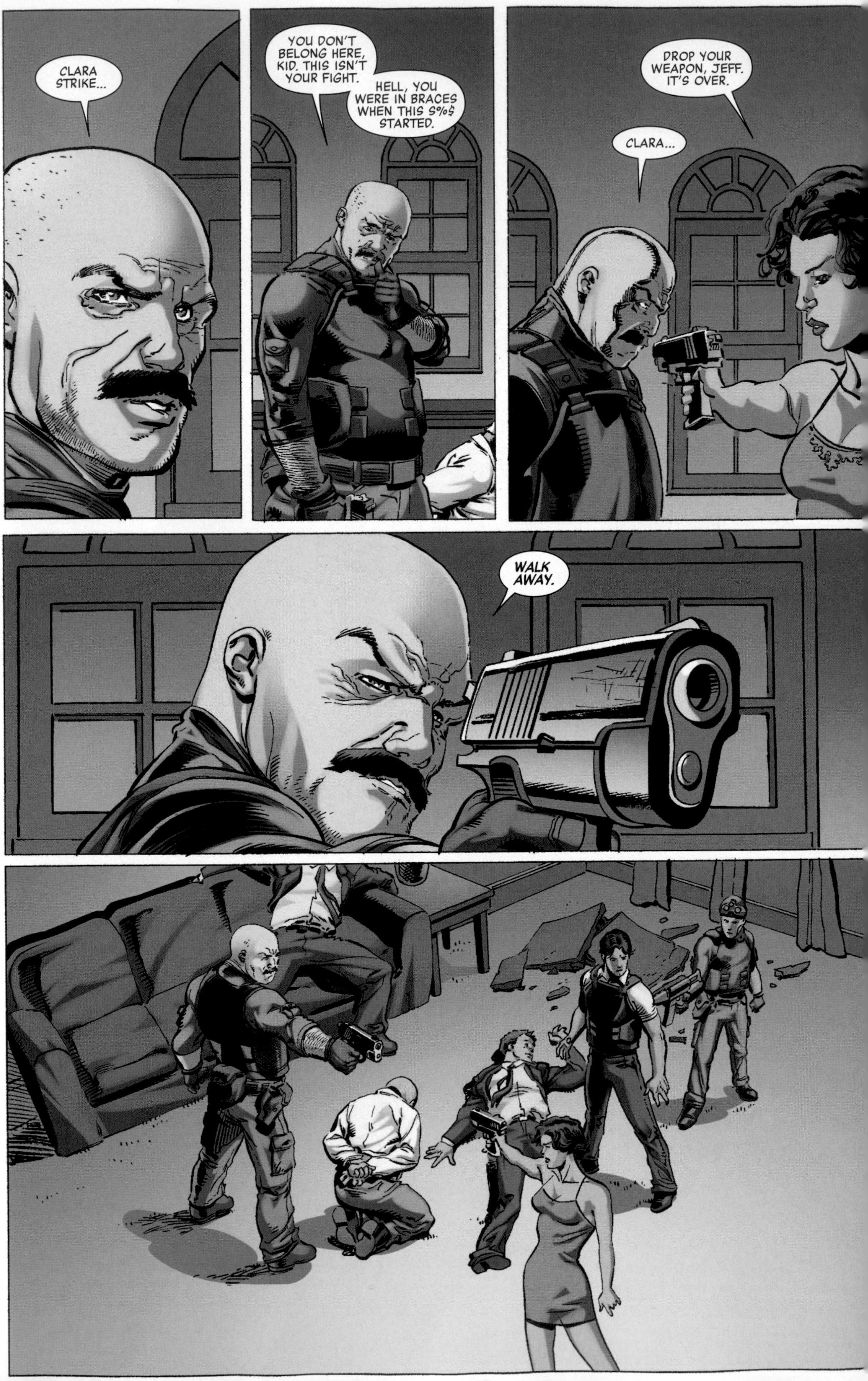
CLARA STRIKE...
YOU DON'T BELONG HERE, KID. THIS ISN'T YOUR FIGHT.
HELL, YOU WERE IN BRACES WHEN THIS $%@$ STARTED.
DROP YOUR WEAPON, JEFF. IT'S OVER.
CLARA...
WALK AWAY.

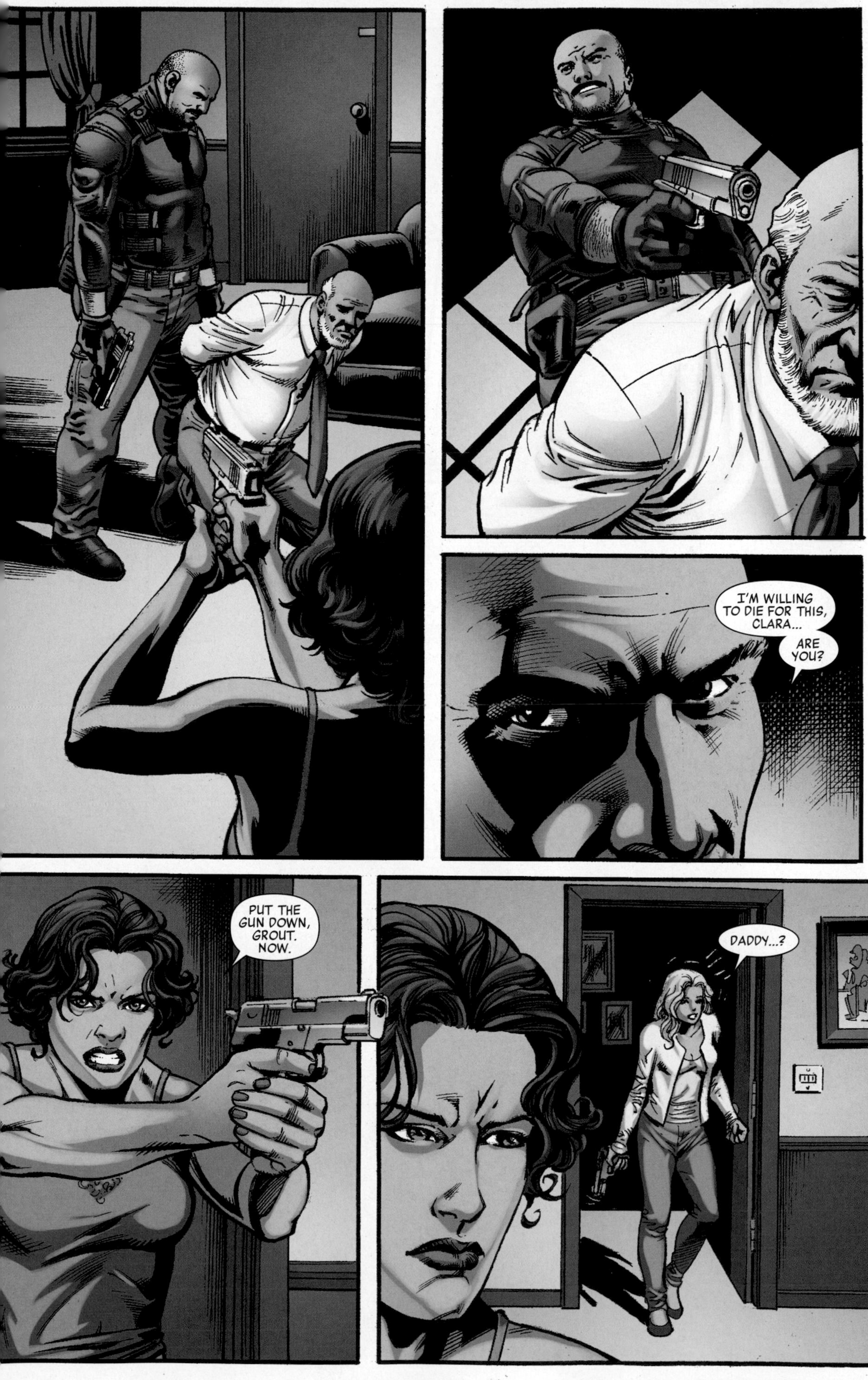
I'M WILLING TO DIE FOR THIS, CLARA...
ARE YOU?
PUT THE GUN DOWN, GROUT. NOW.
DADDY...?

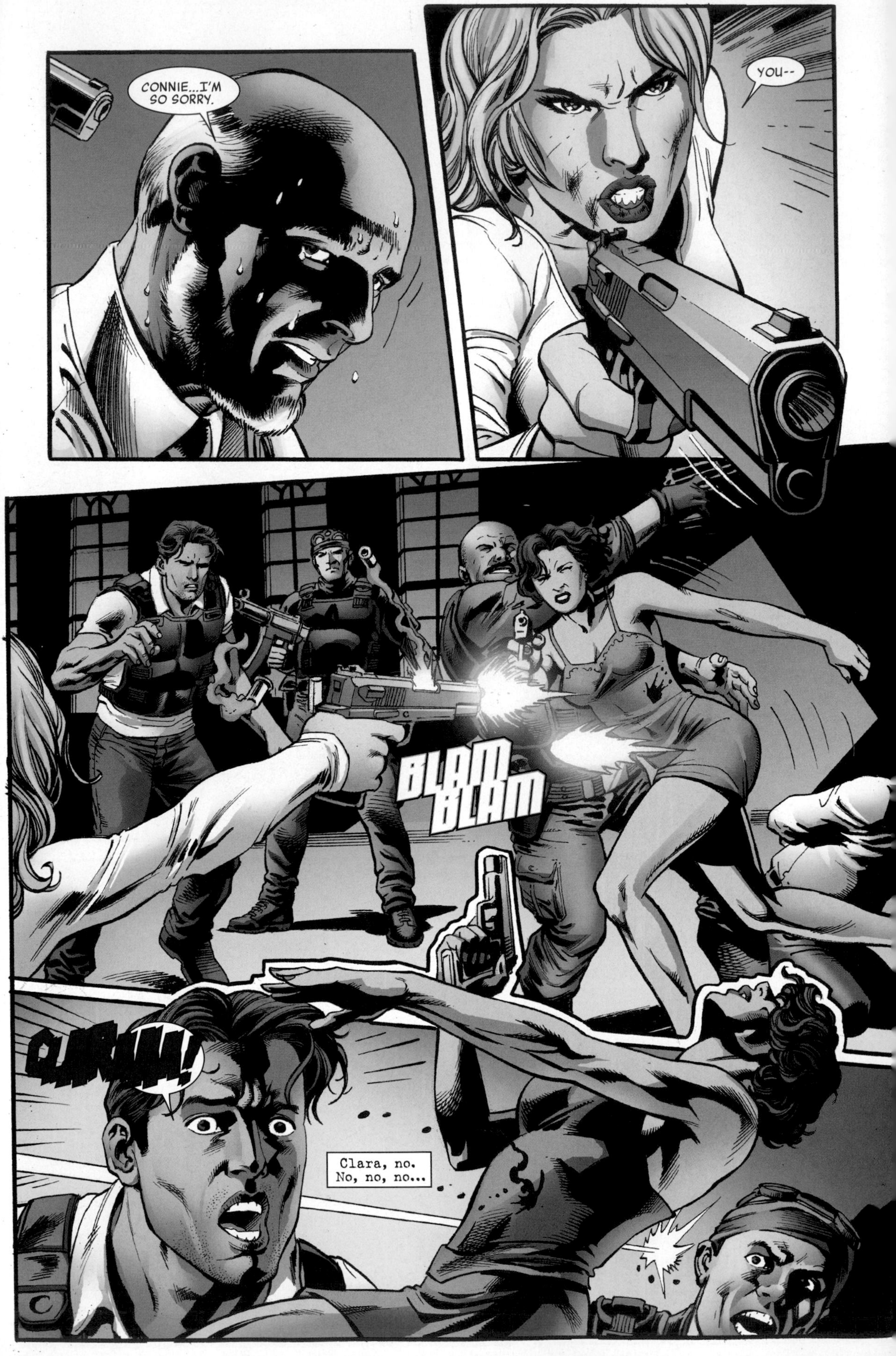
CONNIE...I'M SO SORRY.
YOU--
BLAM BLAM
Clara, no. No, no, no...

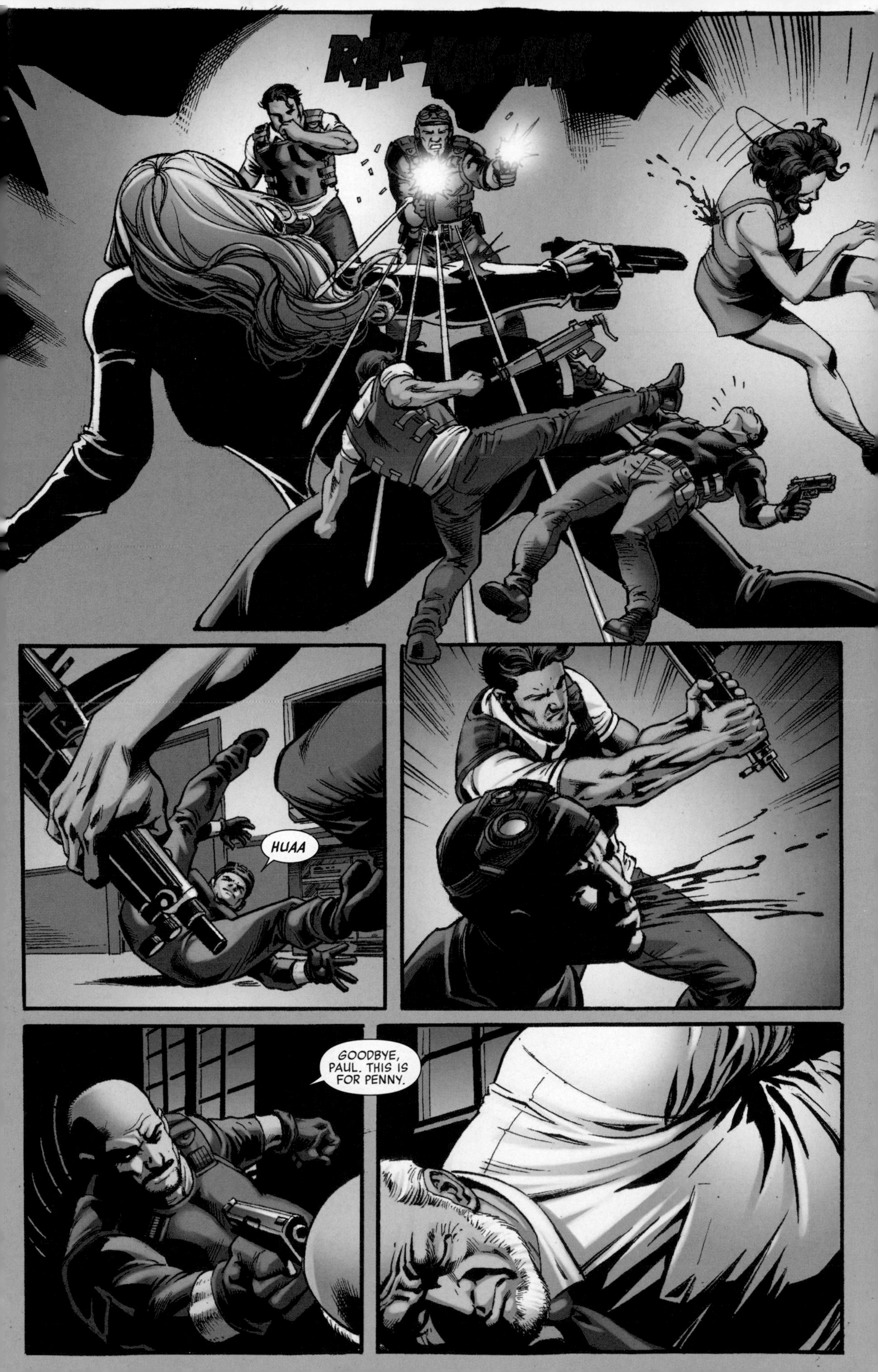
RAK-RAK-RAK
HUAA
GOODBYE, PAUL. THIS IS FOR PENNY.

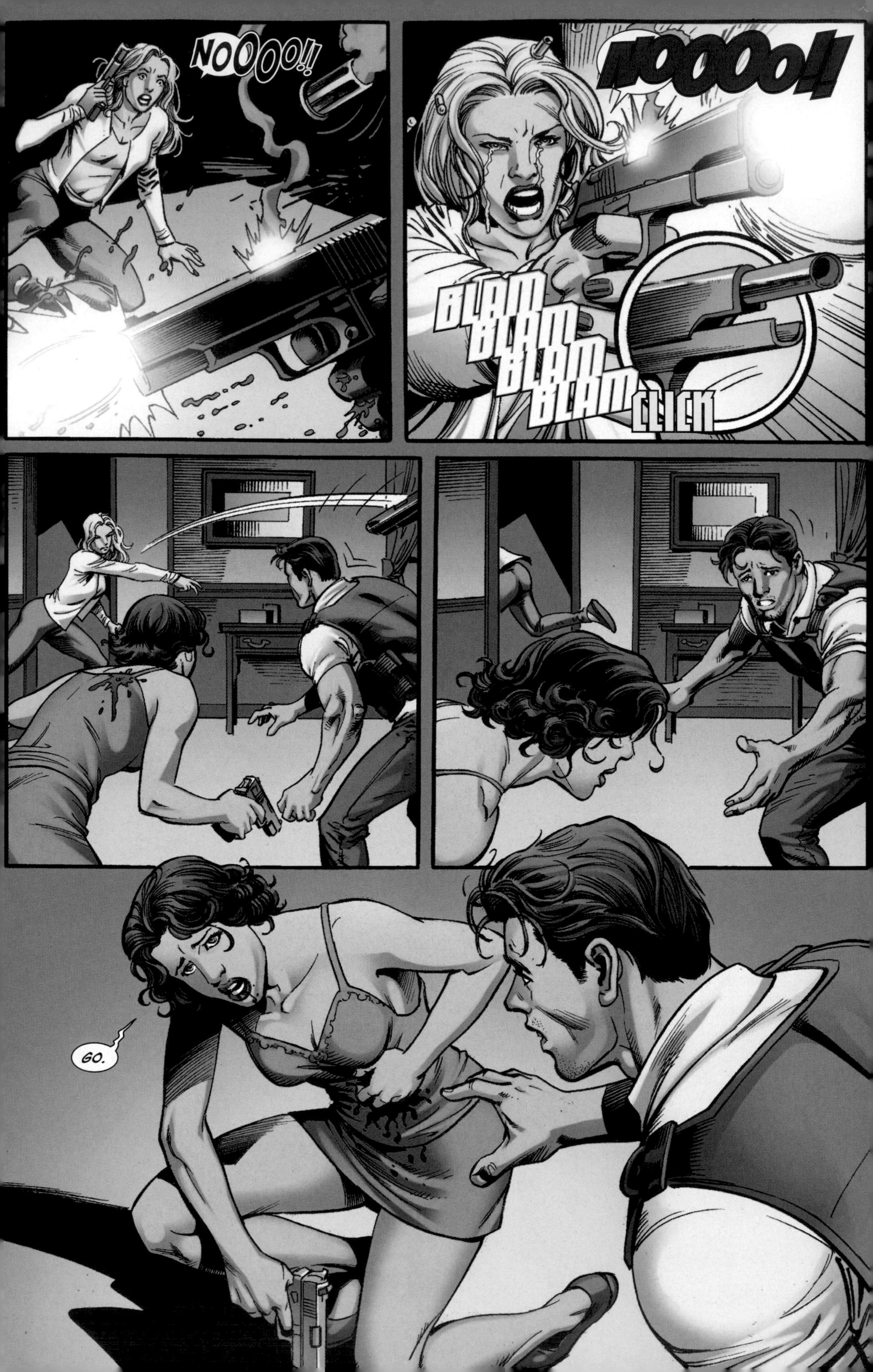
NOOOO!!
NOOOO!!
BLAM
BLAM
BLAM
BLAM
CLICK
GO.

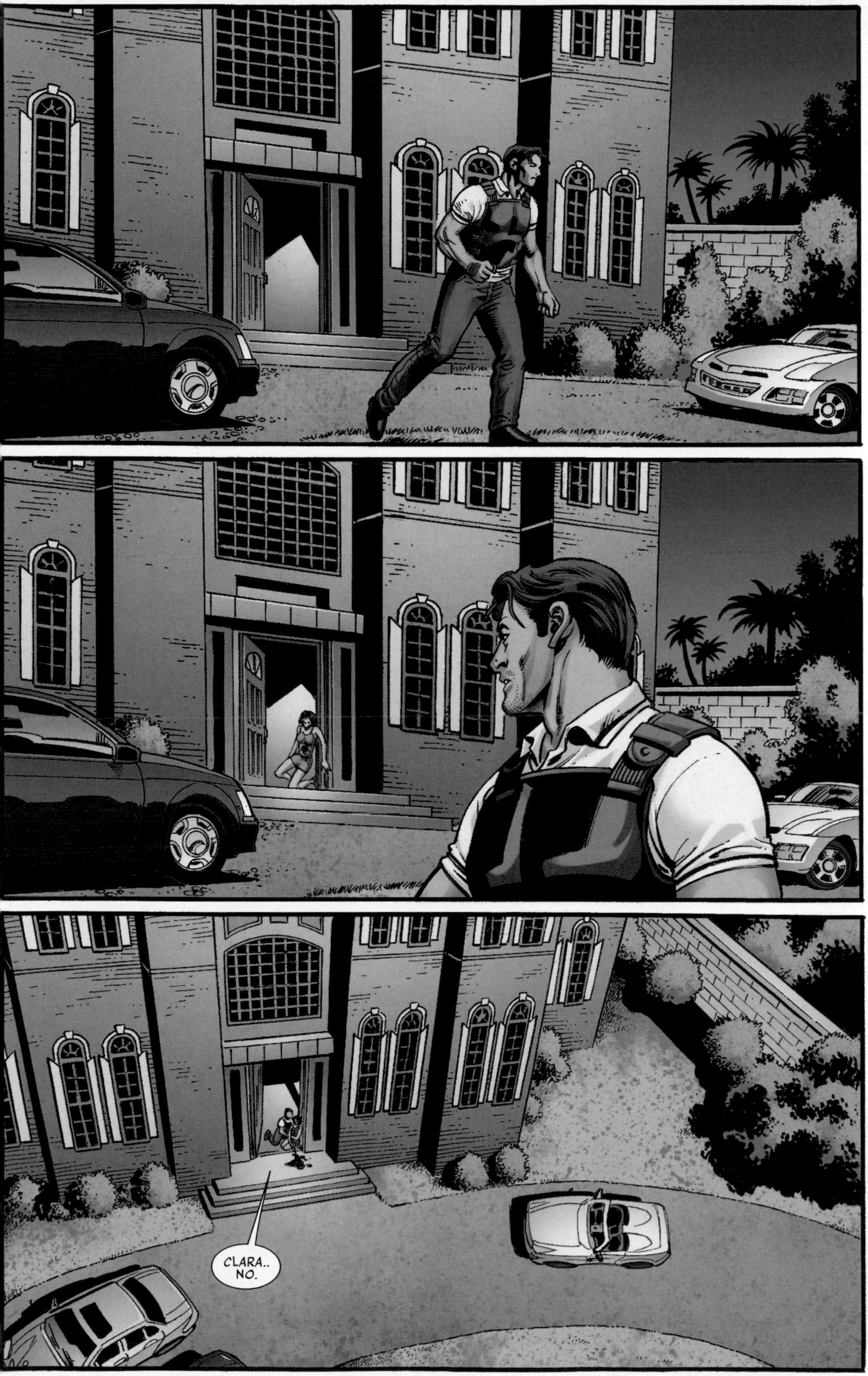
CLARA..
NO.

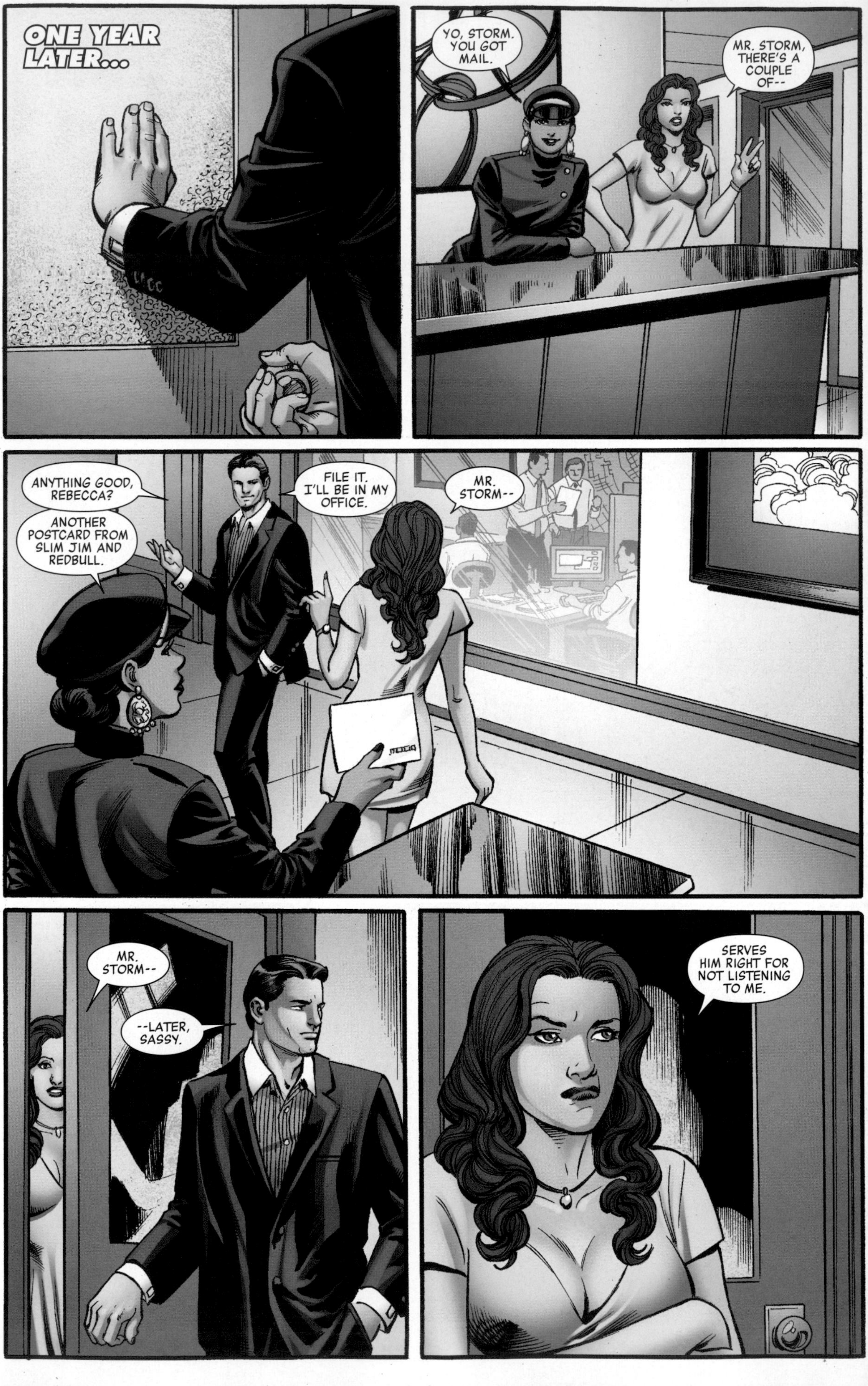
ONE YEAR LATER...
YO, STORM. YOU GOT MAIL.
MR. STORM, THERE'S A COUPLE OF--
ANYTHING GOOD, REBECCA?
ANOTHER POSTCARD FROM SLIM JIM AND REDBULL.
FILE IT. I'LL BE IN MY OFFICE.
MR. STORM--
MR. STORM--
--LATER, SASSY.
SERVES HIM RIGHT FOR NOT LISTENING TO ME.

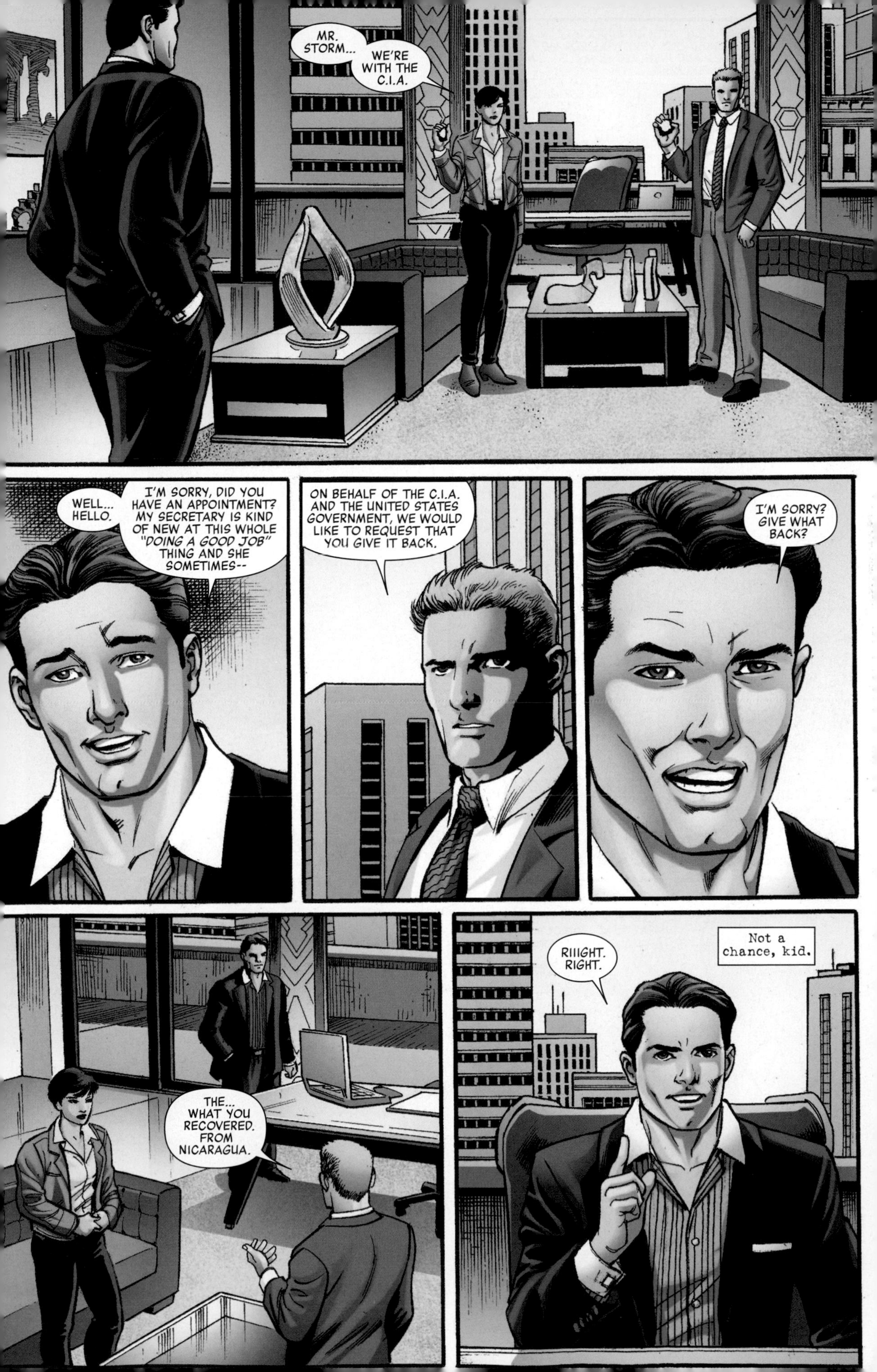
MR. STORM...
WE'RE WITH THE C.I.A.
WELL... HELLO.
I'M SORRY, DID YOU HAVE AN APPOINTMENT? MY SECRETARY IS KIND OF NEW AT THIS WHOLE "DOING A GOOD JOB" THING AND SHE SOMETIMES--
ON BEHALF OF THE C.I.A. AND THE UNITED STATES GOVERNMENT, WE WOULD LIKE TO REQUEST THAT YOU GIVE IT BACK.
I'M SORRY? GIVE WHAT BACK?
THE... WHAT YOU RECOVERED. FROM NICARAGUA.
RIIIGHT. RIGHT.
Not a chance, kid.

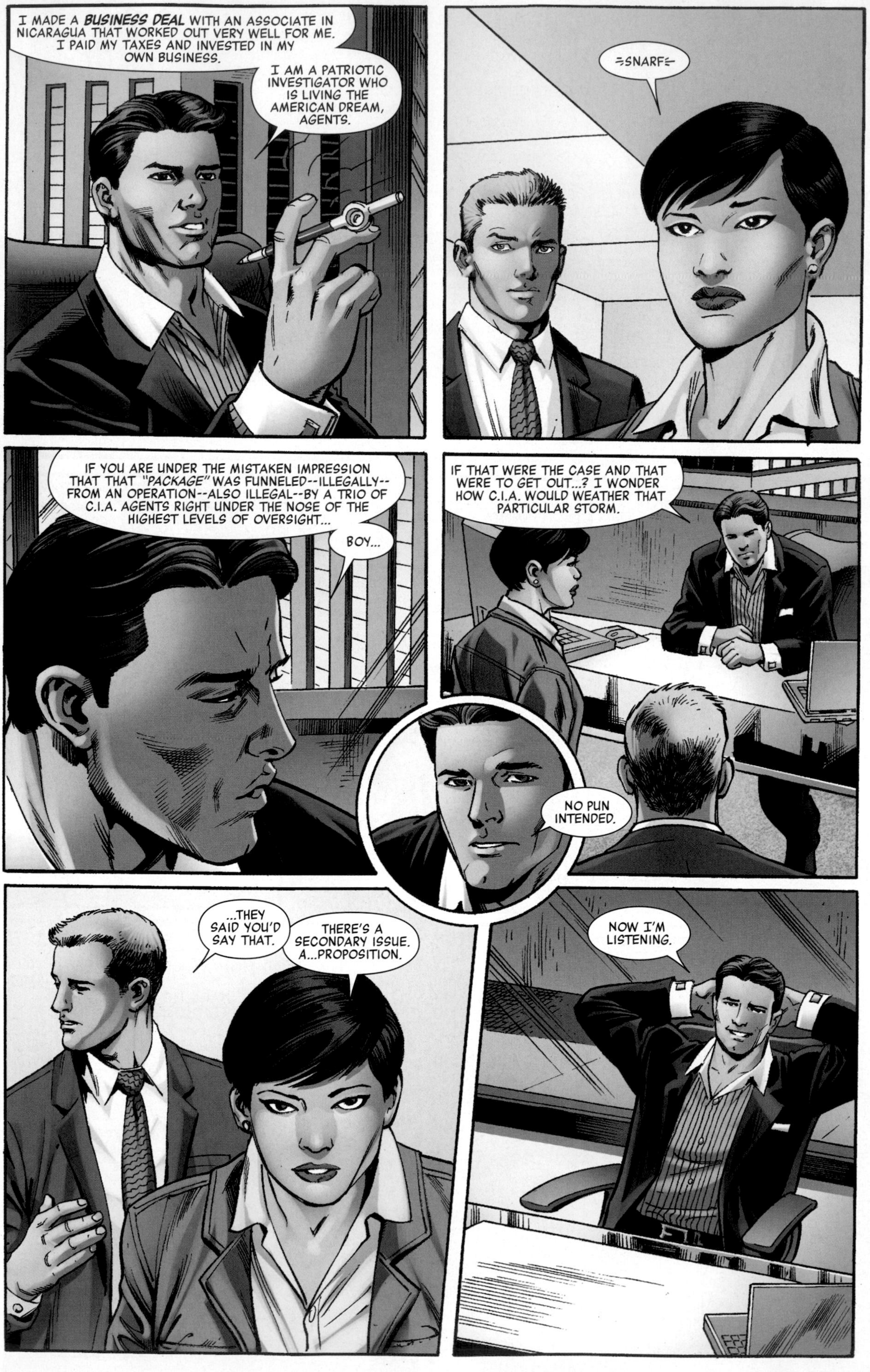

I MADE A BUSINESS DEAL WITH AN ASSOCIATE IN NICARAGUA THAT WORKED OUT VERY WELL FOR ME. I PAID MY TAXES AND INVESTED IN MY OWN BUSINESS.
I AM A PATRIOTIC INVESTIGATOR WHO IS LIVING THE AMERICAN DREAM, AGENTS.
=SNARF=
IF YOU ARE UNDER THE MISTAKEN IMPRESSION THAT THAT "PACKAGE" WAS FUNNELED--ILLEGALLY--FROM AN OPERATION--ALSO ILLEGAL--BY A TRIO OF C.I.A. AGENTS RIGHT UNDER THE NOSE OF THE HIGHEST LEVELS OF OVERSIGHT...
BOY...
IF THAT WERE THE CASE AND THAT WERE TO GET OUT...? I WONDER HOW C.I.A. WOULD WEATHER THAT PARTICULAR STORM.
NO PUN INTENDED.
...THEY SAID YOU'D SAY THAT.
THERE'S A SECONDARY ISSUE. A...PROPOSITION.
NOW I'M LISTENING.

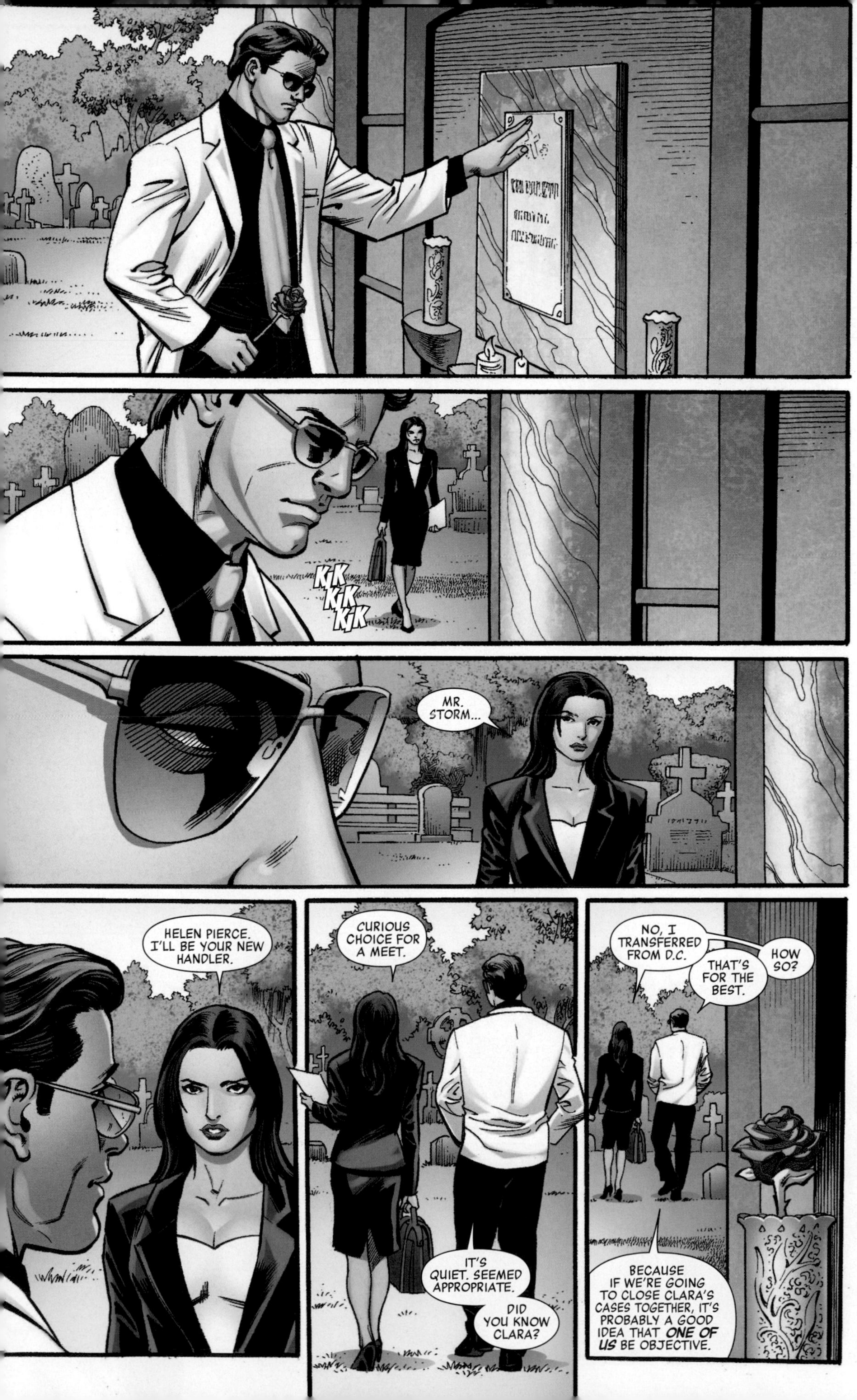

KIK KIK KIK
MR. STORM...
HELEN PIERCE. I'LL BE YOUR NEW HANDLER.
CURIOUS CHOICE FOR A MEET.
IT'S QUIET. SEEMED APPROPRIATE.
DID YOU KNOW CLARA?
NO, I TRANSFERRED FROM D.C.
THAT'S FOR THE BEST.
HOW SO?
BECAUSE IF WE'RE GOING TO CLOSE CLARA'S CASES TOGETHER, IT'S PROBABLY A GOOD IDEA THAT ***ONE OF US*** BE OBJECTIVE.

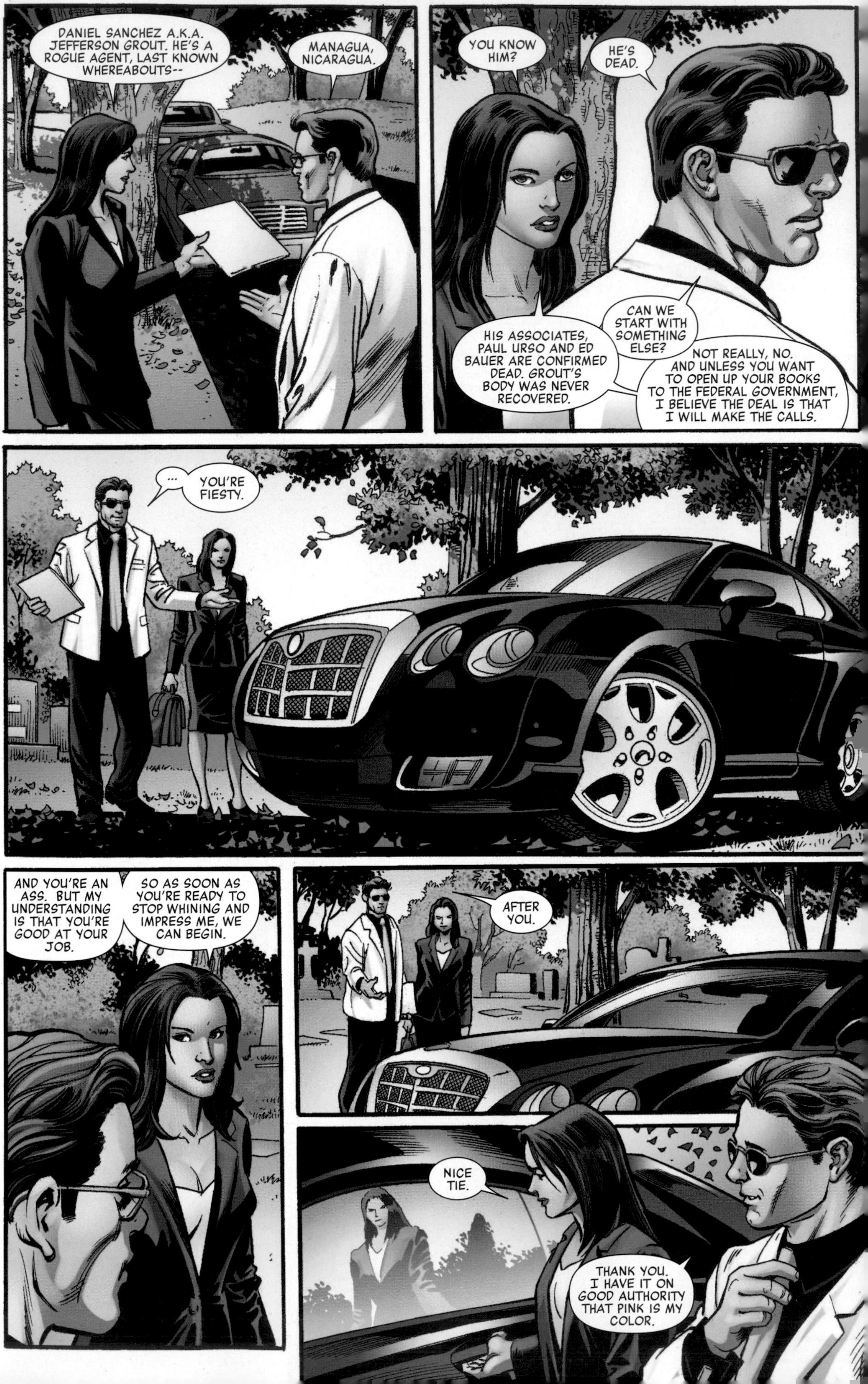
DANIEL SANCHEZ A.K.A. JEFFERSON GROUT. HE'S A ROGUE AGENT, LAST KNOWN WHEREABOUTS--
MANAGUA, NICARAGUA.
YOU KNOW HIM?
HE'S DEAD.
HIS ASSOCIATES, PAUL URSO AND ED BAUER ARE CONFIRMED DEAD. GROUT'S BODY WAS NEVER RECOVERED.
CAN WE START WITH SOMETHING ELSE?
NOT REALLY, NO. AND UNLESS YOU WANT TO OPEN UP YOUR BOOKS TO THE FEDERAL GOVERNMENT, I BELIEVE THE DEAL IS THAT I WILL MAKE THE CALLS.
...
YOU'RE FIESTY.
AND YOU'RE AN ASS. BUT MY UNDERSTANDING IS THAT YOU'RE GOOD AT YOUR JOB.
SO AS SOON AS YOU'RE READY TO STOP WHINING AND IMPRESS ME, WE CAN BEGIN.
AFTER YOU.
NICE TIE.
THANK YOU. I HAVE IT ON GOOD AUTHORITY THAT PINK IS MY COLOR.

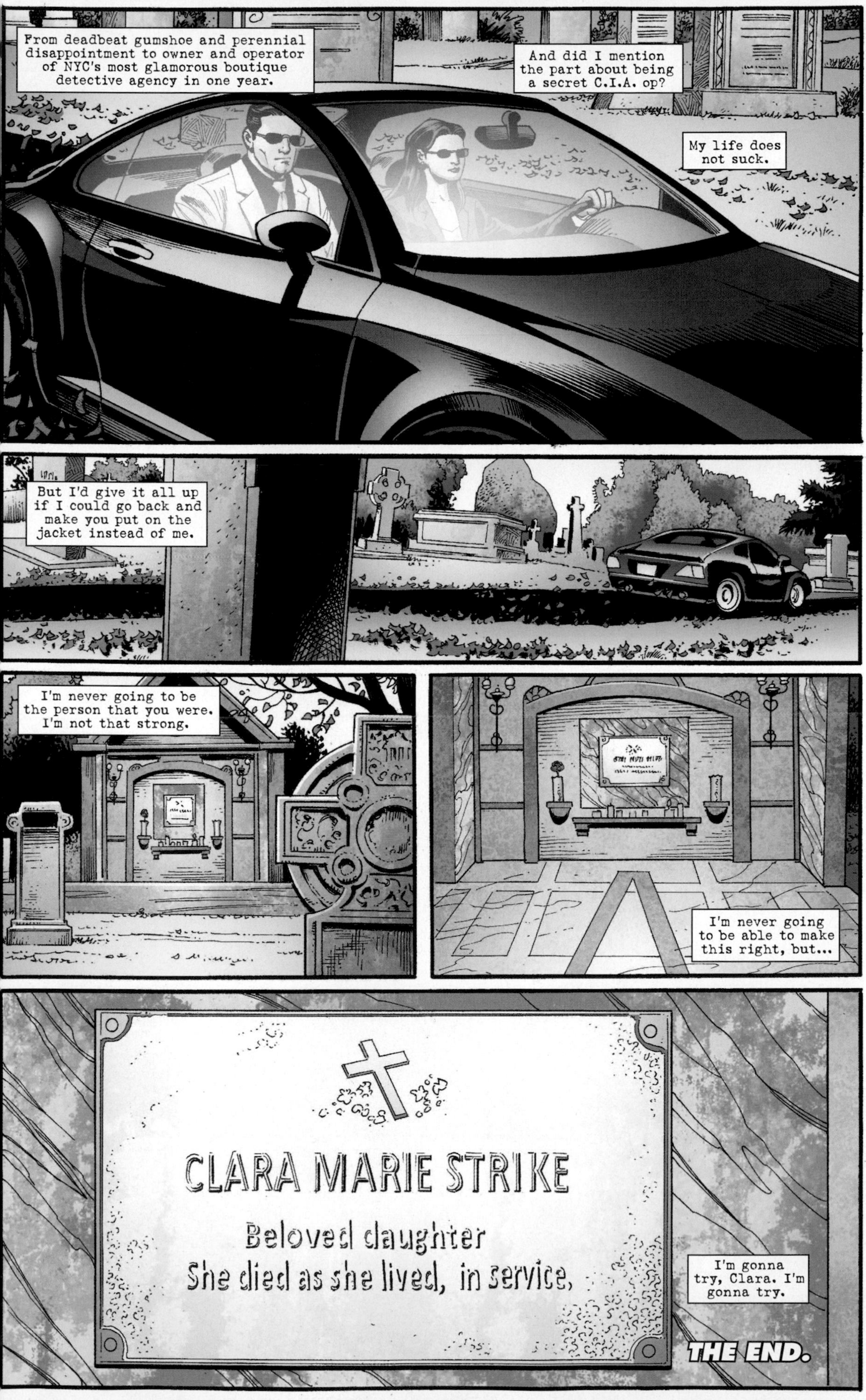
From deadbeat gumshoe and perennial disappointment to owner and operator of NYC's most glamorous boutique detective agency in one year.
And did I mention the part about being a secret C.I.A. op?
My life does not suck.
But I'd give it all up if I could go back and make you put on the jacket instead of me.
I'm never going to be the person that you were. I'm not that strong.
I'm never going to be able to make this right, but...
CLARA MARIE STRIKE
Beloved daughter
She died as she lived, in service.
I'm gonna try, Clara. I'm gonna try.
THE END.

CASTLE

EXTRAS

The evolution of a page in a graphic novel, from script to final art.

32.1 INT. STORM'S APARTMENT KITCHEN. NIGHT.

THE PLACE IS SMALL, NOT THE NICEST APARTMENT ON THE PLANET, BUT IT'S NOT A SQUAT EITHER. HE'S A RELATIVE GROWN UP; HE HAS A RELATIVELY GROWN UP APARTMENT. EXPOSED BRICK WALL, FRAMED MOVIE POSTER FOR _____ ON THE WALL, MAYBE. DEFINITELY NOT DECORATED BY A WOMAN.

ANYWAY, WE'RE IN THE KITCHEN. IN THE FOREGROUND, A KETTLE OF WATER HAS JUST STARTED TO BOIL. NEAR IT SITS AN OPEN CUP 'O NOODLES-TYPE CONTAINER (I'M SURE WE PROBABLY CAN'T CALL THEM CUP 'O NOODLES. CUP 'O RAMEN, MAYBE?). STORM IS VISIBLE IN THE BACKGROUND EATING NOODLES OUT OF A SECOND CONTAINER AND WATCHING THE KETTLE. HE'S HOME. HE'S TAKEN OFF HIS JACKET AND ROLLED UP HIS SLEEVES.

FX: HWEEEEEE [KETTLE]

NO DIALOGUE.

32.2 STORM HOLDS A PIECE OF THE TRAILER PARK MAIL OVER THE STEAM AS HE FILLS THE TWO STYROFOAM NOODLE CUPS.

STORM/CAP: WHAT DO YOU WANT TO BET THE CONTENTS OF THE TRAILER PARK MAIL LOOK REMARKABLY LIKE MY OWN?

32.3 STORM SITS AT A VERY SMALL TABLE EATING NOODLES WHILE HE LOOKS THROUGH THE STOLEN MAIL. THERE SHOULD BE A RESPECTABLE PILE OF PAPER ON THE TABLE.

STORM/CAP: THREE COLLECTION LETTERS, A BUNCH OF JUNK, BILLS... MISS MARIAN KYNDE, I WOULD JUDGE YOU IF YOUR INBOX WASN'T FRIGHTENINGLY REFLECTIVE OF MY OWN.

STORM/CAP: WAIT A MINUTE... DIDN'T YOU ALREADY HAVE A PHONE BILL?

STORM/CAP: A BUSINESS LINE? NOW WE DO HAVE A LOT IN COMMON.

32.4 ON THE PHONE BILL. [DETAIL WHAT WE SHOULD SEE]

STORM/CAP: HO HO HO... WHAT HAVE WE HERE?

32.5 STORM STANDS, HOLDING THE BILL, AND MAKES A PHONE CALL.

STORM: HI, YES—WHO DO I SPEAK TO IF I HAVE A QUESTION ABOUT MY BILL?

STORM: THE NUMBER IS [INSERT NUMBER]

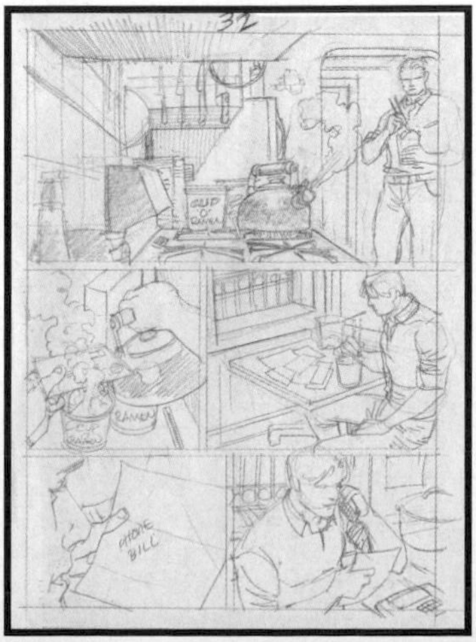
32
CUP 'O' RAMEN
RAMEN
PHONE BILL

Book ROOK/STORM Issue Story Page # 32 Artist(s)

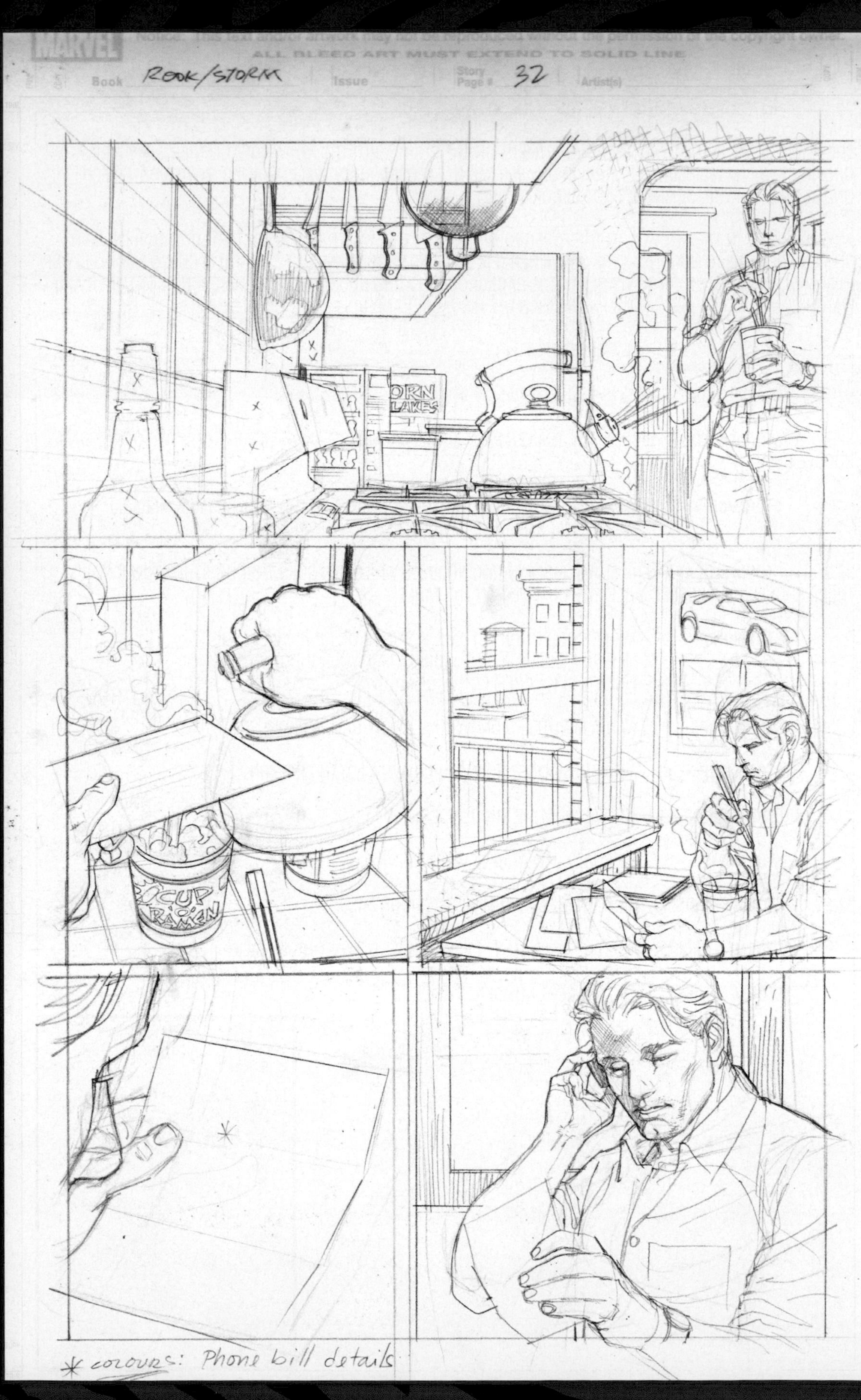
ORN
LAKES
CUP O RAMEN

* colours: Phone bill details

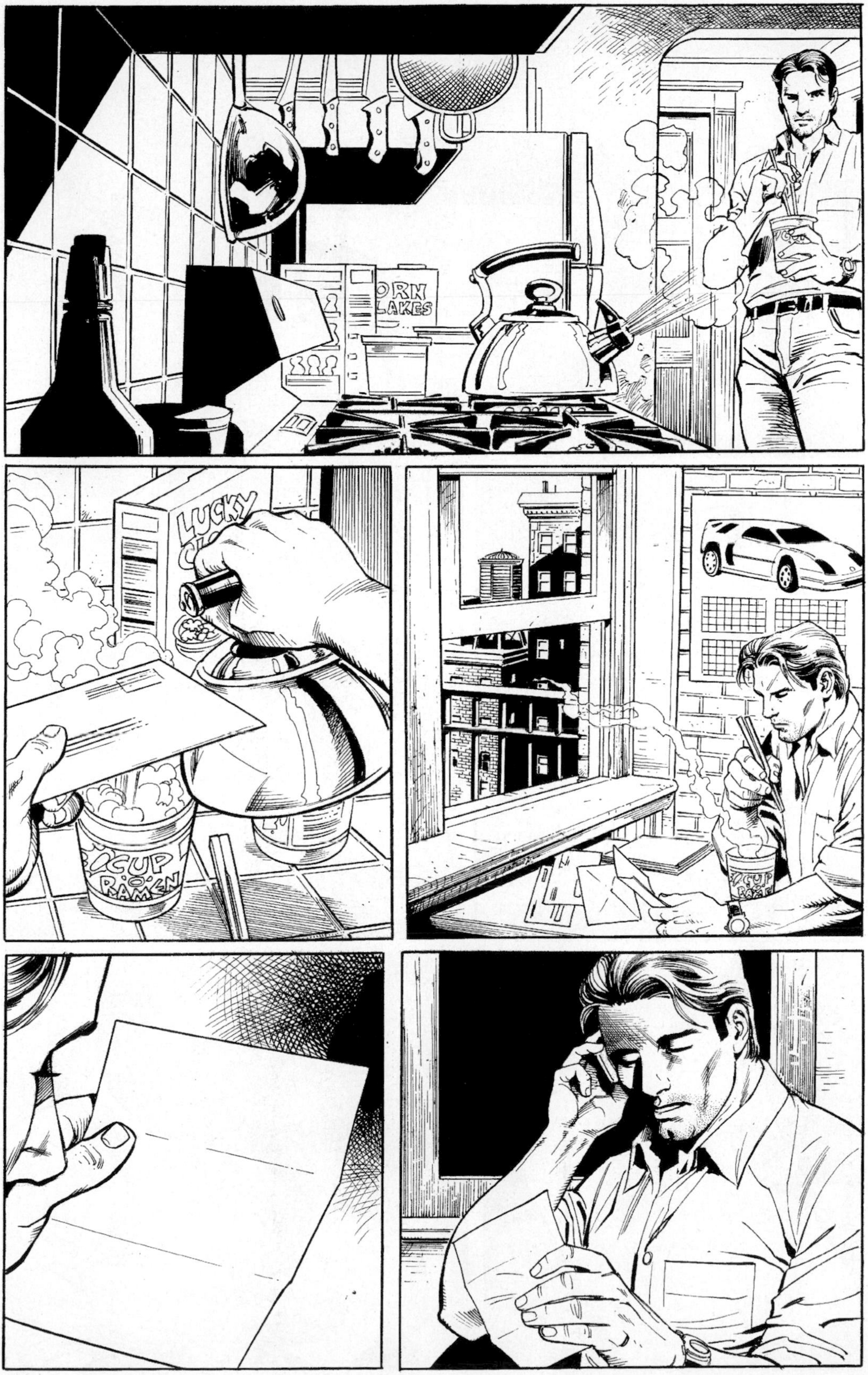

LUCKY
CUP O' RAMEN

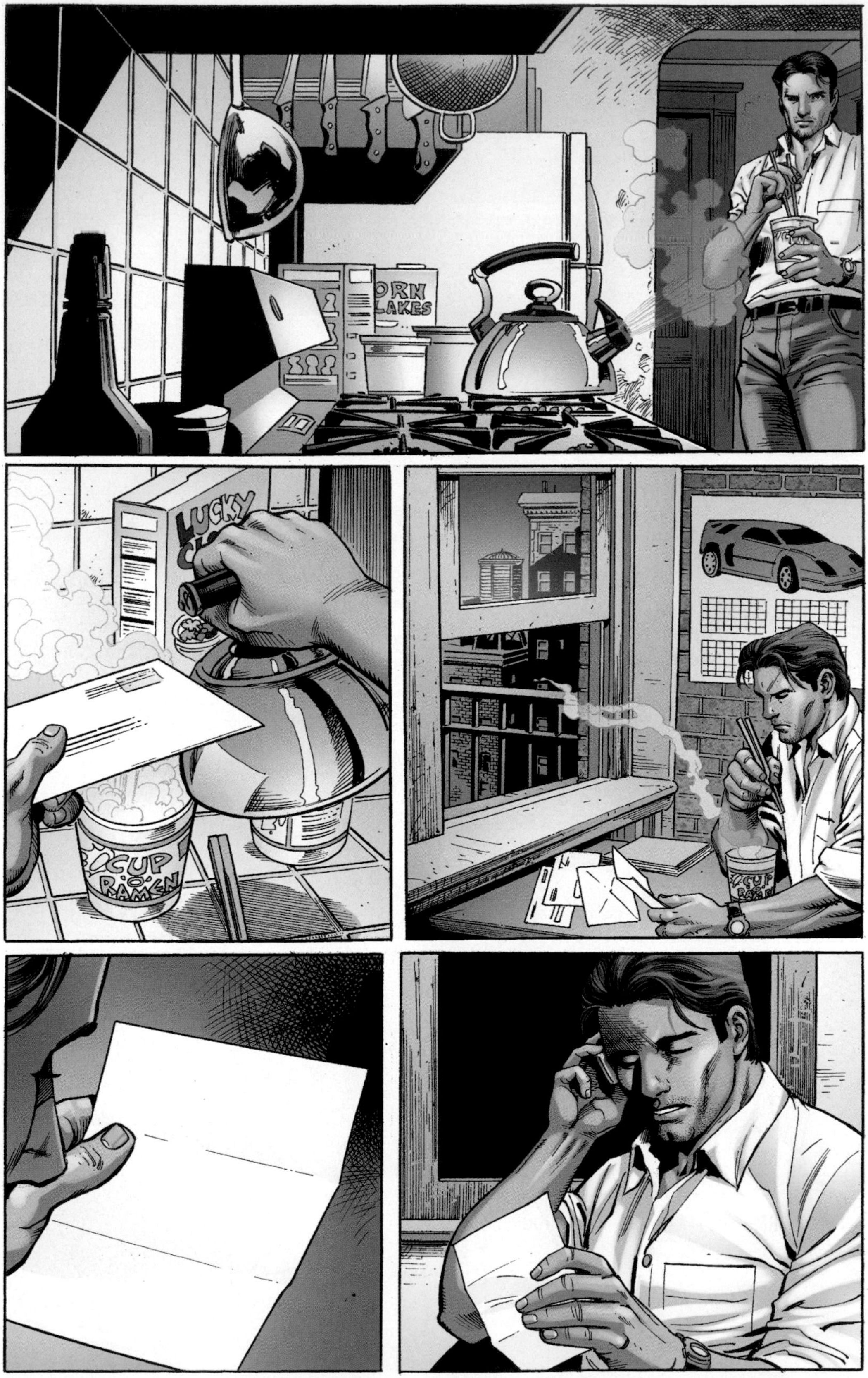
LUCKY
CUP O RAMEN

PAGE 33

IN MY HEAD, THIS PAGE HAS FOUR VERTICAL PANELS THAT EACH FEATURE STORM ROTATED JUST A BIT SO THAT WE MOVE FROM HIM FACING LEFT-ISH IN PANEL ONE TO RIGHT-ISH IN PANEL 4—THE IDEA BEING THAT WE'RE WATCHING HIM DO HIS DANCE HERE, MANIPULATING THE WOMAN ON THE OTHER END OF THE LINE. THIS IS OUR FIRST CHANCE TO SEE STORM BE REALLY GOOD AT HIS JOB/SHOW OFF HIS CHARM. MAKE SURE THERE'S A TWINKLE IN HIS EYE. THE FIFTH PANEL WOULD THEN RUN WIDE ACROSS THE BOTTOM OF THE PAGE.

THAT SAID, I SORT OF SUCK AT PAGE DESIGN AND IT'S WHAT YOU DO FOR A LIVING. SO IF YOU HAVE A BETTER IDEA, GO WITH GOD, MY FRIEND.

33.1 THE FREEZE FRAME MOMENT IS "ARE YOU A PARENT, BY CHANCE?" HE SMILES, RAISES HIS EYEBROWS, SQUINTS A LITTLE.

STORM: YEAH, NO, THAT'S A TYPO I'VE BEEN MEANING TO CORRECT—IT'S MARION, WITH AN O. MAN'S NAME.

STORM: NO, NO WORRIES. HAPPENS ALL THE TIME.

STORM: ARE YOU A PARENT, BY CHANCE?

33.2 BIG GRIN—HE'S GOT HER. FREEZE FRAME IS "KNEW YOU'D UNDERSTAND."

STORM: YEAH, SO, I'M GOING OVER MY BILLS HERE AND WE HAVE A SECOND LINE FOR MY DAUGHTER AND SHE'S BEEN MAKING SOME VERY PECULIAR CALLS AND I'D LIKE TO GET TO THE BOTTOM OF IT.

STORM: KNEW YOU'D UNDERSTAND.

STORM: FIRST, THESE CALLS THAT ARE MARKED BLOCKED—IS THERE ANY WAY TO FIND OUT—

33.3 PATHETIC EXPRESSION. FREEZE FRAME MOMENT IS "THE THINGS THESE KIDS GET INTO..."

STORM: WELL, I WOULDN'T WANT YOU TO GET IN TROUBLE, ON ACCOUNT OF A CONCERNED FATHER.

STORM: MY DAUGHTER, SHE'S SIXTEEN, YOU KNOW?...

STORM: SURE, I'LL HOLD...

STORM: FEDERAL BUILDING? HUH.

STORM: OH RIGHT!—HER UNCLE, MY BROTHER WORKS FOR THE...

33.4 PULLING THE PHONE AWAY FROM HIS FACE AND TALKING AT IT MORE THAN INTO IT.

STORM: THE ________, YES! THANK YOU. GOOD TO KNOW SHE'S KEEPING IN TOUCH WITH THE FAMILY.

STORM: LAST QUESTION, THERE'S A NOTE MADE HERE THAT THE SERVICE PLAN HAS CHANGED...?

STORM: ADDED AN INTERNATIONAL PLAN!

STORM: OF COURSE! RIGHT. YES. SHE'S GOT A FIELD TRIP COMING UP.

STORM: WELL, IT'S IS A VERY PROGRESSIVE SCHOOL. OKAY—THANKS FOR YOUR HELP! GOTTAGOBYE!

33.5 CLOSE ON STORM'S CLOSED-MOUTH SMIRK.

STORM/CAP: GOTCHA.

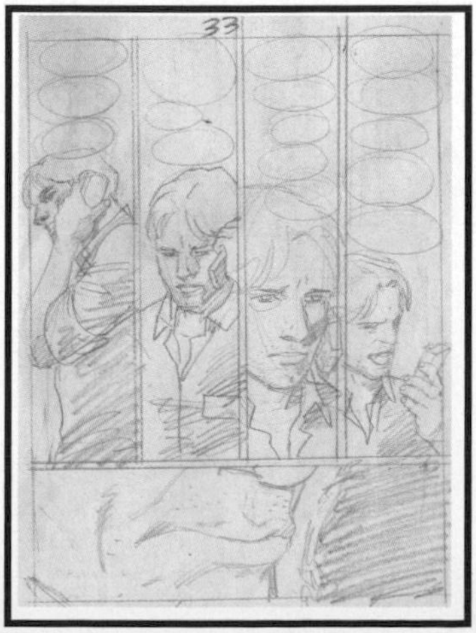

33

ALL BLEED ART MUST EXTEND TO SOLID LINE

Book ROOK/STORM Issue Story Page # 33 Artist(s)

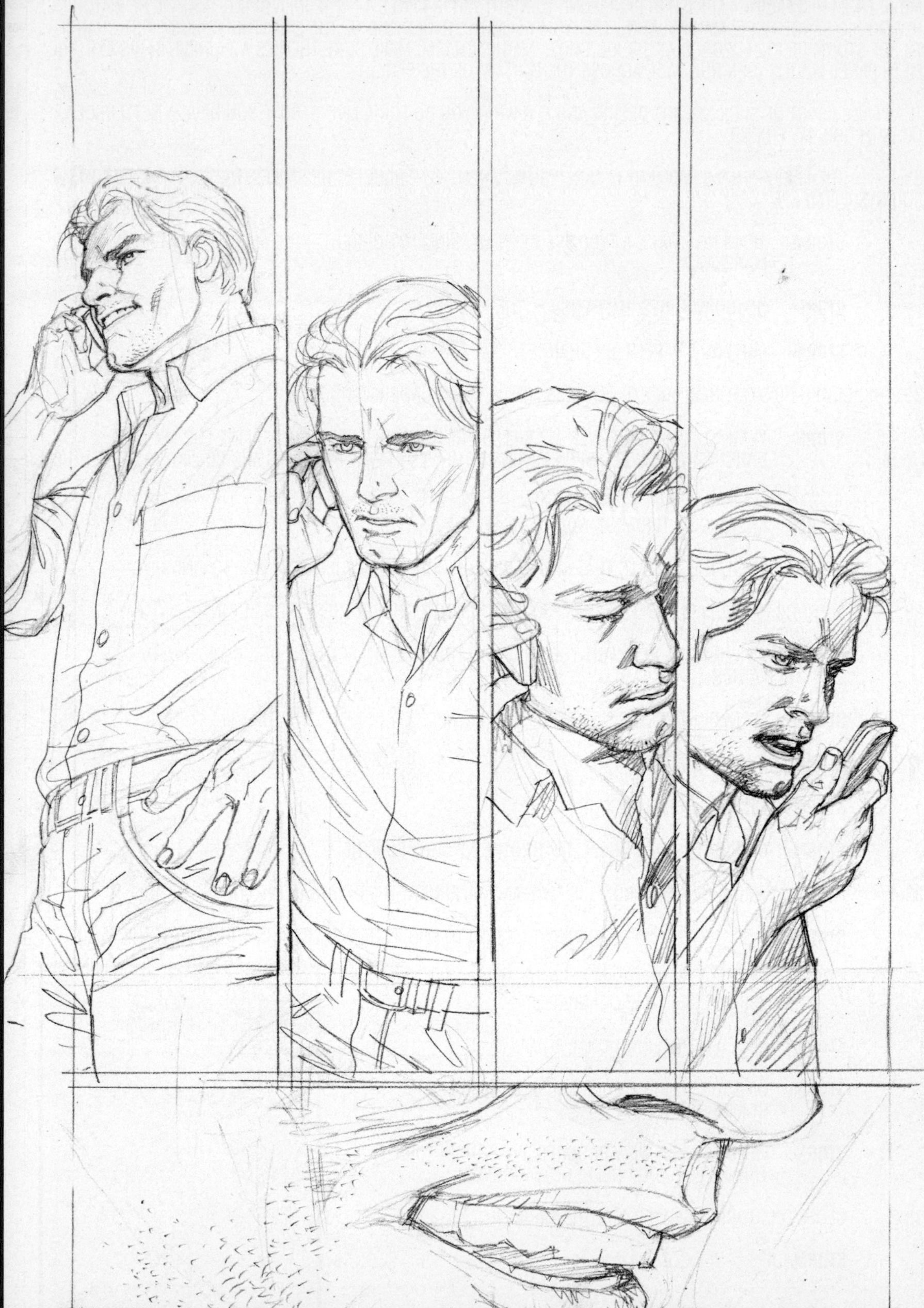

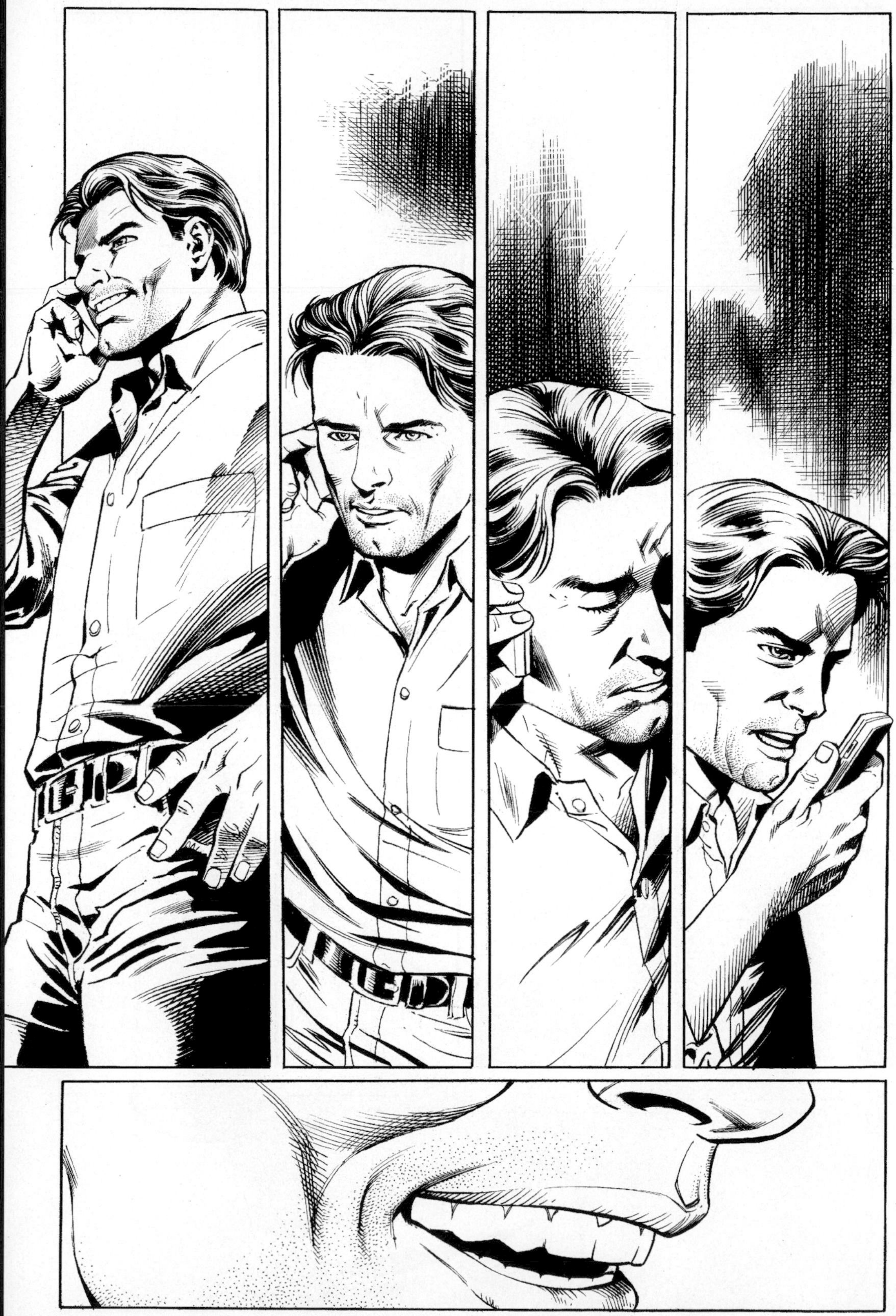

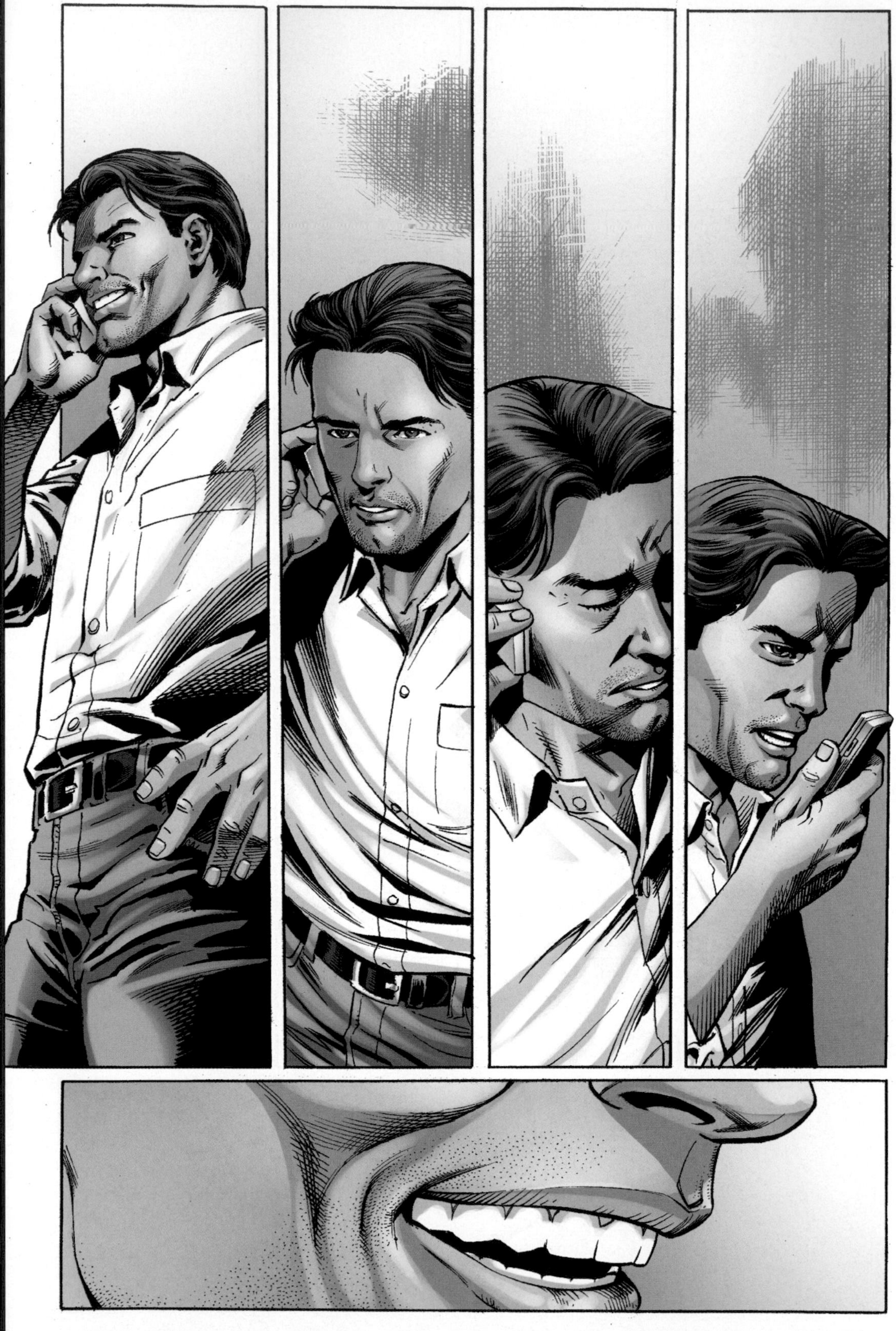

PAGE 34

34.1 INT. APARTMENT STAIRWELL – NIGHT. FROM THE BASE OF THE STAIRS, BY THE EXIT DOOR, LOOKING UP. STORM'S GOT HIS BAG AND HE'S FLYING DOWN THE STEPS, HIS JACKET BILLOWING OUT BEHIND HIM. HE'S TALKING TO HIS DAD ON THE PHONE AS HE GOES.

STORM: DAD, TWO THINGS AND I'LL LEAVE YOU ALONE--

STORM: ONE: IS IT POSSIBLE TO TRACE SOMEONE INTERNATIONALLY IF THEY'VE GOT A US CELL PHONE, AND—

STORM: IF I'VE GOT DATES AND TIMES OF CALLS COMING INTO THE FEDERAL BUILDING THROUGH A MAIN NUMBER, ANY WAY TO TELL WHAT EXTENSION THEY GOT TRANSFERRED TO?

34.2 STORM REACHES FOR THE DOOR WITHOUT REALLY LOOKING AT IT, HE'S LOOKING DOWN(ISH) FOCUSING ON HIS CONVERSATION WITH HIS DAD.

STORM: C'MON! WHEN HAVE I EVER ASKED YOU FOR ANYTHING?

STORM: WHEN TODAY?

34.3 OVER STORM'S SHOULDER AS HE OPENS THE DOOR AND HANGS UP THE PHONE.
WE'RE ON TWO PLAIN CLOTHES COPS, STANDING RIGHT IN FRONT OF THE DOOR AS STORM OPENS IT. THEY'RE JUMPY AND SURPRISED; THEY WERE JUST ABOUT TO OPEN THE DOOR THEMSELVES WHEN STORM CAUGHT THEM OFF GUARD.

IF WE HAD THE LIKENESSES, THESE COPS WOULD OF COURSE BE ESPOSITO AND RYAN. WE DON'T. THEY AREN'T. LET'S MAKE THEM TOMMY TOMBALL AND LUCILLE "PUMPKIN" MERUNKA. TOMMY'S A BIG, AFRICAN AMERICAN TEDDY BEAR OF A MAN. ONLY, YOU KNOW, A TEDDY BEAR WHO MIGHT ACTUALLY THROW A PUNCH. PUMPKIN IS A THICK-BODIED REDHEAD WITH FRECKLES, SMALL EYES AND A BROAD MOUTH.

OR, YOU KNOW, WHATEVER. HAVE FUN.

THIS BEAT FEELS A LITTLE AWKWARD TO ME, SO, AGAIN, IF YOU HAVE A CLEARER VISUAL IN MIND FOR THIS PANEL OR PAGE, PLEASE BE MY GUEST.

STORM: ALL RIGHT, I'M HEADED TO THE OFFICE. CALL ME BACK.

FX: BIP

34.4 ON STORM AS HE TAKES A PUNCH TO THE FACE FROM PUMPKIN. THE WOMAN PACKS A WHOLLUP. HE GETS HIT HARD AND FLYS BACK.

FX: BAM [OR SOMETHING LESS CHEESEY]

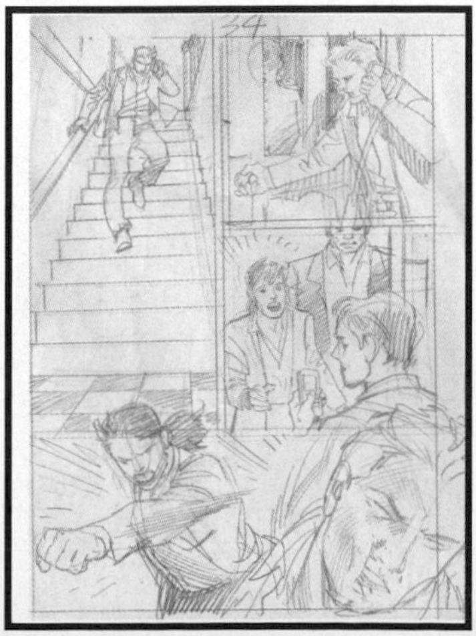

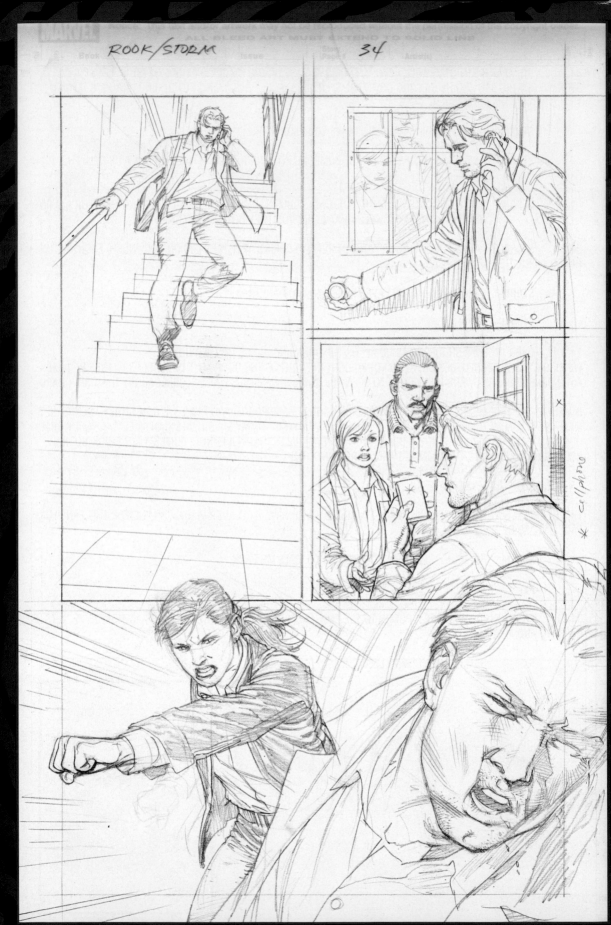

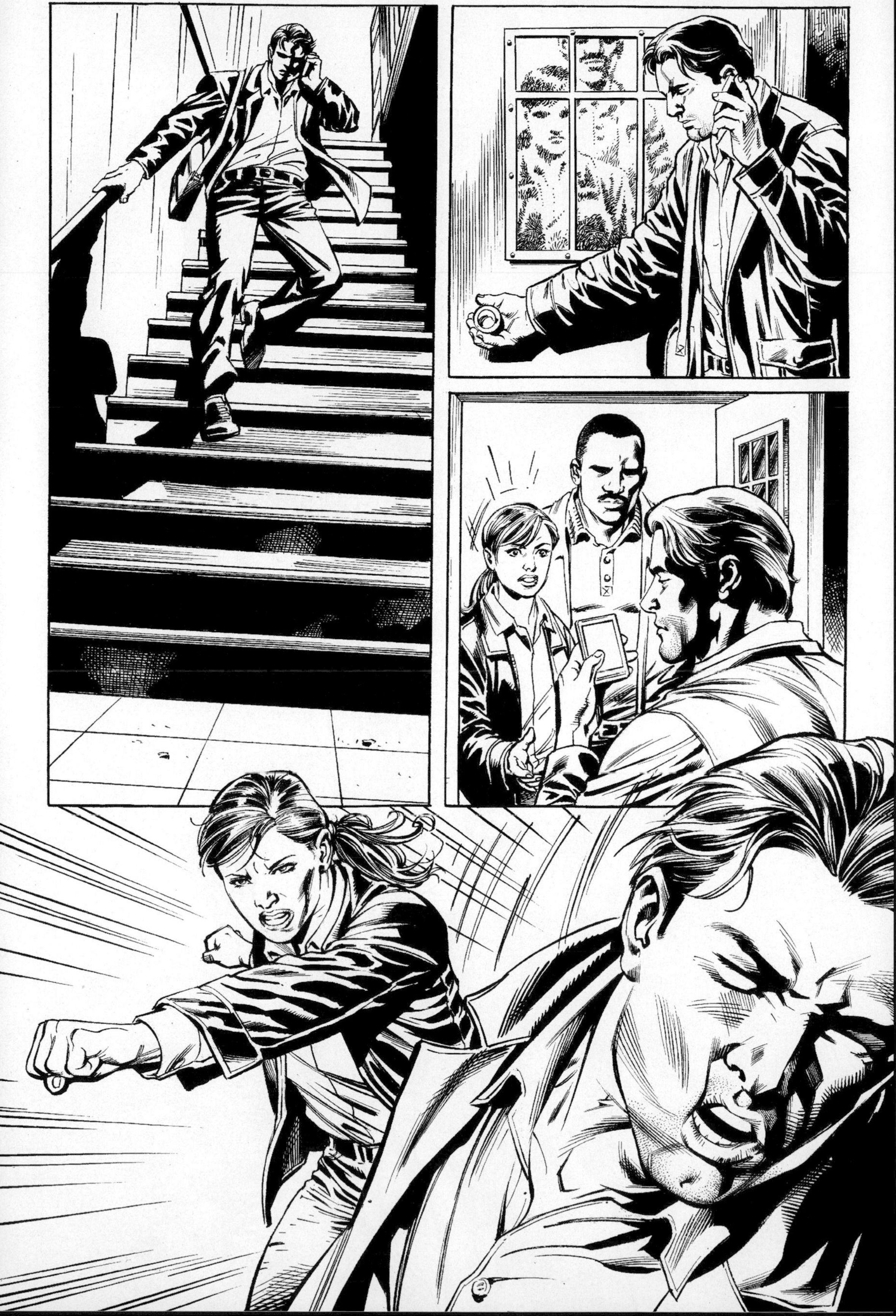

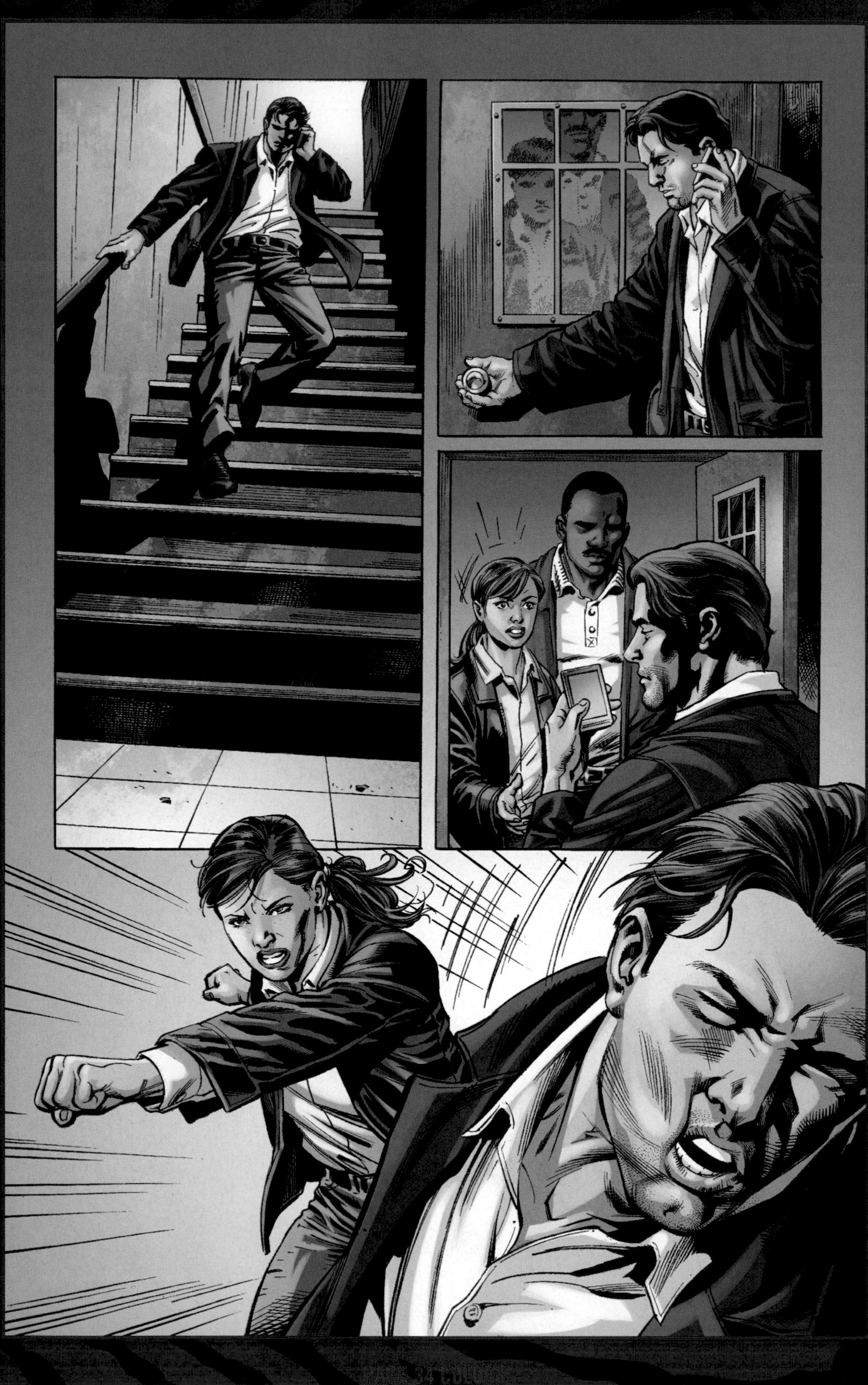
PAGE 34 COLORS

FOLLOW THE EXPLOITS OF DERRICK STORM

DEADLY STORM

While tracking down a missing husband for a desperate wife, private investigator Derrick Storm discovers there's a lot more to the job than he's been led to believe when he discovers the missing husband is actually a rogue CIA operative involved in selling national security secrets to enemy forces. He soon finds himself knee deep in international intrigue when he's recruited by the lovely and dangerous Clara Strike, a CIA agent with a penchant for trouble and adventure.

STORM SEASON

CIA Agent Clara Strike enlists the help of retired NYPD detective Derrick Storm to bug the hotel suite of an African head of state. But this routine mission quickly spirals out of control when Storm overhears a woman's terrifying scream on the wire. Plagued by the victim's helpless cry, Storm—despite Strike's warning, or perhaps because of it—investigates the truth.

A CALM BEFORE STORM

Derrick Storm is looking forward to finally getting out of the game — stocking up his cabin cruiser and heading out into the open Atlantic for good. But his plans are put on hold when, on the eve of a UN summit, the severed head of a Russian diplomat is found bobbing in the backwaters of the Hudson. Storm's CIA handler Clara Strike enlists him to crack a plot of global proportions, pitting the uncanny PI against a legion of eastern bloc mercenaries, and an ex-KGB hit-man known simply as "The Fear."

STORM'S BREAK

A brutal cold snap has practically brought Manhattan to its knees, driving the island's denizens indoors. The city's homeless are driven down, into the bowels of ancient train tunnels and the concrete roots of skyscrapers. It's a world of predators and prey, and when runaway teenage girls start disappearing into this underworld, Derrick Storm isn't afraid to find out why. It doesn't take long before Storm trips to an international human trafficking ring headed by notorious Panama kingpin Marco Juarez. Teaming up with reliable and gutsy CIA agent Clara Strike, these two race to stop one of the world's most vile criminals before he destroys more innocent lives.

STORM WARNING

When Derrick Storm's close friend, attorney Sam Strummel, is murdered in cold blood in a cemetery outside of NYC, Storm launches his own investigation to bring the murderer to justice. While investigating Strummel's business dealings, Storm exposes a murder-for-hire syndicate that has just made him their next target.

UNHOLY STORM

 When the daughters of four high-powered international businessmen are discovered dead in New York City, the NYPD scrambles to bring the murderer to justice. But when a fifth girl is found mutilated in a pool of her own blood, her prestigious French family hires Derrick Storm to run his own investigation and find the real killer. With limited access to evidence, Storm has only one lead — a strange symbol drawn in blood at each of the five crime scenes. While immersing himself in voodoo religion and rituals, Storm enlists the help of the beautiful and daring Clara Strike, his CIA handler. Together they uncover a deep web of deception under the guise of mysticism and devotion. And in a race against time, this most unlikely pair unlock the mystery behind a network of international assassins capable of creating a global catastrophe.

GATHERING STORM

While packing his bags for a much-needed vacation, Storm gets a call from CIA Agent Clara Strike with an urgent mission. Storm must help protect the Swiss Ambassador's daughter against a formidable foe: a former KGB officer who is known for killing his victims with undetectable poison. When the mission is compromised, Clara fears that there is a mole in the CIA. In a bold move, Clara decides to put Storm undercover at Langley in order to smoke out the guilty party. Unexpectedly, Storm does more than just that; he uncovers a conspiracy that goes to the top levels of the agency and threatens Clara's livelihood.

STORM RISING

On a quest to recover a rare sapphire stolen from one of Manhattan's elite, Derrick Storm comes face to face with Bentley Silver: notorious jewel thief and rival womanizer. As the two men compare their conquests, they form an unlikely union in order to bring down a Parisian thief who threatens to undermine Silver's livelihood and Storm's bank account. A trail of stolen jewels leads Storm and Bentley to an underground international society, which is shrouded in secrecy and has a deadly mission.

DRIVING STORM

Storm faces his toughest case to date when CIA Agent Clara Strike asks him to clear her sister Susan's name after she's accused of murdering her husband. Strike insists that it was police incompetence and tainted evidence that led to her sister's arrest. Storm takes the case, only to realize that the police conspiracy against Susan isn't just Clara's hunch, it's a stone wall of silence even he may not be able to get past. And the closer he gets to the truth, the more danger he puts Susan in, leading Storm to a terrible choice – prove her innocence or save her life.

STORM'S LAST STAND

An ex-con out for vengeance, an old lover looking for closure, and a hardened cop hoping to find peace of mind all come crashing into Storm's life when a man they all know jumps off the Brooklyn Bridge. Or was he pushed? Now these former foes must work together to solve a crime that brings up their complicated past history and some memories better left forgotten. Storm must protect his reputation, heart, and possibly his life while unlocking the mystery behind his friend's death. In the midst of this, CIA Agent Clara Strike calls on Storm to help with what she deems, an "easy" task. But when this mission leads to Clara's abduction by MI5 agents, Storm must balance his two identities and cases while trying to save Clara's life.

STORM FALL

Storm is finally feeling like he has his life back: a few open and shut PI cases that lack any danger or intrigue and no recent calls from CIA Agent Clara Strike. But when her lack of contact begins to concern him, Storm begins to search for the woman who he has begun to care for as more than just a colleague. But what Storm unravels quickly turns his world upside down. Is Clara the CIA agent she claimed to be or a rogue spy operating outside of the law? Just when he begins to scratch the surface of the truth, his bank account is drained and a murder of a rival PI is pinned on him. Storm must take on his most challenging client yet: himself. Is this the work of Clara or one of his many enemies? Storm has to comb through his entire career as a PI and as a secret CIA operative: every criminal he put away, every crime he solved, every life he affected, in order to find out who would do this to him. Will he find the culprit pulling the puppet strings or will this be the end of Derrick Storm?

OTHER BOOKS BY THE AUTHOR

RICHARD
CASTLE
HELL HATH
NO FURY

HELL HATH NO FURY

Taking a sabbatical from his college teaching job, Adam Parel has moved his family to the remote Oregon town of Jessup to finish his first novel. At first, Jessup seems ideal. Adam's wife and sons make friends quickly and there's enough quiet for Adam to get his work done. But as he researches his new hometown, Adam becomes convinced there's something sinister going on beneath Jessup's peaceful façade. People have gone missing here for decades and Adam eventually discovers the horrifying reason why: an obsessive cult that will stop at nothing to keep their sacred region 'pure.' As Adam struggles to escape with his family, he soon finds himself hunted by bloodthirsty fanatics for whom killing is the only way of living.

RICHARD
CASTLE
FLOWERS FOR
YOUR GRAVE

FLOWERS FOR YOUR GRAVE

Four murders in and the NYPD are still desperate for a lead on the serial killer that the tabloids are calling 'The Florist.' Struggling journalist Leroy Fine knows if he cracked this story he could get back everything he's lost – his job, his wife, his self-respect. So when Leroy uncovers a piece of evidence the cops have overlooked, he begins his own private investigation into the twisted and deadly world of The Florist. But as Leroy gets closer to discovering the killer's identity, he soon realizes he's put himself and everyone he loves in mortal danger. Now Leroy must decipher the Florist's riddles and unmask his identity… or end up the latest flower-covered corpse on the Ledger's front page.

RICHARD
CASTLE
AT DUSK
WE DIE

AT DUSK WE DIE

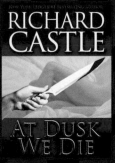

Still residing in the same tiny Texas town where he grew up, Ben Meltzer's life is a peaceful one. He runs the local drugstore and has a growing family with his high school sweetheart. So when the Satan's Creed motorcycle gang drive into town, he hardly pays them any mind. But after the entire town is ravaged by the Creed in a single night, he and his family are forced to flee for their lives and pray for the dawn. Because the Satan's Creed are no ordinary biker gang – they're ravenous vampires come to feed. As Ben attempts to keep his family safe, he

RICHARD
CASTLE
A SKULL AT
SPRINGTIME

A SKULL AT SPRINGTIME

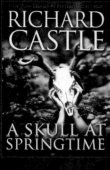

Looking for a way to pay for her college after her father's death, Rachel Lyons is spending the summer planting trees in the clearcut forests of remote Washington. It's a lucrative but lonely job and Rachel soon finds the monotony draining. That is, until she stumbles upon a half-buried skeleton deep in the woods – a discovery that leads her to uncover an entire field of corpses. When Rachel's attempts to contact authorities are thwarted, it quickly becomes clear that she isn't alone out here. As she struggles to escape back to civilization, Rachel must struggle to stay alive or risk becoming yet another one of the skeletons beneath the dirt.

NEW YORK LEDGER #1 BESTSELLING AUTHOR
RICHARD
CASTLE
A ROSE FOR
EVERAFTER

A ROSE FOR EVERAFTER

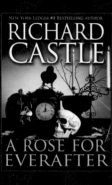

At the Blessed Sacrament School for Girls, Sister Mary Grace leads her young charges in daily Morning Prayer, asking the Lord their souls to keep. But the young women of Riverbend are starting to disappear, only to be found in shallow graves, wrapped in shrouds of white and grasping a red rose in their cold dead hands. Who could be killing the town's virgin daughters? And why is he burying them alive? When Sister Mary Grace starts investigating, she discovers a trail of evidence that leads from the local rectory to the upper echelons of the archdiocese – and ultimately to a secretive organization whose provenance may be very far from godly.

New York Ledger's #1 Best Seller
RICHARD
CASTLE
WHEN IT COMES
TO SLAUGHTER

WHEN IT COMES TO SLAUGHTER

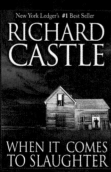

The neo-hippie community of Fair Haven, Vermont, had never experienced a single murder in its nearly 40-year history – until one moonless night a week ago, when five members of the Akin family were brutally hacked to death and found hanging from meat hooks. Suddenly, the town's tiny two-man police force – Chief Derek Olson and Deputy Ana Ruiz – find themselves thrust into a nightmare world. They wrestle with a dearth of evidence and a populace becoming more paranoid by the second as rumors abound of a scarecrow-like creature with hatchets for hands prowling the countryside. When a second family is butchered in the same gruesome fashion, Olson and Ruiz begin to suspect that many of their townsfolk are not the radical peaceniks they claim to be – the majority, in fact, harbor dark, violent pasts that may finally be coming home to roost.

RICHARD
CASTLE
KISSED
AND KILLED

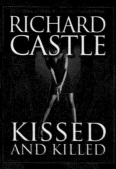

KISSED AND KILLED

Rookie detective Alexandra Jones grew up fast in the mean streets of the Bronx. But nothing could prepare her for the spate of murders currently plaguing the five boroughs: Someone is killing the city's richest men by cutting off their tongues and – in a final coup de grace – lopping off their privates. Jones' street-smart investigative skills soon lead her to the dark underbelly of the fashion industry, where beauty is a commodity easily bought and sold. It becomes clear that the killer is amongst those tossed aside after their youth has been used and abused. But as she sinks deeper into the fashion underworld, Jones discovers she's become the latest target in the killer's quest. Can she uncover the murderer in time or will she end up as yet another victim of their lethal rage?

RICHARD
CASTLE
HEAT WAVE

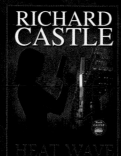

HEAT WAVE

Mystery sensation Richard Castle introduces his newest character, NYPD Homicide Detective Nikki Heat. Tough, sexy, professional, Nikki Heat carries a passion for justice as she leads one of New York City's top homicide squads. She's hit with an unexpected challenge when the commissioner assigns superstar magazine journalist Jameson Rook to ride along with her to research an article on New York's Finest. PulitzerPrize-winning Rook is as much a handful as he is handsome. His wise-cracking and meddling aren't her only problems. As she works to unravel the secrets of the murdered real estate tycoon, she must also confront the spark between them. The one called heat.

THE NEW YORK TIMES BESTSELLING AUTHOR OF HEAT WAVE
RICHARD
CASTLE
NAKED
HEAT

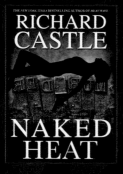

NAKED HEAT

When New York's most vicious gossip columnist, Cassidy Towne, is found dead, Heat uncovers a gallery of high profile suspects, all with compelling motives for killing the most feared muckraker in Manhattan. Heat's investigation is complicated by her surprise reunion with superstar magazine journalist Jameson Rook. The residue of their unresolved romantic conflict and crackling sexual tension fills the air as Heat and Rook embark on a search for a killer among celebrities and mobsters, singers and hookers, pro athletes and shamed politicians. This new, explosive case brings on the heat in the glittery world of secrets, cover-ups, and scandals.

RICHARD
CASTLE
NEW YORK CITY
HEAT
RISES

HEAT RISES

The bizarre murder of a parish priest at a New York bondage club is just the tip of an iceberg that leads Nikki Heat to a dark conspiracy that reaches all the way to the highest level of the NYPD. But when she gets too close to the truth, Nikki finds herself disgraced, stripped of her badge and out on her own with nobody she can trust. Except maybe the one man in her life who's not a cop. Reporter Jameson Rook. In the midst of New York's coldest winter in a hundred years, there's one thing Nikki is determined to prove. Heat Rises.

ABOUT THE AUTHOR

Much of what I'm about to tell you is not true. It is, however, exactly as I remember it.

Chapter One : The Early Years

I was born during a howling thunderstorm on the first of April, shortly after midnight. According to the doctor, as I took my first breath the heavens shuddered with a thunderclap unlike any he had ever heard before… or since. Needless to say, after a birth like that, people expected great things. But I wasn't quite ready for the pressure, so I spent the next few years sucking my thumb and spitting up on people.

Given my birthdate, my mother called me her April Fools' baby, and every birthday she'd sit me down and solemnly tell me that I was adopted. The minute she had me going, she'd yell, "April Fools!" and we'd both laugh and laugh, and then she'd gently remind me that she had no idea who my father was. You'd expect this to bother me, but I kind of liked not knowing who he was. In my imagination he was something cool, like an astronaut, or a jungle explorer, or at the very least an insurance actuary assessing the risks of being an astronaut or jungle explorer. I suppose that making up stories about my father's identity was how I found my way to telling stories. I'd gotten a taste for it, and I liked it!

My first novel (still unpublished), was written at the age of six and three-quarters, and was the aptly titled *Booger Man, the Man Made of Boogers.* It was released to my immediate circle of literary peers to very harsh critical reaction. Undaunted by the negative press, I set about writing something a little less "gross" (to quote Suzy Fitzsimmons). The result was: *Why is the Sky Red and Other Questions Martian Kids Ask their Parents?* Sales of *"Why"* were most likely hurt by my inability to determine where to put the question mark in the title.

With a mediocre reaction to "Why" I set a new course, dipping my toe into the waters of non-fiction literature, starting with a slim tome entitled: *Where Did My Finger Go? (It's up my nose!)*, which enumerated all the places I had, to that point, stuck my finger. *"Finger"* was quickly followed by a junior self-help volume titled: *How to Trick Grown-ups into Giving You Things (Like Extra Helpings of Dessert)*, which proved to be extraordinarily popular among my classmates.

But, ultimately, I left the world of non-fiction. I just felt too constrained by having to service the facts. I wanted to stretch my imagination, so I returned to my storytelling roots, penning the imaginative thriller: *The Moon is Watching You Sleep! I Think It's Planning on Doing Something Horrible to You!* When my school chums dragged themselves into class from a fearful and sleepless night, I knew I had arrived. I was, at long last, a manipulator of human emotion. I felt drunk with power. (Though at that age I had never been drunk, so I guess it's more appropriate to say I felt "sugar-rushed" with power.)

During this period of time, my mother was trodding the boards on the Great White Way, so the New York City Public Library became my unofficial and unpaid babysitter. While my mother would work, I would curl up in the stacks and read the classics: Edgar Allen Poe, Arthur Conan Doyle, and Carolyn Keene. (What can I say? Nancy Drew was hot.) My education had begun.

And then, just like that, I hit puberty and suddenly lost all interest in reading.

The next seven years was a mélange of utterly pedestrian experiences that would be completely unremarkable, if I hadn't later suffused them with plot lines from Archie comics. Consequently, I have some wonderful stories about the malt shop and riding around in an old jalopy.

Coming Soon:

Chapter Two – Edgewyck Academy and Beyond: Learning the Dark Arts.
 And I get my first novel published!